BOOK I
ORGANIZING THINKING
GRAPHIC ORGANIZERS

SANDRA PARKS AND HOWARD BLACK

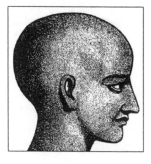

© 1992
CRITICAL THINKING PRESS & SOFTWARE
(formerly Midwest Publications)
P.O. Box 448 • Pacific Grove • CA 93950-0448
Phone 800-458-4849 • FAX 408-393-3277
ISBN 0-89455-354-2
Printed in the United States of America

CONTENTS

CHAPTER 4 – SOCIAL STUDIES 134

CHAPTER 5 – MATHEMATICS 183

CHAPTER 6 – SCIENCE 224

SANDRA PARKS (formerly Sandra Black) received an M.A. in Curriculum from the University of South Florida and did doctoral studies at Indiana State University. She provides staff development to schools across the country and serves as an educational consultant to the National Center for Teaching Thinking. She also conducts National Curriculum Study Institutes annually for the Association for Curriculum Development. Sandra Parks is the founding president of the Indiana Association for the Gifted.

HOWARD BLACK received an M.A. in Mathematics from Indiana State University and did doctoral studies at both Indiana State and Michigan State universities. He taught physics at Indiana University for 28 years and in 1978 received the Distinguished Teaching Award from that university. He currently teaches math and general studies at Bethune-Cookman College in Daytona Beach, Florida, where he was given the 1990 Award for Excellence in Teaching.

The authors appreciate the cooperation of administrators, teachers, and students in the academic excellence programs of Dade County (Florida) Public Schools. We also appreciate the efforts of the students and teachers at Bachmon Elementary School in Salt Lake City, Utah, who contributed to the classroom effectiveness of *Organizing Thinking* by field-testing these lessons. Special thanks to Kathi Anderson and Principal James DeNeff.

INTRODUCTION

COMPONENTS OF *ORGANIZING THINKING*

ORGANIZING THINKING PROVIDES:

prepared lessons (student materials and lesson plans) for infusing thinking skills instruction into content learning

suggestions for class discussion topics on content lessons and thinking processes

identification of numerous content objectives to apply thinking skills instruction across the curriculum

master graphics to prepare a transparency collection for explaining concepts and guiding classroom discussion

tools for process writing instruction

ORGANIZING THINKING

Organizing Thinking is a handbook of lessons which integrate the teaching of thinking skills into elementary school instruction. The central feature of all lessons is the use of graphic organizers to illustrate how information is related. These graphic organizers depict key skills (compare and contrast, sequence, part/whole relationships, classification, and analogy) and involve students in active thinking about textual information to promote clearer understanding of content lessons. Diagrams serve as "mental maps" to depict complex relationships in any subject and at any grade level. Thus, graphic organizers become a metacognitive tool to transfer the thinking processes to other lessons which feature the same relationships.

The use of graphic organizers encourages students to see information as components of systems or as contrasting concepts, rather than as isolated facts. Once information and relationships have been recorded on graphic organizers, students then use the pictorial outline to form more abstract comparisons, evaluations, and conclusions. These "diagrammatic outlines" help students organize their thinking for writing, oral or visual presentations, and problem solving.

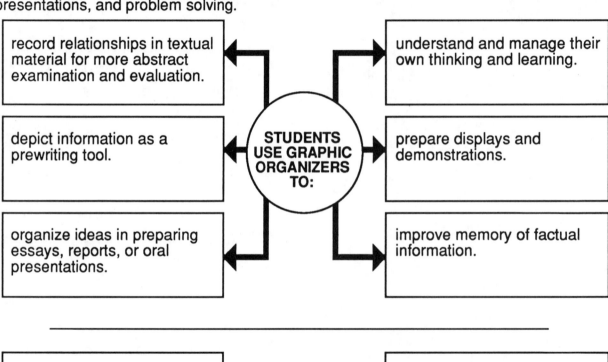

record relationships in textual material for more abstract examination and evaluation.

depict information as a prewriting tool.

organize ideas in preparing essays, reports, or oral presentations.

STUDENTS USE GRAPHIC ORGANIZERS TO:

understand and manage their own thinking and learning.

prepare displays and demonstrations.

improve memory of factual information.

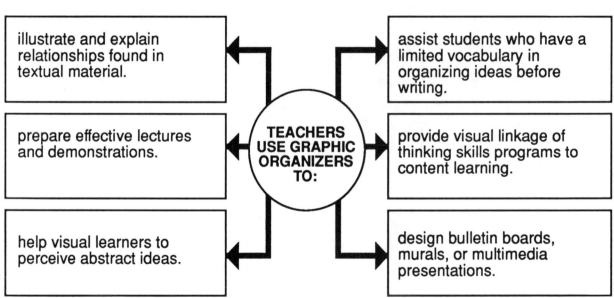

illustrate and explain relationships found in textual material.

prepare effective lectures and demonstrations.

help visual learners to perceive abstract ideas.

TEACHERS USE GRAPHIC ORGANIZERS TO:

assist students who have a limited vocabulary in organizing ideas before writing.

provide visual linkage of thinking skills programs to content learning.

design bulletin boards, murals, or multimedia presentations.

Lessons in *Organizing Thinking* are designed to supplement text material and to accompany corresponding content objectives. *Organizing Thinking* features graphs and diagrams of relationships commonly employed in language arts, mathematics, social studies, science, art, and music instruction. Each lesson includes a lesson plan, background information which can be reproduced for student use, and the completed graphic organizer containing suggested answers. Since a photocopy machine will not reproduce light blue print, the completed graphic organizer also serves as a blank diagram for student use.

LESSON PLAN FORMAT

THINKING SKILL: Identifies the thinking process employed in the lesson so that teachers and students use appropriate terms.

CONTENT OBJECTIVE: Identifies the content objective of the lesson. *Organizing Thinking* lessons supplement the corresponding content lesson and are taught as the lesson appears in course outlines or text material. Some lessons are appropriate to introduce concepts; others are designed to review or extend content lessons.

DISCUSSION: Suggests techniques for using graphic organizers in discussion, provides dialogues to explain, model or extend lessons, and summarizes inferences, interpretations, or conclusions which result from discussion.

WRITING EXTENSION: Provides suggestions for essay questions, summary writing, or creative writing tasks. Questions may be used as essay items on unit tests or as a class Think/Pair/Share activity.

THINKING ABOUT THINKING: Provides suggestions to help students reflect about their own thinking and learning. THINKING ABOUT THINKING questions may be used for class discussion or as a Think/Pair/Share activity.

SIMILAR CONTENT LESSONS: Identifies other lessons in the same content area which feature the same thinking process and the same graphic organizer.

COMPLETED GRAPHIC: Provides answers for the lesson.

TEXT PASSAGE AND WORKSHEET: Provides lesson material (background information and a blank graphic) to be reproduced for student use.

SUGGESTIONS FOR CLASS DISCUSSION

The discussion section of each lesson suggests techniques for using the graphic organizer in classroom discussion, dialogues to clarify key concepts within the lesson, and results of the discussion (interpretations, inferences, or conclusions). The class discussion is guided by using a transparent graphic organizer on an overhead projector. The TECHNIQUE of visually guided discussion focuses students' attention on the information and relationships in the lesson. It becomes a visual tool for recording student responses, picturing the content of the lesson and recording each individual's contribution to the discussion.

DIALOGUE suggestions offer models for expressing thought processes when discussing key concepts. Sample dialogues appear in "screened" bold type. The WRITING EXTENSION and metacognitive questions (THINKING ABOUT THINKING) may also be used to stimulate class discussion or as a Think/Pair/Share activity. Dialogues extend students' understanding of the content beyond the given lessons and prompt them to form interpretations, inferences, or conclusions.

The purposeful use of graphic organizers should lead students to understand significant factors in a lesson. The RESULT paragraph expresses the main point of the discussion: a clarification, interpretation, inference, or conclusion drawn from the lesson.

USING GRAPHIC ORGANIZERS AS A PREWRITING TOOL

The lessons in *Organizing Thinking* are designed to teach primary students how to write thoughtful essays and accurate descriptions. Students follow these steps in each lesson:

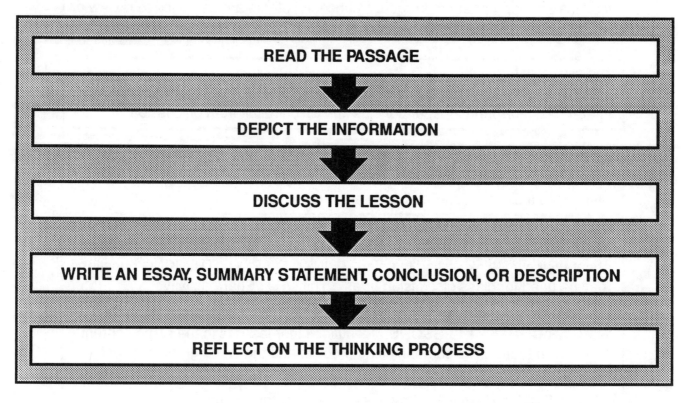

Students transfer information from texts or discussion to a graphic organizer. The graphic organizer serves as a "visual outline" of information for writing descriptions or essays. Provide a blank graph for the prewriting step until students are confident enough to organize concepts independently. Although primary students write brief passages, their writing should contain the significant information from the graphic organizer. Encourage students to state how the information is related. Students may also draw their own organizational graphs and diagrams. To demonstrate the use of a graphic organizer, select a section from a text and illustrate it on a transparency of the graphic organizer.

        © 1992 CRITICAL THINKING PRESS & SOFTWARE • P.O. Box 448, Pacific Grove, CA 93950

Introduce one type of graphic organizer at a time. Teach students explicitly how to write the answers to essay questions and use them on your unit tests. Use a completed graph as your answer key to help score essay tests quickly. Don't hesitate to give language-limited students essay questions. Although primary students may write sparse answers, their essays demonstrate their knowledge and their emerging organizational skills.

METACOGNITIVE QUESTIONS

Metacognition refers to knowledge about, awareness of, and control over one's thinking and learning. Metacognitive questions, labeled THINKING ABOUT THINKING, are designed to help students become more aware of their thinking processes, and more deliberate and reflective about how well the process works. Students in the primary grades can think about their thinking easily. They may, however, need more prompting to recognize a particular process than older students would.

According to Swartz and Perkins (*Teaching Thinking: Issues and Approaches*. Pacific Grove, CA: Critical Thinking Press & Software, 1990) metacognitive strategies include:

1. Awareness of the thinking process
   - Using thinking terms—e.g., "predicting," "uncovering assumptions," etc.—to mark the presence of these thinking activities
2. Strategic use of the thinking process
   - Providing a list of components or a series of steps for students to follow in doing a certain type of thinking
   - Verbal prompting of students to go through a series of steps in their thinking
   - Asking students to describe retrospectively what they did in thinking about a particular issue or problem
   - Having students "think out loud" while other students listen to the thinking processes going on and note the steps in the process.
3. Reflective use of the thinking process
   - developing rules for good thinking
   - recommending to others ways to think
   - correcting ineffective thinking

Metacognitive questions prompt students to make their thinking processes explicit and to evaluate the effectiveness of the process. Metacognition facilitates transfer and promotes the clear understanding of the lesson. In *Organizing Thinking* these questions refer primarily to the use of graphic organizers as a thinking strategy and as an effective tool in comprehending information. For additional background and examples of metacognitive questioning in creative thinking, critical thinking, and decision making, see *Teaching Thinking: Issues and Approaches*.

Teachers find that students recognize the usefulness of graphic organizers easily and use them independently. Metacognition about this technique is best reflected in students' design of their own graphic organizers, specialized to the particular task. Encourage students to develop graphic organizers for *Organizing Thinking* lessons and text lessons.

The Think/Pair/Share lesson in the study skills chapter illustrates the value of metacognitive discussion between students. Think/Pair/Share discussion is helpful to primary students, particularly those with language limitation. This peer-teaching technique improves the quality and frequency of student participation in class discussion, models reflective, self-correcting thinking, and can be used with any lesson for clarity and understanding. The WRITING EXTENSION and THINKING ABOUT THINKING questions in each lesson may also be used as a topic for a Think/Pair/Share discussion.

CURRICULUM APPLICATIONS

Each *Organizing Thinking* lesson plan identifies numerous primary lessons in the same discipline in which the demonstrated thinking process and graphic organizer can be used to clarify the content. Teachers and thinking skills curriculum committees may use these application references in identifying curriculum opportunities for the meaningful integration of thinking skills instruction.

DIRECTIONS FOR PREPARING AND USING MASTER GRAPHS

To prepare a transparency which you may often reuse, reproduce the master graph on acetates with your photocopy or transparency master machine. Remember to use washable markers when recording information for each lesson. To reuse the transparency, wipe off the markings with a damp cloth. Store your "library" of transparencies in pocket folders in a ringed notebook.

The blank master graph may be reproduced as a student worksheet and used several ways:

- If you are working with students who have a limited attention span you may direct students to fill in their worksheets as you develop the lesson on the transparency.
- Students may use the graphs as a study tool to examine complex passages.
- Students may use the graphs to organize picture displays of ideas within a passage.

To prepare your own lessons, examine your texts for examples of the relationships depicted on the graphs: **compare/contrast, part/whole, sequence, classification, analogy.** Select the appropriate graphic organizer and write in the expected answers to create an answer key. Use the blank lesson format form to prepare your lesson plan. It is not necessary to represent every example of the relationships in this fashion since over-use of any technique can cause it to become less effective. The use of graphic organizers is especially effective in complex lessons that contain significant concepts which may be unclear or confusing to students.

The graphic organizers become a familiar visual outline for organizing information. Use them as a basis for bulletin board design. Such displays offer students a colorful reminder of current lessons and the thinking processes involved. Students may also use the graphic organizers in design projects, displays, media presentations, science fair exhibits, report writing, and speech preparation. Place a file of blank graphs where students may take them as needed.

BRIDGING *BUILDING THINKING SKILLS* TO CONTENT OBJECTIVES

For teachers who use *Building Thinking Skills*® or other thinking skills programs, *Organizing Thinking* links thinking skills instruction to specific content lessons. Each graphic organizer can be used to teach a *Building Thinking Skills*® lesson and subsequently to apply the same process to teach a content lesson. The graphic organizer serves as a visual cue to remind students of the thinking process and to transfer that process to a particular content application.

CHAPTER 1—BLACKLINE MASTER GRAPHS

LESSON PLAN FORM		COMPARE AND/OR CONTRAST DIAGRAMS
	INTERVAL GRAPHS	
TRANSITIVE ORDER GRAPHS		FLOWCHART DIAGRAMS
	CENTRAL IDEA GRAPHS	
BRANCHING DIAGRAMS		CLASS RELATIONSHIPS DIAGRAMS
	MATRIX DIAGRAMS	

LESSON PLAN FORM

TITLE _____

THINKING SKILLS _____

CONTENT OBJECTIVE _____
_____

DISCUSSION _____
_____
_____
_____
_____
_____
_____
_____
_____
_____
_____
_____
_____

WRITING EXTENSION _____
_____
_____
_____
_____

THINKING ABOUT THINKING _____
_____
_____
_____
_____

SIMILAR CONTENT LESSONS _____
_____

 © 1992 CRITICAL THINKING PRESS & SOFTWARE • P.O. Box 448, Pacific Grove, CA 93950

COMPARE AND/OR CONTRAST DIAGRAMS

TWO PEOPLE

- Backgrounds
- Historical periods
- Achievements
- Ideals
- Challenges

TWO PLACES

- Locations
- Land forms
- Significance
- Natural resources
- Development

TWO THINGS

- Parts
- Measurements
- Kinds
- Uses
- Origins
- Operation
- Significance

TWO CULTURES

- Geographic locations
- Histories
- Economic systems
- Political systems
- Leaders
- Technologies
- Values
- Art

USE COMPARE AND/OR CONTRAST DIAGRAMS TO EXAMINE

TWO STORIES

- Significant characteristics
  - conflicts
  - ideals
  - characters
  - styles
  - organization
  - significance of titles
  - novelty

TWO EVENTS

- Participants
- Leaders
- Significance
- Causes
- Consequences
- Historical periods

TWO ORGANISMS

- Types
- Habitats
- Life requirements
- Structures

USING COMPARE AND CONTRAST DIAGRAMS

RATIONALE FOR COMPARE AND CONTRAST ACTIVITIES

The compare and contrast process is a helpful technique for clarifying and understanding concepts. Concepts may include objects, organisms, people, or ideas. The comparison step (HOW ALIKE?) allows learners to relate a new concept to existing knowledge. The more similarities the learner can identify, the more clearly the new concept will be understood and remembered. The contrast step (HOW DIFFERENT?) allows learners to distinguish the new concept from similar concepts. This promotes clear understanding and memory by eliminating confusion with related knowledge.

The compare and contrast process should become a regular habit for students and teachers when examining new vocabulary words. After a student gives a definition, the teacher may ask, "How is that like…," followed by "How is that unlike…." This completes clarification in three steps:

1. Definition of the concept

2. Identification with a similar concept that the student already knows

3. Distinction from the concept in step two.

The number of responses in the "How Alike" or "How Different" steps will vary. Each lesson may not contain the same number of similarities and differences contained on the master graph. Several blanks are provided on the diagram to encourage students to consider as many similarities or differences as possible.

USE THE COMPARE AND CONTRAST DIAGRAM TO:

- Compare and contrast two terms or ideas.
- Organize thinking to respond to essay questions.
- Clarify the meaning of terms in reviewing for a test.

TO USE THE COMPARE AND CONTRAST DIAGRAM:

1. Write the two concepts in the blanks at the top.

2. Discuss with students the definition and significant characteristics of each concept as you record it. This discussion confirms that students have sufficient background to make the rest of the exercise meaningful.

3. Record phrases which express similarities on each "HOW ALIKE" line. Note that these phrases commonly begin with "both," confirming that the characteristic is shared by both concepts.

4. Record phrases which express differences on each "HOW DIFFERENT" line. Each difference between the two concepts should relate to the same quality, but should point up the difference between the two terms. Establish this pattern:

"**With regard to** (quality), (concept one and its distinctions), **but** (concept two and its distinctions)."

5. Ask students to explain what the distinction between the two concepts means or how the concepts will be used differently.

NOTE: The overlapping classes diagram may also be used to describe similarities and differences.

COMPARE AND CONTRAST DIAGRAM

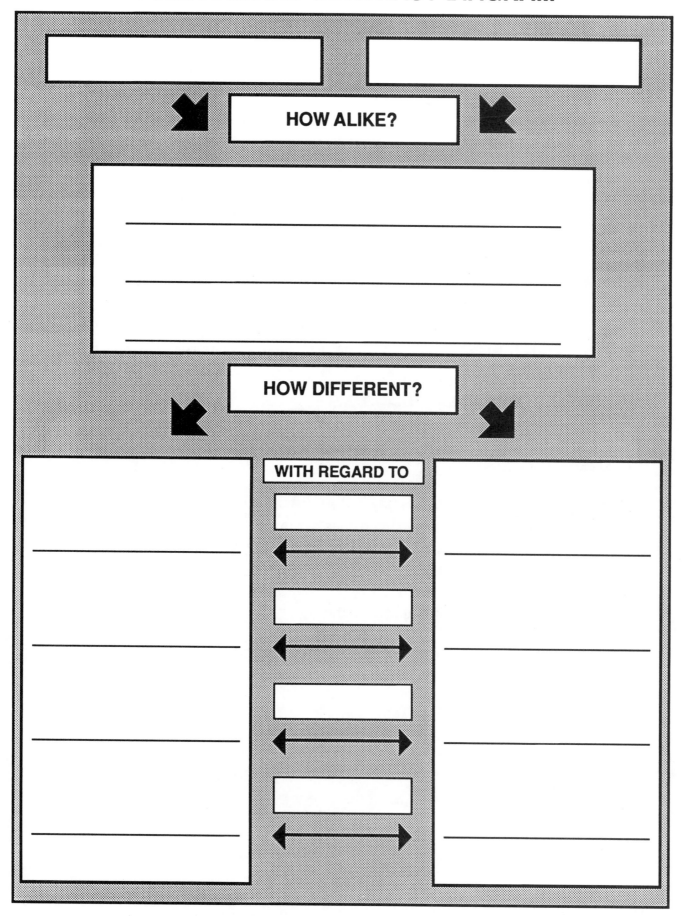

HOW ALIKE?

HOW DIFFERENT?

WITH REGARD TO

USING COMPARE OR CONTRAST DIAGRAMS

RATIONALE FOR COMPARE OR CONTRAST ACTIVITIES

Use the compare or contrast graph when only one of the two processes is significant. To compare concepts, use the graph to emphasize shared traits, such as showing analogous relationships between figures of speech. Use the diagram to illustrate many characteristics which two objects, organisms, or ideas share and how each expresses that characteristic. Students recognize that many connections are being expressed in a few metaphoric words.

To contrast concepts, use the diagram to emphasize differences and to eliminate confusion by separating a new term from similar ones. "Contrast" emphasizes subtle differences which might otherwise be overlooked.

For clarity, begin each discussion by identifying the characteristics being differentiated. Then describe how that characteristic is different for each term. Establish this pattern:

"With regard to (quality), (item one and its distinctions), **but** (item two and its distinctions)."

For example: **"With regard to** body shape, a cat has short ears and a long tail, **but** a rabbit has long ears and a short tail."

The number of responses in the "How Alike" or "How Different" steps will vary. Several blanks are provided on the diagram to encourage students to consider as many similarities or differences as possible.

USE COMPARE OR CONTRAST DIAGRAMS TO:

- Compare or contrast two concepts.
- Organize thinking to prepare writing assignments.
- Analyze metaphors.

TO USE THE COMPARE OR CONTRAST DIAGRAM:

1. Write the two terms or concepts in the blanks at the top.
2. Identify the characteristic being compared or contrasted. Write it in the center column.
3. Discuss how that characteristic applies to the first term and write the answer in the left column.
4. Discuss how that characteristic applies to the second term and write the answer in the right column.
5. Encourage students to draw inferences about the significance of the differences between these two terms or concepts.

COMPARE OR CONTRAST DIAGRAM

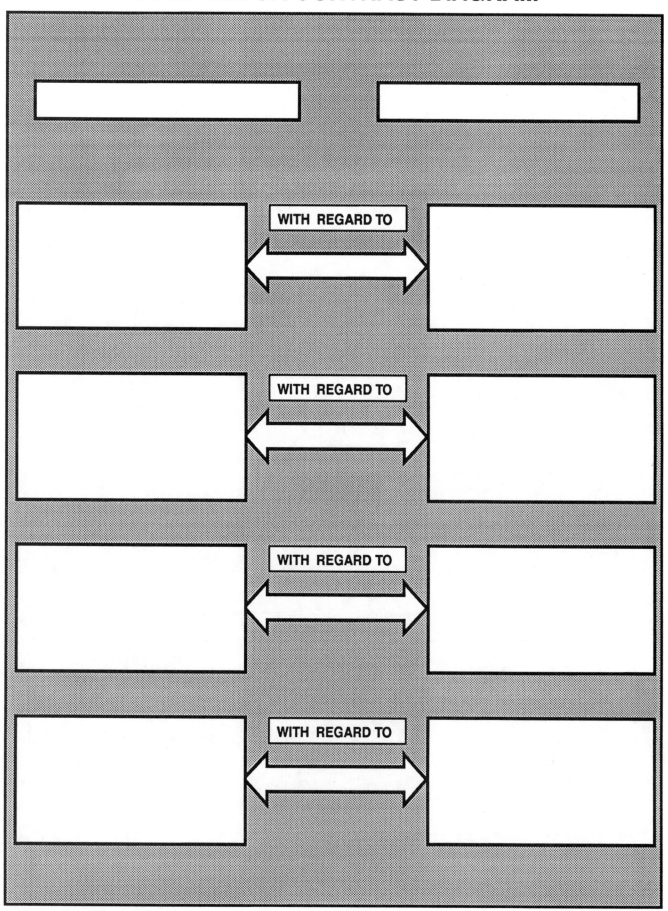

WITH REGARD TO

WITH REGARD TO

WITH REGARD TO

WITH REGARD TO

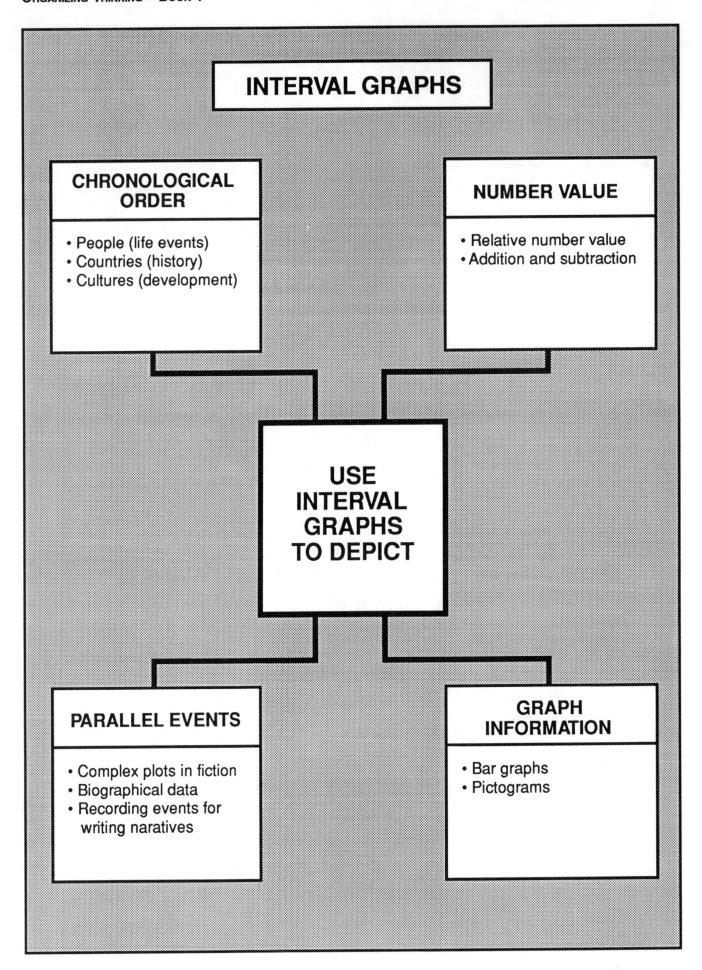

INTERVAL GRAPHS

CHRONOLOGICAL ORDER

• People (life events)
• Countries (history)
• Cultures (development)

NUMBER VALUE

• Relative number value
• Addition and subtraction

USE INTERVAL GRAPHS TO DEPICT

PARALLEL EVENTS

• Complex plots in fiction
• Biographical data
• Recording events for writing naratives

GRAPH INFORMATION

• Bar graphs
• Pictograms

USING THE INTERVAL GRAPH

RATIONALE FOR USING INTERVAL GRAPHS

Interval graphs can be used to depict value and order in a variety of forms. For example, time lines are frequently featured in text materials to show events in chronological order. Number lines are used to explain addition and subtraction processes.

Since interval graphs are primarily used to record quantitative data, students may use the information on the graph to interpret trends, correlations or simultaneous values. To depict two trends or to correlate a series of events, use a parallel interval graph to organize information. To depict simultaneous values of two variables, use a grid graph with perpendicular scales.

USE INTERVAL GRAPHS TO:

- Record and correlate events with given dates.
- Depict positive and negative number values.
- Depict correlations or parallels between events occurring at the same time.
- Depict simultaneous values of two variables.

TO USE THE INTERVAL GRAPH:

1. Select the appropriate type of interval graph: time line, parallel interval graph, or grid graphs.
2. Decide the range (years, values, etc.) that the total graph should cover and select appropriate intervals. The master graph contains ten intervals.
3. Label the lines of the graph.
4. Record the data.
5. Interpret significant trends or conclusions suggested by the data .

TO DESIGN A TIME LINE WITH MORE OR FEWER THAN TEN INTERVALS:

1. Determine the range of dates or values and mark at each end of the graph.

   Example: *To record events from 1775 to 1800, record 1775 at the left end and 1800 at the right end of the line.*

2. Subtract the smaller value from the larger value to calculate the range value.

   The range value of this example is determined by 1800 – 1775 = 25 years (range).

3. Decide the practical number of intervals for this data.

   For this example, five intervals should be sufficient. Note that six (6) marks are needed to produce five intervals.

4. Divide the range value by the number of intervals to get the interval value.

   25 years ÷ 5 intervals = 5 years per interval (interval value).

5. Add the interval value to the smaller limit of the range to determine the value of the second mark.

   1775 + 5 = 1780 value (year) of the second mark.

6. Repeat this process until you have labeled all the marks on the graph.

| 1775 | 1780 | 1785 | 1790 | 1795 | 1800 |

TIME LINE

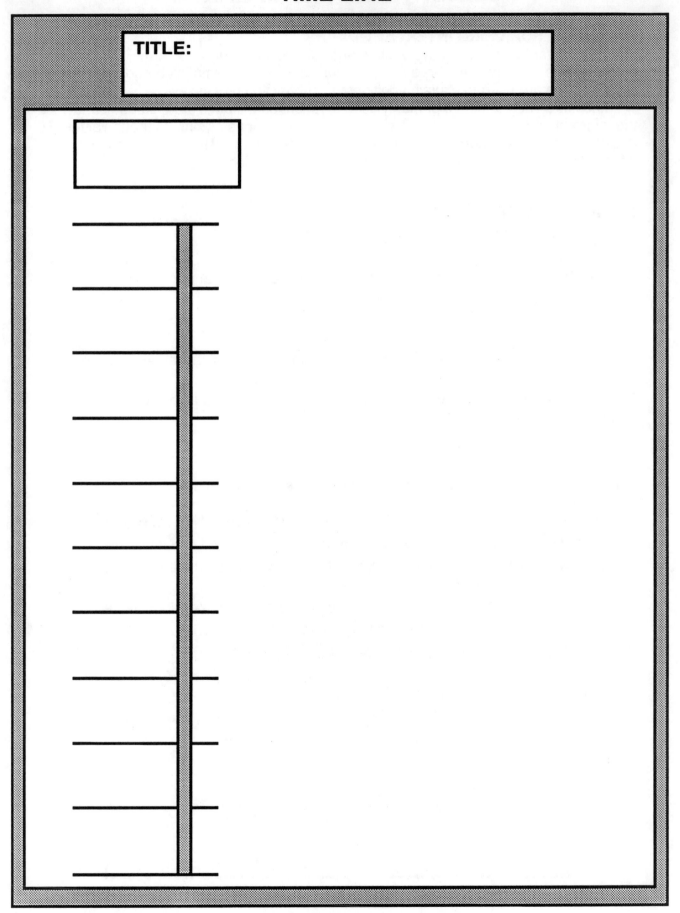

TITLE:

PARALLEL TIME LINE

TITLE

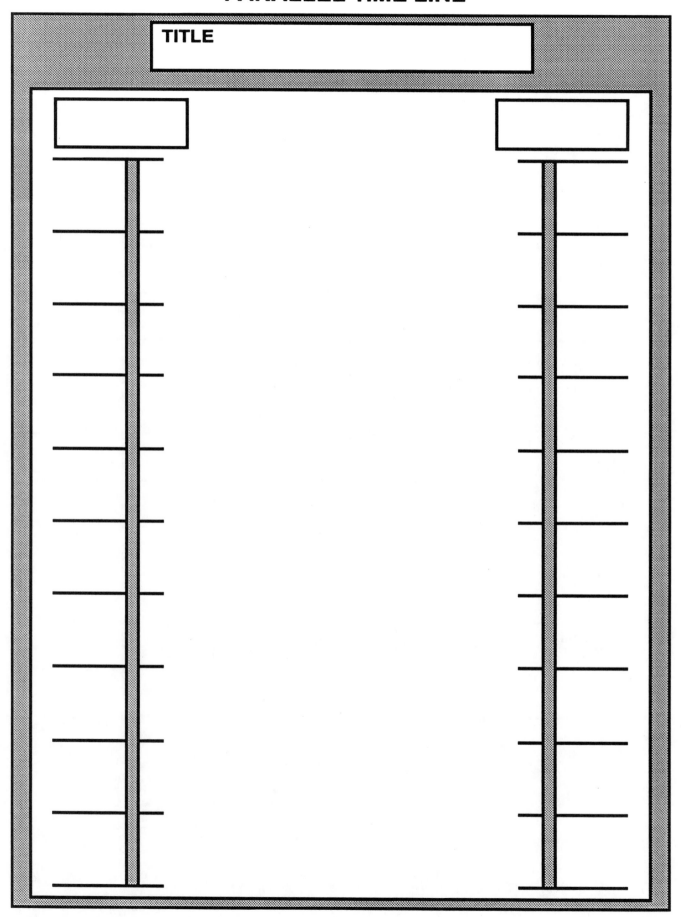

PARALLEL TIME LINE

GRID GRAPH

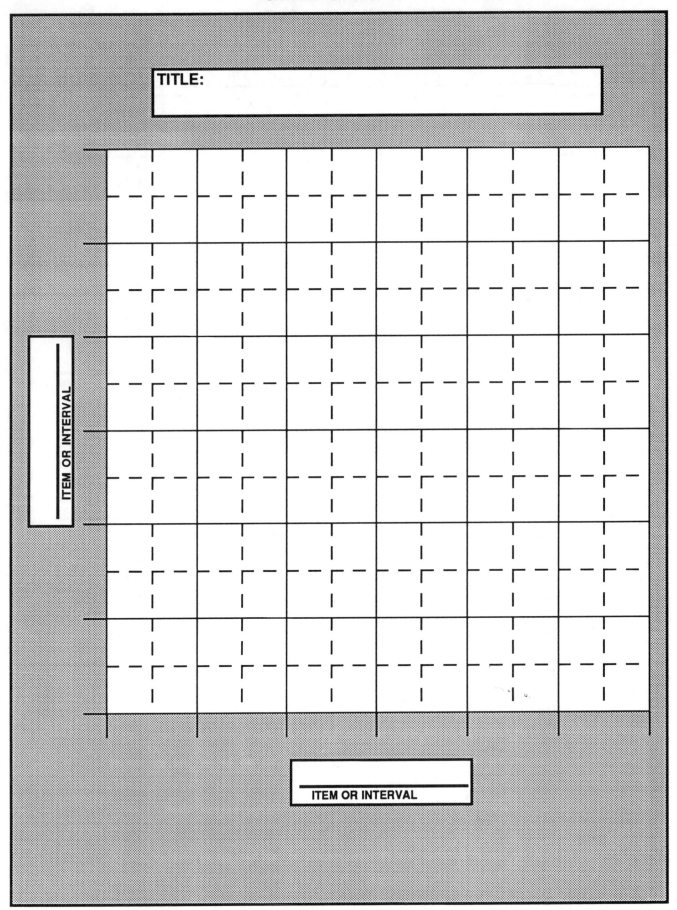

TITLE:

ITEM OR INTERVAL

ITEM OR INTERVAL

TRANSITIVE ORDER GRAPHS

PEOPLE

- Backgrounds
- Historical periods
- Achievements

EVENTS

Order of:

- Occurence
- Significance

NUMBER VALUE

- Relative number value

USE TRANSITIVE ORDER GRAPHS TO RECORD

DECISION MAKING

Prioritizing:

- Goals
- Options
- Time uses
- Personal values

OBJECTS

- Size
- Origins
- Development
- Significance
- Operation

ORGANISMS

- Size
- Development
- Significance
- Life cycles

USING TRANSITIVE ORDER GRAPHS

RATIONALE FOR USING TRANSITIVE ORDER GRAPHS

Transitive order graphs are useful for recording inferred order from written passages. Readers can use the graph to keep track of relative position, rank, order, or quantity. Since this graph is used to record the information given, an item's relative position may change as the text identifies intervening items. Thus, using a pencil or erasable marker is recommended.

USE TRANSITIVE ORDER GRAPHS TO:

- Record order by inference from text materials.

TO USE THE TRANSITIVE ORDER GRAPH:

1. Indicate the factor or characteristic being ranked.
2. Indicate the direction of the transitive order and list the limits; i.e., youngest to oldest, earliest to latest, largest to smallest.
3. Enter items on the lines as information is given in the written passage. Use a pencil or erasable marker in order to change answers easily.
4. Change item order, if necessary, as text material identifies intervening items.
5. You may use the margin to record proposed position, until text information confirms the relative order.

USING CYCLE GRAPHS

RATIONALE FOR USING CYCLE GRAPHS

Cycle graphs are transitive order graphs which depict repeating chronological order or interrelationship. Cycle graphs are useful in recording information to show time or direction cycles or to emphasize the repetitive characteristic of a trend. The directional arrows in the diagram may point in either direction to depict the relationship.

USE CYCLE GRAPHS TO:

- Record cyclical occurrence.
- Depict interrelationship.

TO USE THE CYCLE GRAPH:

1. Divide a circle into the number of parts in the process to be shown.
2. Enter events in order.
3. Use arrows to indicate the direction of flow.
4. Interpret significant trends or conclusions that the information suggests.

TRANSITIVE ORDER GRAPHS

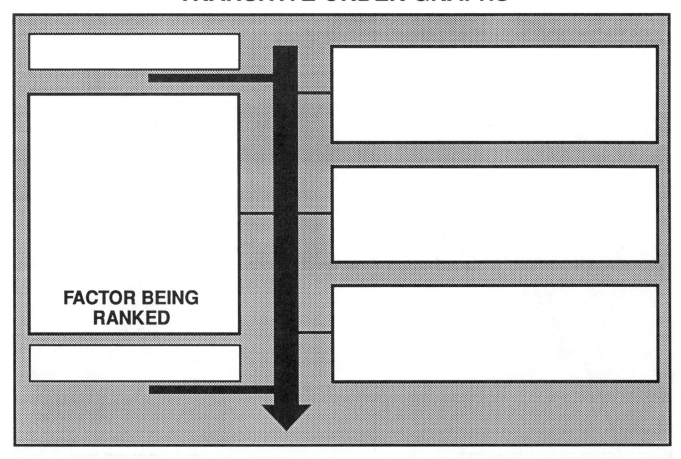

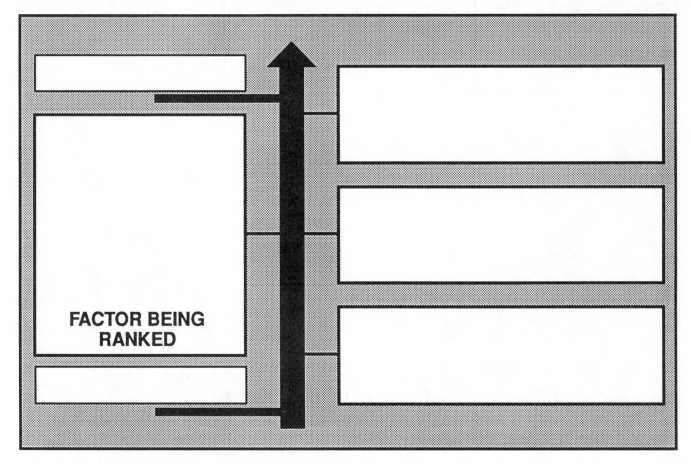

CYCLE GRAPH

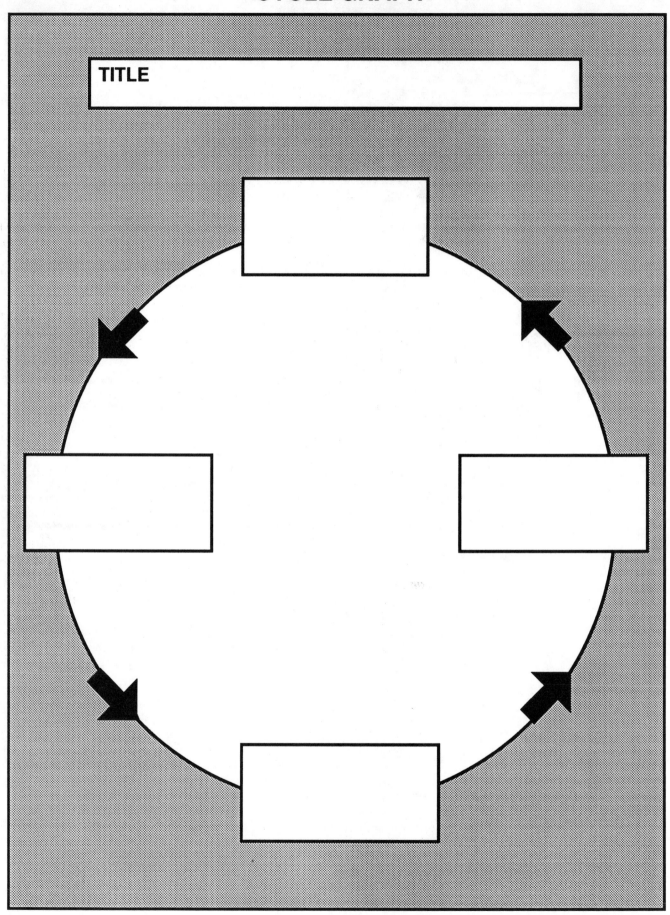

TITLE

CYCLE GRAPH

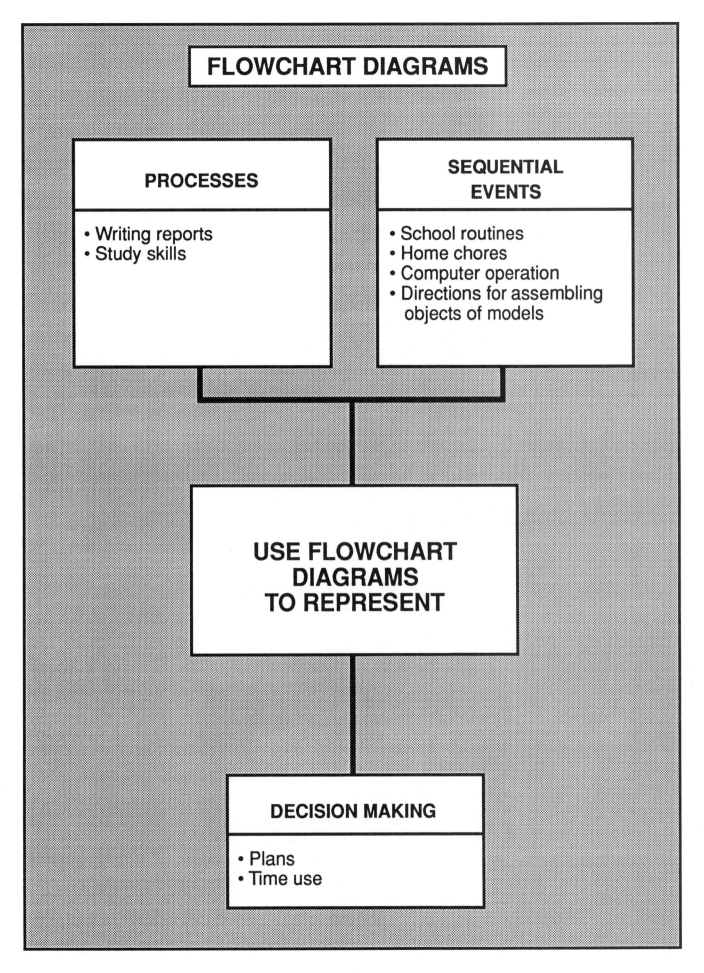

FLOWCHART DIAGRAMS

PROCESSES
- Writing reports
- Study skills

SEQUENTIAL EVENTS
- School routines
- Home chores
- Computer operation
- Directions for assembling objects of models

USE FLOWCHART DIAGRAMS TO REPRESENT

DECISION MAKING
- Plans
- Time use

USING FLOWCHART DIAGRAMS

RATIONALE FOR USING FLOWCHARTS

A flowchart is a diagram that represents a sequence of events, actions, or decisions. Flowcharts have also become a useful tool for computer programmers. Programmers use a standard set of symbols so that the reader may quickly understand the **flow** of thought represented by the **chart**.

Flowchart symbols include:

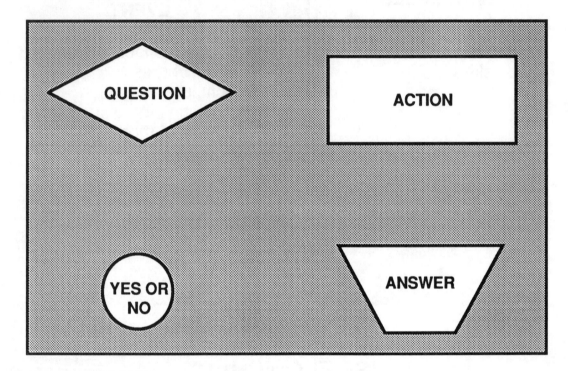

USE FLOWCHARTS TO:

- Sequence events in plots, historical eras, or laboratory instructions.
- Picture stages in the development of organisms, social trends, or legislative bills.
- Write instructions.
- Depict social or natural cycles.
- Plan a course of action.
- Solve mathematics and scientific problems.
- Depict the consequences of decisions.

TO USE A FLOWCHART:

1. Reproduce the decision diagram and flowchart template to create enough symbols to depict the steps or decisions in a lesson.
2. Cut apart the reproductions of the master graphic. Rearrange the symbols to form a flowchart with careful attention to decisions, actions, and answers.
3. Label each symbol to show the steps or decision points.
4. Leave some symbols blank to lead students to predict decisions, consequences, or alternatives.

STEPS

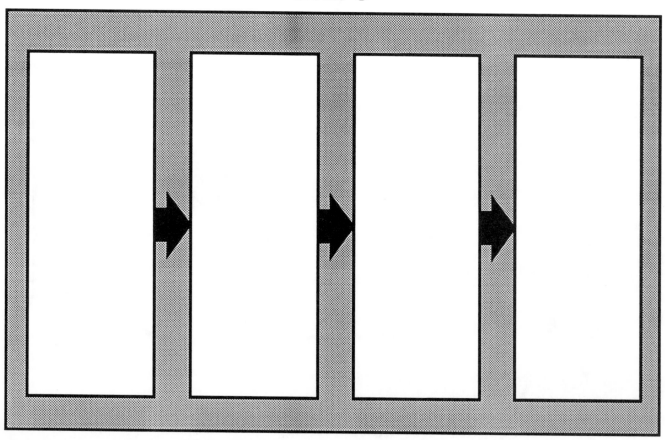

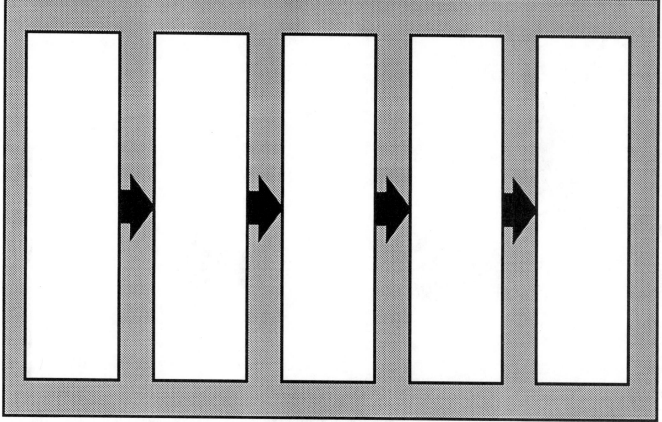

DECISION DIAGRAM

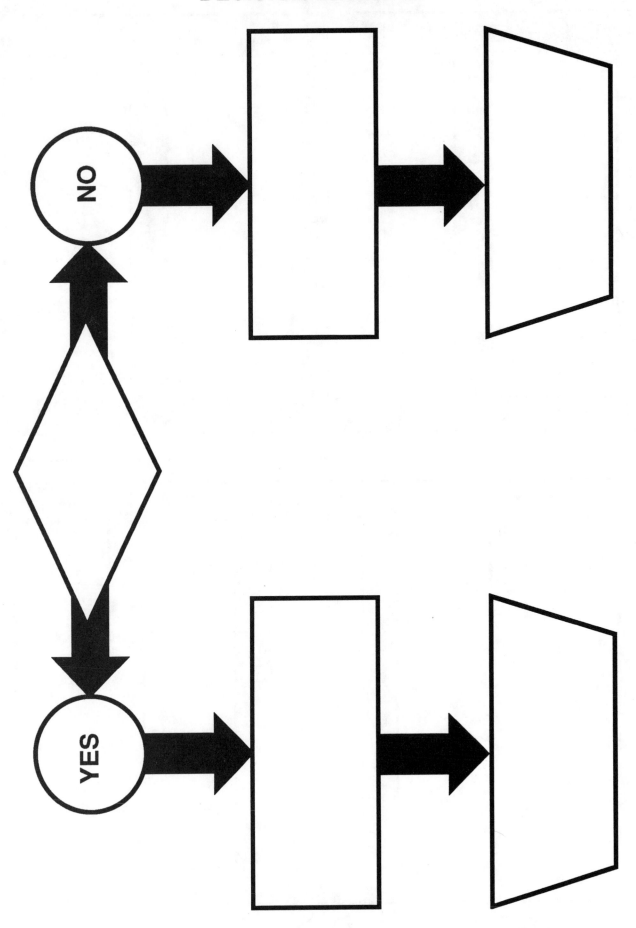

FLOWCHART TEMPLATE

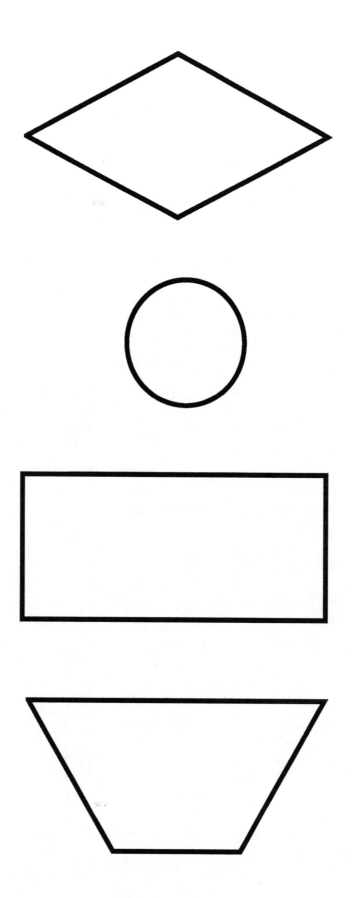

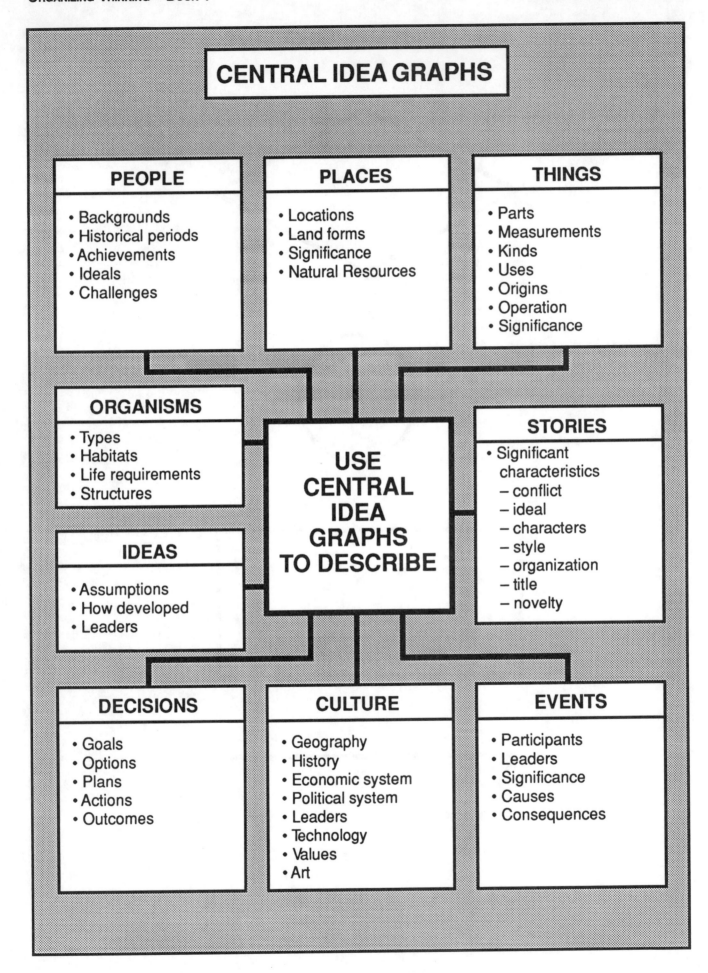

CENTRAL IDEA GRAPHS

PEOPLE
- Backgrounds
- Historical periods
- Achievements
- Ideals
- Challenges

PLACES
- Locations
- Land forms
- Significance
- Natural Resources

THINGS
- Parts
- Measurements
- Kinds
- Uses
- Origins
- Operation
- Significance

ORGANISMS
- Types
- Habitats
- Life requirements
- Structures

USE CENTRAL IDEA GRAPHS TO DESCRIBE

STORIES
- Significant characteristics
  – conflict
  – ideal
  – characters
  – style
  – organization
  – title
  – novelty

IDEAS
- Assumptions
- How developed
- Leaders

DECISIONS
- Goals
- Options
- Plans
- Actions
- Outcomes

CULTURE
- Geography
- History
- Economic system
- Political system
- Leaders
- Technology
- Values
- Art

EVENTS
- Participants
- Leaders
- Significance
- Causes
- Consequences

USING THE CENTRAL IDEA GRAPH

RATIONALE FOR CENTRAL IDEA ACTIVITIES

The central idea graph (sometimes called "webbing") is used to depict the parts of a whole, results of an event, or factors leading to a central theme. Students often perceive the supporting points as disconnected fragments of information, rather than as a conceptual whole. Use this graph to prompt students that supporting data are related to the central idea and are not isolated facts.

Central idea graphs are useful as a reading comprehension tool, a review aid, or a guide for designing exhibits or displays. In creative thinking and decision making activities, use them to depict alternatives, consequences, or related terms. These graphs can be used to depict a variety of relationships: part/whole, events/consequences, causes/effects, class/subclass, and concepts/examples. Because this graph is so versatile it is commonly used as a prewriting tool. Several variations of the central idea graph are featured in the writing lessons.

The number of "arms" will vary. Four blanks have been provided to encourage students to consider many divisions, examples, or alternatives.

USE CENTRAL IDEA GRAPHS TO:

- Depict a main idea and supporting details.
- Depict parts of a given object, system, or concept.
- Depict general classes and subclasses of a system.
- Depict factors leading to or resulting from a given action.
- Depict alternatives or creative connections in decision making and creative thinking.

TO USE THE CENTRAL IDEA GRAPH:

1. Write the central idea in the circle. Write each supporting detail on an "arm" of the diagram. Each "arm" may also branch to illustrate examples or subcategories.

2. To depict factors contributing to or resulting from a given event, mark each "arm" as an arrow. Direct the arrows toward the central idea to illustrate multiple causes; direct them away to illustrate multiple consequences or effects.

3. In decision making, enter the issue in the circle and brainstorm with students as many options or alternatives as they can suggest. Use the same graph to generate criteria that should apply to the most desirable solution. Examine each alternative regarding the proposed criteria.

4. To generate creative images or applications, write the subject in the circle. Brainstorm related ideas record them on the "arms." Each "arm" may branch to generate new connections. Examine the richness of ideas that the connections bring to the central idea. Select "arms" which are unusually imaginative or descriptive and use the ideas recorded there to create metaphors.

CENTRAL IDEA GRAPHS

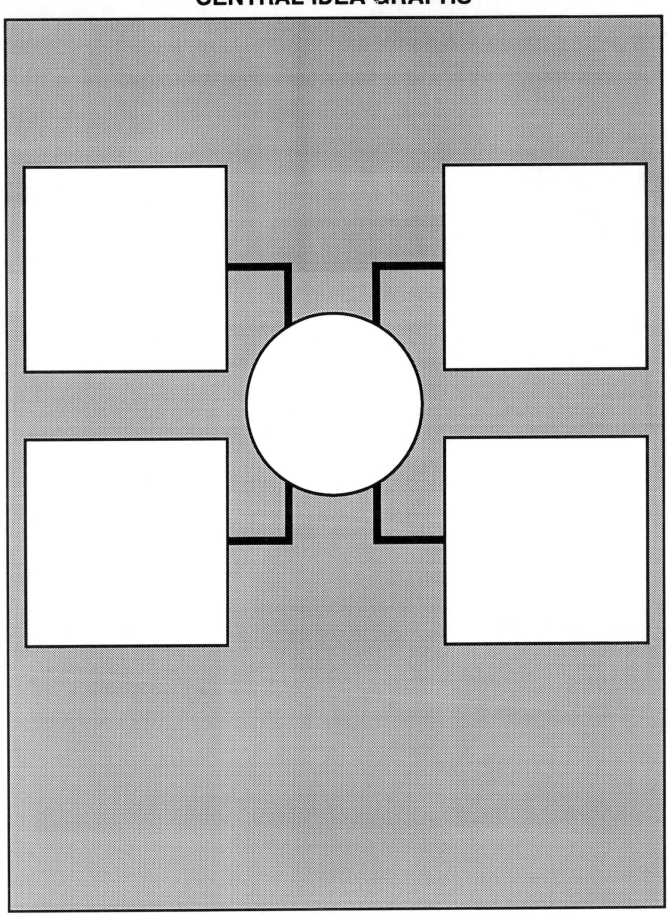

© 1992 Critical Thinking Press & Software • P.O. Box 448, Pacific Grove, CA 93950

CENTRAL IDEA GRAPHS

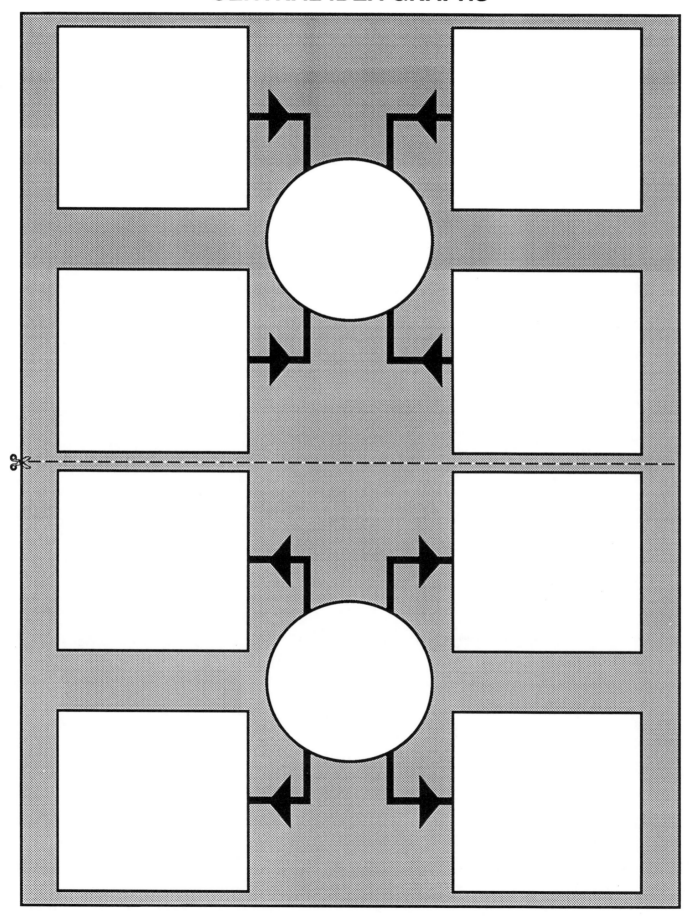

WEB DIAGRAM

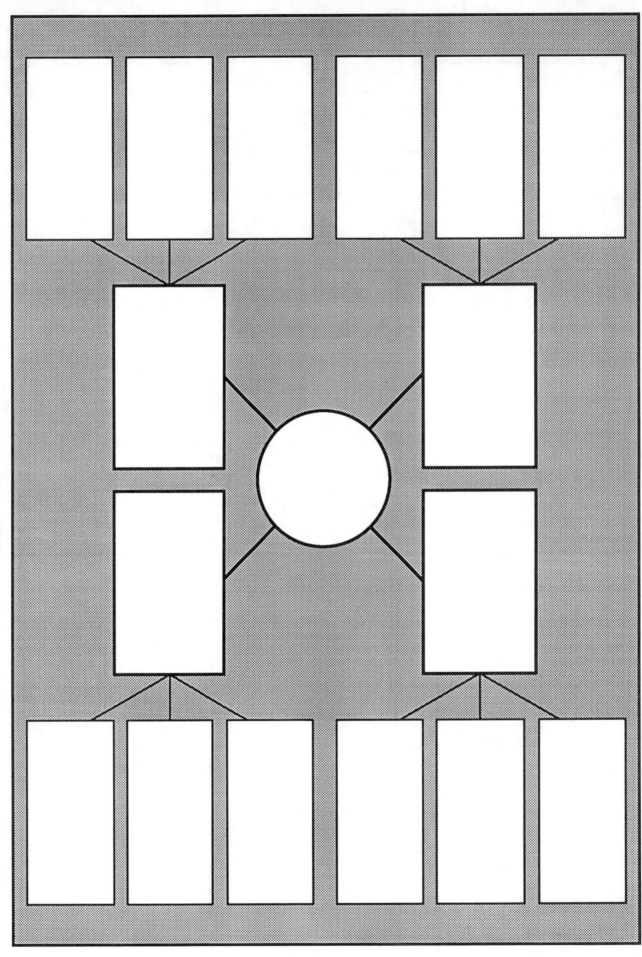

ARCH DIAGRAM: REASONS AND CONCLUSIONS

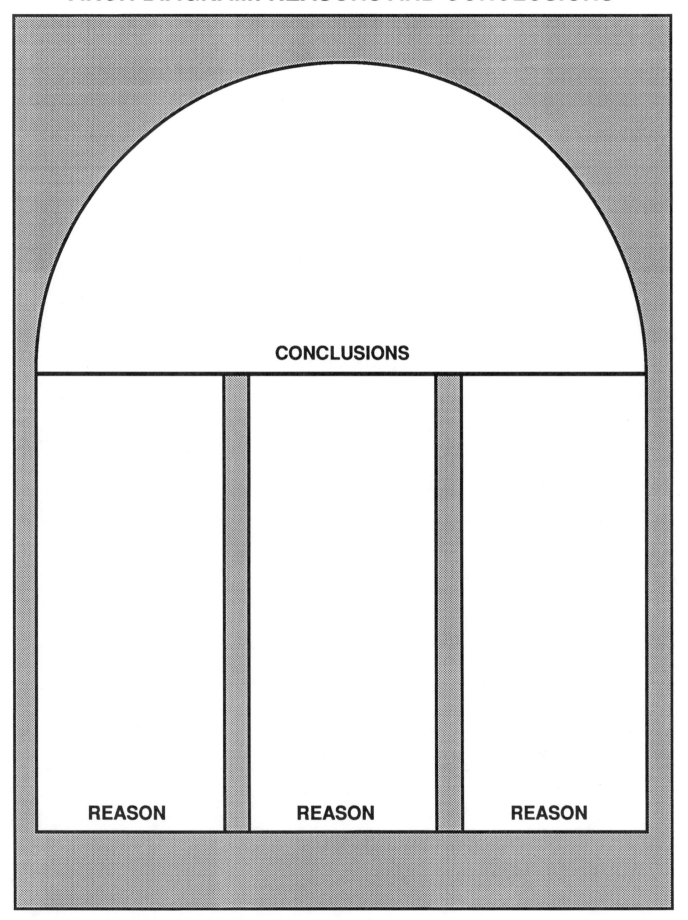

CONCLUSIONS

REASON   **REASON**   **REASON**

ARCH DIAGRAM:
MAIN IDEA AND SUPPORTING DETAILS

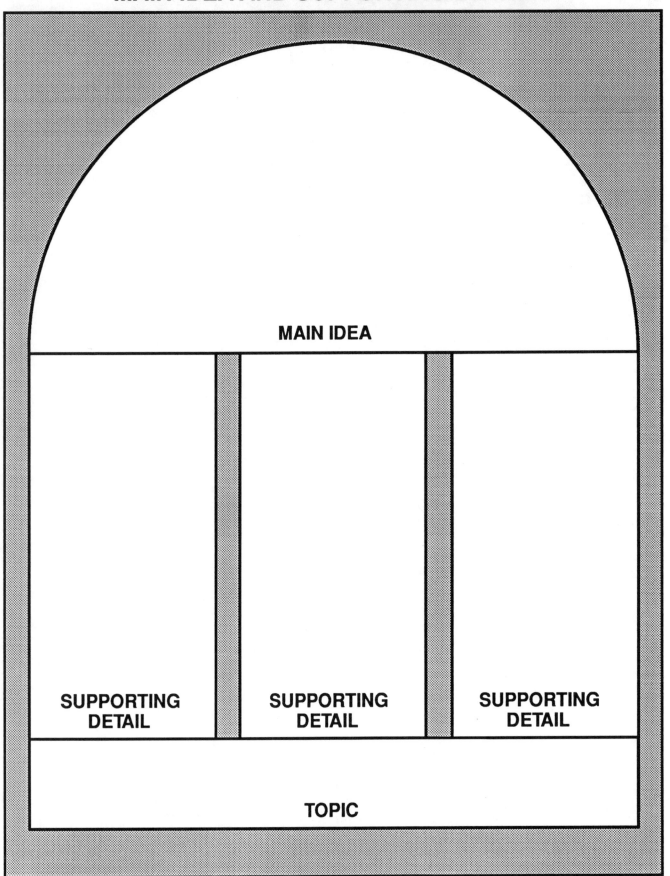

MAIN IDEA

SUPPORTING DETAIL **SUPPORTING DETAIL** **SUPPORTING DETAIL**

TOPIC

BRANCHING DIAGRAMS

FAMILY TREES

- Royal families
- Historical families
- Personal History

HIERARCHICAL RELATIONSHIPS

- Biological chains
- Evolutionary chains

ORGANIZATION CHARTS

- School organization
- Government organization

USE BRANCHING DIAGRAMS TO DEPICT

CLASS/SUBCLASS

- Organisms
- Sets/Subsets

SYSTEMS

- Parts
- Kinds
- Uses
- Origin

ORGANISMS

- Structure
- Phyla
- Habitat
- Life requirements
- Physiology

USING THE BRANCHING DIAGRAM

RATIONALE FOR BRANCHING ACTIVITIES

Branching diagrams are useful for recording information about class and subclasses, hierarchical relationships, family trees, and complex systems, allowing elaborate systems of relationship to be represented visually.

This diagram, like others in this series, prompts students to depict complex relationships as they read ideas in texts, newspapers, and magazines. In this way students learn the content and the technique simultaneously. Many textbooks give students the completed diagram as a quick and effective means of illustrating complex relationships. However, providing the completed diagram for the learner does not offer the student the opportunity to recognize complex relationships in a passage without assistance. A student who completes the diagram independently is more likely to learn to identify complex relationships in a passage.

Use the branching diagram to depict many subdivisions or sub-classes of a broader category. Use the central idea graph to describe individual terms or categories which are not further subdivided.

USE BRANCHING DIAGRAMS TO:

- Break categories into smaller classes.
- Depict family trees and hierarchical relationships.
- Illustrate systems.

TO USE THE BRANCHING DIAGRAM:

Note: The master graphs contain two or three subdivided classes. To create additional master graphs with a different number of subdivisions, use the blank graph most similar to what you need (having the correct number of subdivisions in the correct locations). Use correction fluid to white out unneeded labels, branches, or boxes. Draw additional branches and boxes by tracing others.

1. Start with the broadest category and the classes into which it can be sorted.

2. Draw a branching diagram, labeling boxes containing the broad category.

3. Determine the characteristic for dividing each class of the broad category.

4. Determine the number of subclasses required by that division.

5. Draw and label each subclass of each category.

6. Determine whether each class can be subdivided and draw appropriate branches.

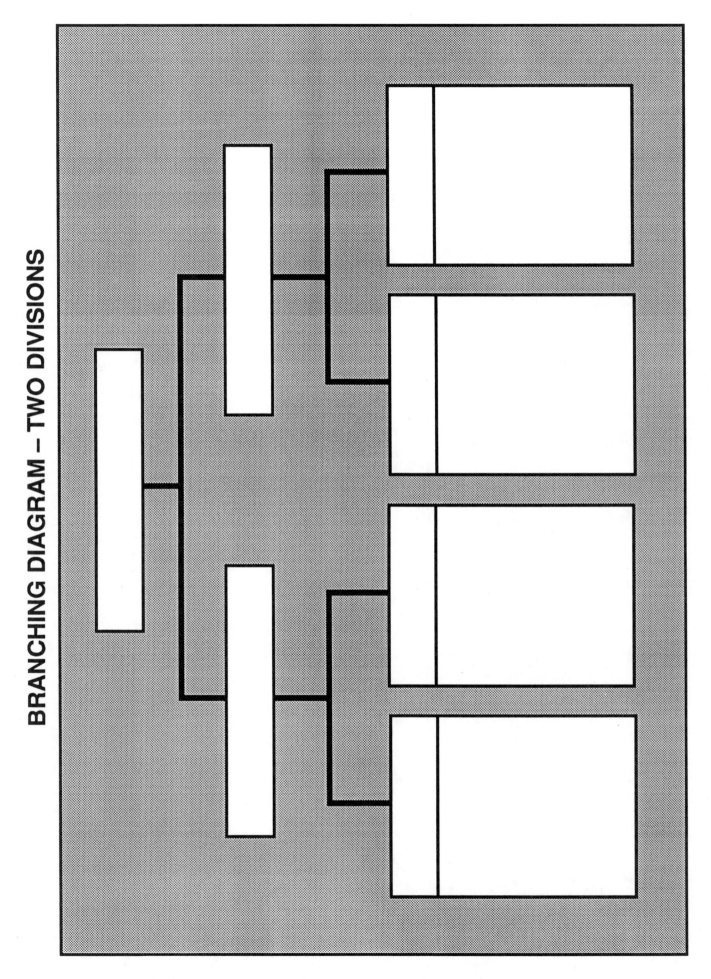

BRANCHING DIAGRAM – TWO DIVISIONS

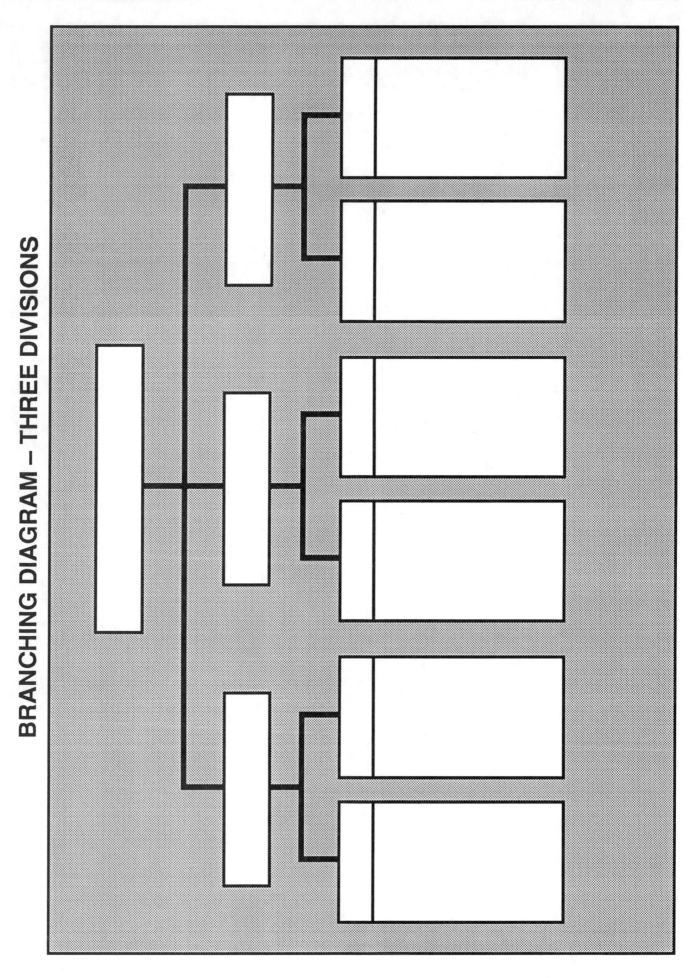

BRANCHING DIAGRAM – THREE DIVISIONS

CLASS RELATIONSHIPS DIAGRAMS

LOGICAL REASONING CONCEPTS

- Connectives (*and, or, not,* and *if…then*)
- Quantifiers (*all, none,* and *some*)

CLASS RELATIONSHIPS

- *Includes* or *is included in*
- *Some…are*
- *No (none)…are*

USE CLASS RELATIONSHIPS DIAGRAMS TO ILLUSTRATE

COMPARISON RELATIONSHIPS

- People
- Places
- Things
- Organisms

MATHEMATICAL CONCEPTS

- Factoring
- Types of polygons

USING THE CLASS RELATIONSHIP DIAGRAM

RATIONALE FOR CLASS RELATIONSHIP ACTIVITIES

Class relationship diagrams, also called Venn diagrams or Euler circles, are used to illustrate the relationship between or among classes. These diagrams are also used to show the union of two sets, to demonstrate the meaning of logic connectives ("and," "or," "not," and "if...then") and to depict class membership in arguments involving class logic.

Using class relationship diagrams involves two steps. First, use the diagram to illustrate relationships in content (from a passage to a diagram). Then, practice translating the relationship into English sentences using the logic connectives "and," "or," "not," and "if...then," and the logic quantifiers "all," "some," and "none."

USE THE CLASS RELATIONSHIP DIAGRAM TO:

- Depict class membership.
- Depict class logic arguments.
- Depict the union of two or more sets.
- Depict comparison and or contrast of two things, organisms, people, or ideas.

TO USE CLASS RELATIONSHIP DIAGRAMS:

1. Clarify the characteristics of the compared sets .
2. Decide which type of class-relationship diagram illustrates the relationship of the compared sets.

RELATIONSHIPS INVOLVING TWO CLASSES

Bull's Eye Diagram

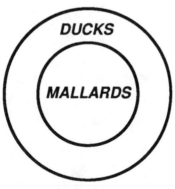

a. If one class includes or is included in another class, then a "bull's eye" diagram expresses that relationship. For example, compare the class "mallards" to the class "ducks," you would select a "bull's eye" diagram, using the outer circle to represent "ducks" and the inner circle to represent "mallards." This relationship can be stated, "All mallards are ducks."

b. If some, but not all, members of one class are also members of another, then an overlapping diagram expresses that relationship. For example: to compare the classes "wild birds" to the class "ducks," you would select an overlapping diagram, using one circle to represent "wild birds" and the other to represent "ducks". This relationship can be stated many ways: "Some ducks are wild birds." "Some wild birds are ducks." "Some ducks are not wild birds." "Some wild birds are not ducks."

Overlapping Diagram

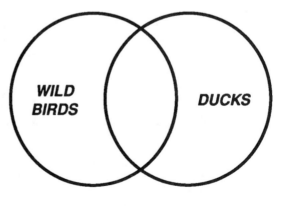

Disjoint Set Diagram

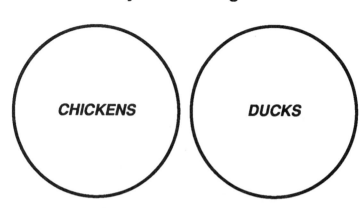

c. If no members of one class are members of another, then a disjoint set diagram illustrates that relationship. For example: to compare the class "chickens" with the class "ducks," you would select a disjoint set diagram. One circle represents the class "chickens" and the other represents the class "ducks." This relationship can be stated, "No ducks are chickens" or "No chickens are ducks."

RELATIONSHIPS INVOLVING THREE CLASSES

d. Complex "bull's eye" diagrams are used to depict class arguments. For example:
   All ducks are wild birds.
   All mallards are ducks.
   Therefore, all mallards are wild birds.
To illustrate this argument, use a "bull's eye" diagram to show that all mallards must be included in the larger class "wild birds."

Complex Bull's Eye Diagram

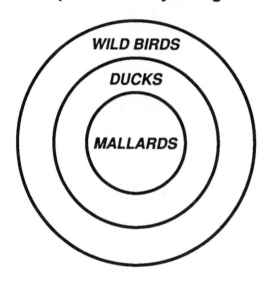

Overlapping Sets of Three Classes

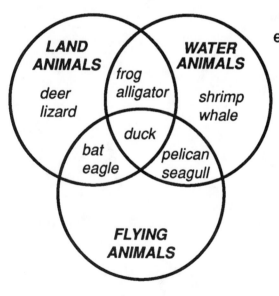

e. A three-set overlapping diagram expresses relationships between and among three classes if some, but not all, members of one class are members of one or both of the others. For example: to depict the classes "land animals," "water animals," and "flying animals," you would use the three-set diagram to show characteristics of the animals. A duck is described as a land animal **and** a water animal **and** a flying animal.

INCLUDES OR IS INCLUDED IN

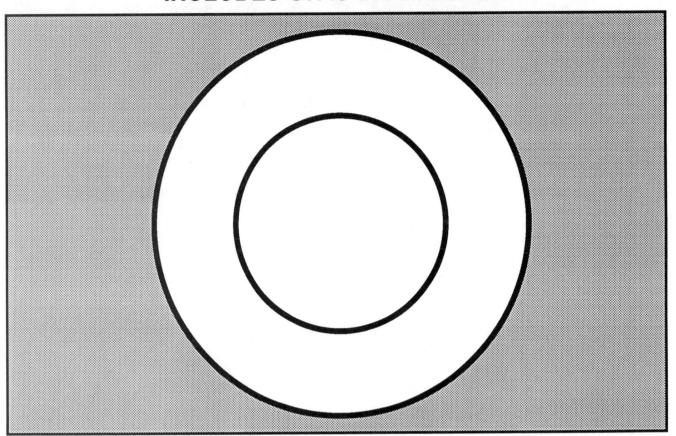

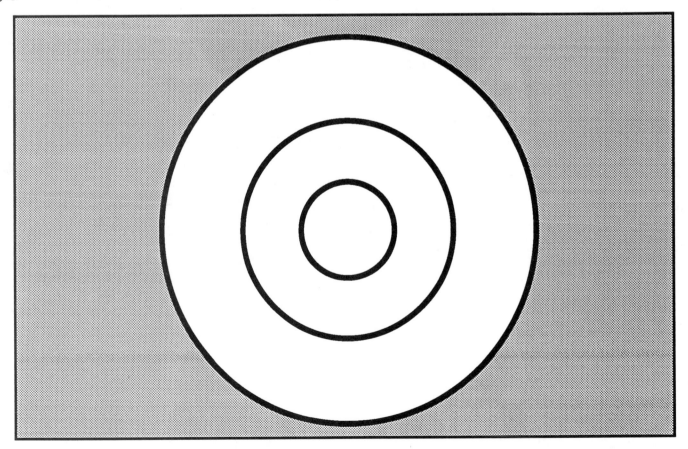

INCLUDES OR IS INCLUDED IN

OVERLAPPING CLASSES –"SOME . . . ARE"

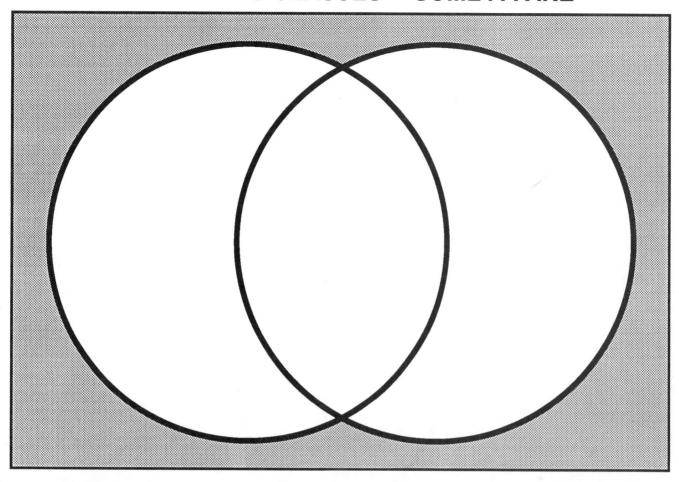

DISJOINT CLASSES –"IS SEPARATE FROM"

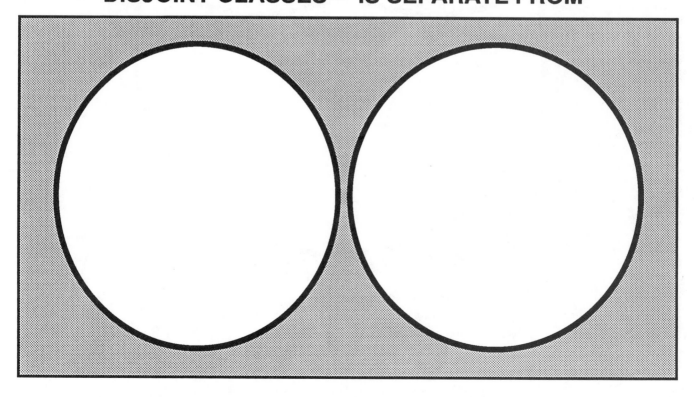

OVERLAPPING CLASSES – THREE CLASSES

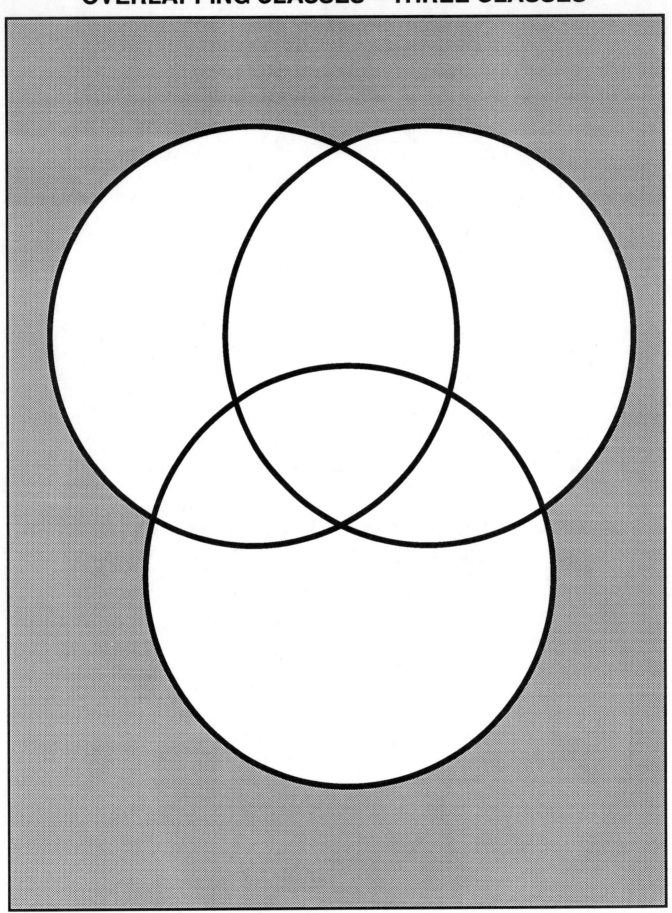

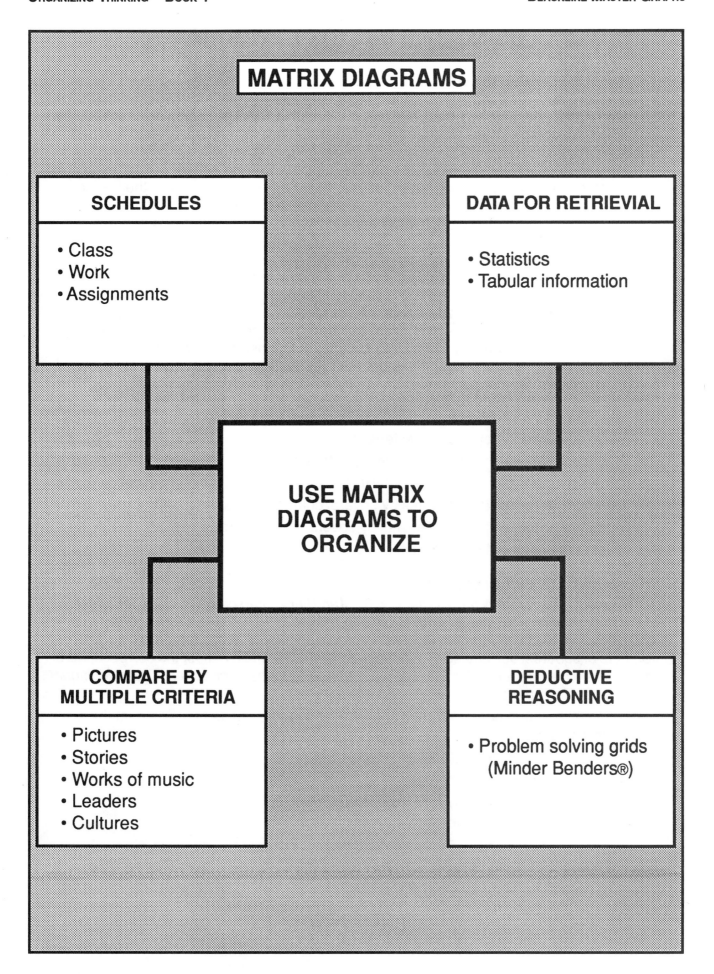

USING THE MATRIX DIAGRAM

RATIONALE FOR MATRIX ACTIVITIES

Matrix diagrams are used to record and cross-reference information by two characteristics. Common matrices include bus, train, and airline schedules, mileage charts, class schedules, and statistical reports. These diagrams allow data to be quickly and easily read and understood.

Matrix diagrams allow students to organize information from written passages and to record inferences from pictures, passages, or artifacts. The learner may then examine significant similarities and differences and draw defensible conclusions from the information. The *matrix diagram* is also useful when applying the same criteria to compare several pictures, pieces of music, stories, historical events, or leaders.

Students may use a completed *matrix diagram* as a guide to prepare a descriptive speech or paper. The debate lessons include the use of a matrix to organize claims and evidence for debate arguments.

In most of the lessons in this handbook, students complete a *matrix diagram* from information given in written passages. Many text books give students the completed matrix, a quick and effective means of illustrating complex relationships. However, providing the completed diagram for the learner does not offer the student the opportunity to recognize complex relationships independently.

USE MATRIX DIAGRAMS TO:

- Record information by two characteristics.
- Report information in schedules, charts, or tables.
- Organize information in order to draw inferences or to form generalizations.
- Compare literary or artistic works by several characteristics.
- Compare historical figures or events by several characteristics.
- Illustrate number patterns or functions.

TO USE THE MATRIX DIAGRAM:

The matrix diagram may have as many vertical and horizontal squares as the characteristics of the data require. The master graphs contain a three-by-three and a four-by-four matrix, since these are the most common formats. To create additional diagrams containing different numbers of squares, use copies of master graphs which contain almost the correct number of squares. Use correction fluid to white out unneeded labels, or boxes. Draw additional boxes by tracing others.

1. Determine the number of horizontal and vertical squares needed to represent the concepts and criteria.

2. Label each row and column.

3. Record information in each square.

4. Draw comparisons or conclusions from the information.

MATRIX DIAGRAM – 3 x 3

	_____	_____	_____
_____			
_____			
_____			

MATRIX DIAGRAM – 4 x 4

MATRIX DIAGRAM – 4 x 4

CHAPTER 2 — LANGUAGE ARTS LESSONS

DESCRIBING SIZE (matrix chart)		NOUNS AND VERBS (compare and contrast diagram)
	STATEMENTS AND QUESTIONS (compare and contrast diagram)	
PARTS OF SPEECH (branching diagram)		NEWSPAPERS AND MAGAZINES (compare and contrast diagram)
	HISTORY OR FICTION? (class relationships diagram)	
TYPES OF BOOKS (flowchart)		AESOP'S FABLES (flowchart)
	CHARLOTTE'S WEB DESCRIBING A CHARACTER (central idea graph)	
CHARLOTTE'S WEB DRAWING INFERENCES (matrix chart)		CHARLOTTE'S WEB REASONS AND CONCLUSIONS (central idea graph, arch diagram)
	CHARLOTTE'S WEB DESCRIBING THE PLOT (transitive order graph)	
DESCRIBING A STORY (central idea graph)		"THE STEAM SHOVEL" (contrast graph)
	DESCRIBING A GOOD SPEECH (branching diagram)	
I'M LISTENING (matrix chart)		DESCRIBING CLASS RELATIONSHIPS (class relationships diagram)
	MAIN IDEA AND SUPPORTING DETAILS (central idea graph, arch diagram)	

DESCRIBING SIZE

THINKING SKILL: Cross-classification.

CONTENT OBJECTIVE: Using the matrix, students will identify words which describe small, medium, and large buildings, containers, and fish.

DISCUSSION: TECHNIQUE—Use a transparency of the matrix to record student responses as the class reviews accurate definitions. Ask each student reporting an answer to use the word in a sentence. For young students or language-limited students, cut out an enlarged and hand-colored copy of the items in the picture dictionary on pages 53 and 54 to create a bulletin board display of the completed matrix. Affix the pictures in the appropriate boxes of the matrix. Use actual objects to describe and compare container size.

DIALOGUE—Ask students to identify what type of object should go in each cell of the matrix. Use that criterion to search the choice list for appropriate examples.

What kind of word should we list in the first box? (small building) **Which words on the list describe small buildings?** (cabin, hut, and shed)

This process encourages students to look systematically for significant characteristics rather than guessing or randomly writing words in the cells.

You may use this opportunity to identify students' knowledge of size connotations in common words. Encourage students to add additional terms in each category to describe small, medium, and large buildings, containers, and fish.

Ask students to identify other objects, actions, or characteristics for which size is significant. Examples may include: time or weight units of measure, adjectives or adverbs describing relative quantity, value of money, or rates of speed. For additional examples of comparing terms by degree of meaning, see the *Building Thinking Skills®* series.

Size may be a significant characteristic in conveying meaning. Not understanding size may result in humorous or misleading explanations.

Why is it important that we know the size of something to picture it in our minds and describe it to other people accurately? Give an example of a funny or unfortunate mistake that might occur if you used the wrong size term. (Example: suppose a mother said, "Drink your gallon of milk before you leave the table.")

Take this opportunity to compare a cup, a pint, a quart, and a gallon. (Note that the sizes in fluid measures for a cup, pint, quart, gallon, and barrel are printed on the pictures.) Use actual concrete objects whenever possible so students can gain tactile appreciation of size differences. Young students may not be able to visualize and distinguish between standard units of volume (cup, pint, quart, and gallon) and words used to describe large or small volumes which may vary in volume (glass, pitcher, and tub). Students may not realize that a "cup" may refer to an eight fluid ounce measuring cup or to the quantity in another container which holds that same volume. Children may classify a gallon as either an average or large container depending on their ability to lift a gallon of milk. Compared to a barrel, however, a gallon is an average container.

Identify films, stories or poems in which size is a key factor in its appeal ("The Three Bears," "Jack and the Beanstalk," *Honey I Shrunk the Kids, Alice in Wonderland.*)

RESULT—In order to picture a building, a container, or a fish accurately, we must understand its size compared to similar things.

WRITING EXTENSION

- **Write a short story that contains a large building, a large container, or a large fish. Rewrite the story using a small building, a small container, or a small fish. How does your story seem different when you change the size? How do the words you used to describe large things change when you describe small things?**

THINKING ABOUT THINKING

- **How did using the diagram help you understand the correct terms for different sizes?**
- **Suggest another lesson in which using a diagram like this would help you understand what you are learning.**
- **Design another diagram that would help you picture the relative size of objects.** (Suggestion: Students may find that the transitive order diagram illustrates degree in objects, actions, or characteristics. A transitive order diagram has been provided for the volume comparison.)

SIMILAR LANGUAGE ARTS LESSONS

- To illustrate works of fiction and nonfiction, types of periodicals, and types of media.
- To illustrate parts of speech, plural and singular forms.
- To solve deductive reasoning problems (*Mind Benders*®).
- To classify punctuation or spelling rules.

DESCRIBING SIZE

DIRECTIONS: Write each word in the box which best describes it.

> apartment building, barrel, cabin, cup, fast-food restaurant,
> gallon, glass, guppy, house, hut, laundromat, minnow,
> perch, pint, quart, school, shark, shed, shopping center,
> supermarket, trout, tuna

	building	container	fish
small	small building cabin hut shed	small container cup glass pint	small fish guppy minnow
average size	average size building fast-food restaurant laundromat house	average size container quart gallon	average size fish perch trout
large	large building apartment building school shopping center supermarket	large container barrel	large fish shark tuna

PICTURE DICTIONARY

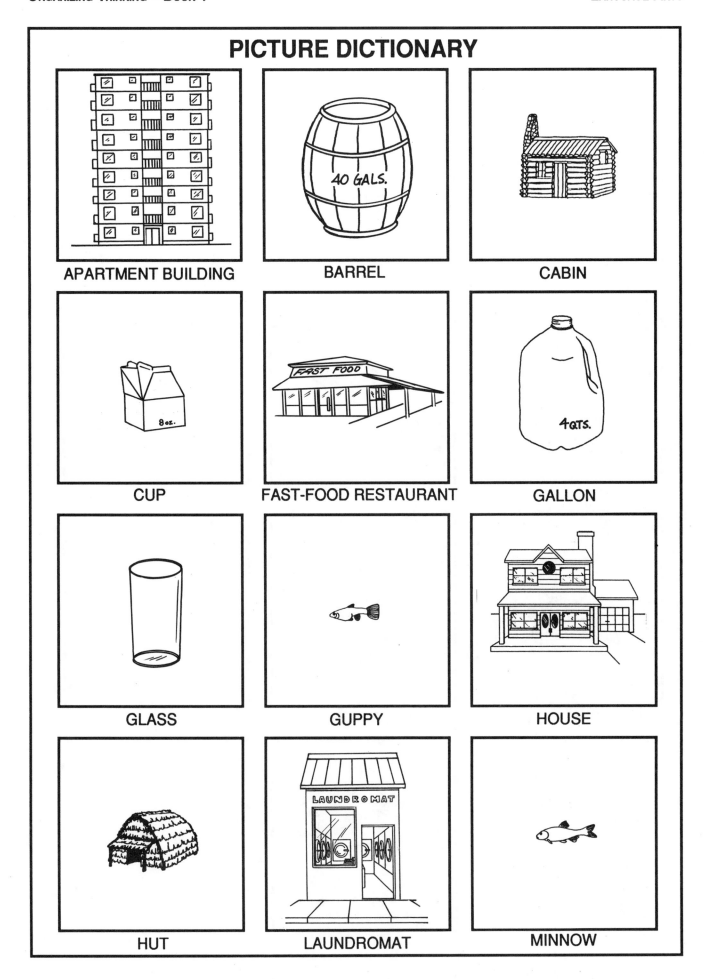

APARTMENT BUILDING   BARREL   CABIN

CUP   FAST-FOOD RESTAURANT   GALLON

GLASS   GUPPY   HOUSE

HUT   LAUNDROMAT   MINNOW

PICTURE DICTIONARY

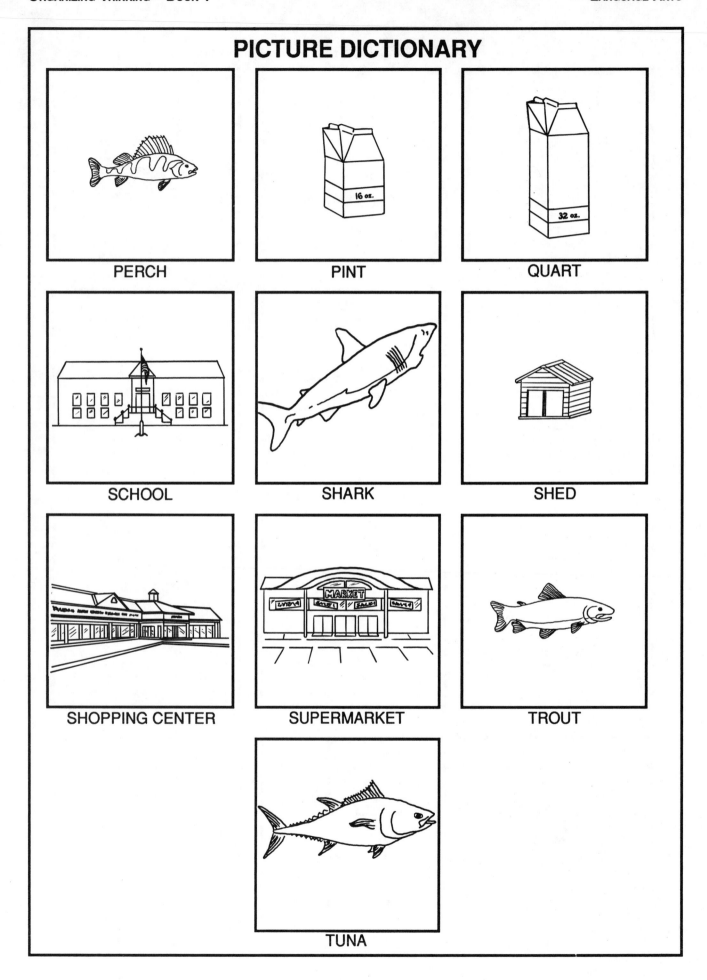

PERCH

PINT

QUART

SCHOOL

SHARK

SHED

SHOPPING CENTER

SUPERMARKET

TROUT

TUNA

NOUNS AND VERBS

THINKING SKILL: Compare and contrast

CONTENT OBJECTIVE: Students will use the compare and contrast diagram to differentiate between nouns and verbs.

DISCUSSION: TECHNIQUE—Use the transparency of the diagram to record student responses regarding nouns and verbs. Encourage your students to identify additional similarities or differences.

DIALOGUE—As students report differences between nouns and verbs, discuss those differences by naming the quality that is different. Establish this pattern: "**With regard to** (quality), (item one and its distinction), **but** (item two and its distinction)." For example,

"**With regard to what they tell, nouns name people, places, or things, but verbs name actions.**"

Help students understand why it is important to be able to identify nouns and verbs.

Why is it important to find the nouns and verbs in a sentence? (To check to see that one has written a complete sentence with verbs which have the right number and tense; to be sure that the reader understands what pronouns like "it," "they," or "you" refer to.)

RESULT— Knowing the difference between nouns and verbs helps a writer decide whether a sentence is complete and whether the ideas in a sentence are clear.

WRITING EXTENSION
• **Describe how nouns and verbs are alike and how they are different.**
• **Why is it important to find nouns and verbs in a sentence?**

THINKING ABOUT THINKING
• **How did using the diagram help you understand the differences between nouns and verbs? How did it help you organize your thoughts before you began to write?**
• **Suggest another lesson in which comparing and contrasting would help you understand what you are learning.**
• **Design another diagram that would help you distinguish between nouns and verbs.** (Students may find that the overlapping classes diagram depicts the differences between nouns and verbs easily.

SIMILAR LANGUAGE ARTS LESSONS
• To compare reality and fantasy, types of books, types of periodicals or media.
• To compare types of sentences, plural and singular forms, or parts of speech.
• To compare characters or plots between stories or plays.
• To clarify terms in vocabulary enrichment lessons (synonyms and antonyms).

NOUNS AND VERBS

DIRECTIONS: **Use the diagram to show how nouns and verbs are alike and how they are different.**

Nouns and verbs are kinds of words that appear in sentences. Nouns name people, places, things, or ideas. Verbs name the action in a sentence. Verbs may describe actions in the past, present, or future. Both nouns and verbs may change spelling to describe more than one.

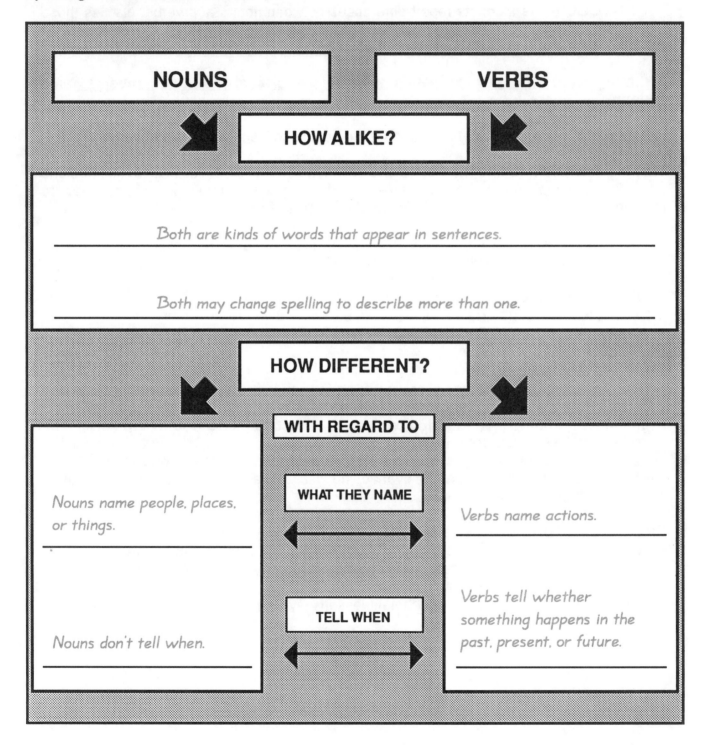

NOUNS

VERBS

HOW ALIKE?

Both are kinds of words that appear in sentences.

Both may change spelling to describe more than one.

HOW DIFFERENT?

WITH REGARD TO

WHAT THEY NAME

Nouns name people, places, or things.

Verbs name actions.

TELL WHEN

Nouns don't tell when.

Verbs tell whether something happens in the past, present, or future.

STATEMENTS AND QUESTIONS

THINKING SKILL: Compare and contrast

CONTENT OBJECTIVE: Students will use the compare and contrast diagram to differentiate between statements and questions.

DISCUSSION: TECHNIQUE—Use a transparency of the diagram to record student responses regarding statements and questions. Encourage students to identify additional similarities or differences.

DIALOGUE—As students report differences between statements and questions, discuss those differences by naming the quality that is different. Establish this pattern: **"With regard to** (quality) , (item one and its distinction), **but** (item two and its distinction)." For example,

"With regard to what they are used for, statements give information, but questions ask for information."

Distinguishing the word patterns and punctuation in statements and questions alerts the listener or reader to think differently. Knowing the difference tells the listener or reader whether to receive, evaluate, or express information. Ask students for classroom examples of statements and questions. Identify situations in which someone was confused because that person believed that a statement was a question or vice versa.

Why is it important to know whether a sentence is a statement or a question? (To know whether the speaker is giving or asking for information. Sometimes a speaker asks a question in the form of a statement. For example, "I won the race?" or "You want to watch television?" Either the tone of a speaker's voice or a writer's use of a question mark tells the listener or reader whether the sentence is a question or a statement.)

RESULT—Being able to recognize written punctuation, sentence structure, and/or voice tones alerts the reader or listener as to whether s/he should receive, evaluate, or express information.

WRITING EXTENSION
- **Describe how statements and questions are alike and how they are different.**
- **Why is it important to know the difference between statements and questions?**

THINKING ABOUT THINKING
- **How did using the diagram help you understand the differences between statements and questions? How did it help you organize your thoughts before you began to write?**
- **Suggest another lesson in which comparing and contrasting would help you understand what you are learning.**
- **Design another diagram that would help you distinguish between statements and questions.** (Students may find that the overlapping classes diagram depicts the difference between statements and questions easily.)

SIMILAR LANGUAGE ARTS LESSONS
- To compare reality and fantasy, types of nonfiction, types of periodicals or media.
- To compare types of sentences, plural and singular forms, or parts of speech.
- To compare characters or plots between stories or plays.
- To clarify terms in vocabulary enrichment lessons (synonyms and antonyms).

STATEMENTS AND QUESTIONS

DIRECTIONS: Use the diagram to show how statements and questions are alike and how they are different.

Statements and questions are kinds of sentences and tell whole thoughts. Both contain a subject and a verb and end with a punctuation mark. Both are used to give or get information. Paragraphs can have both.

Statements give information about people, places, things, or ideas. They always end with a period. The whole verb usually follows the subject; for example, "The motor is running."

Questions ask for information about people, places, things, or ideas. They always end with a question mark. The subject usually comes between parts of the verb; for example, "Is the motor running?"

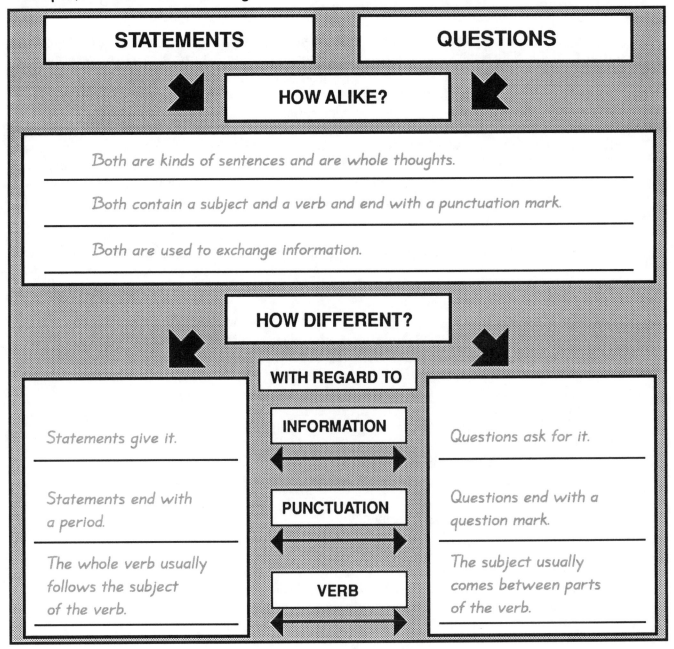

STATEMENTS		QUESTIONS

HOW ALIKE?

Both are kinds of sentences and are whole thoughts.

Both contain a subject and a verb and end with a punctuation mark.

Both are used to exchange information.

HOW DIFFERENT?

WITH REGARD TO

	INFORMATION	
Statements give it.		Questions ask for it.
Statements end with a period.	**PUNCTUATION**	Questions end with a question mark.
The whole verb usually follows the subject of the verb.	**VERB**	The subject usually comes between parts of the verb.

© 1992 CRITICAL THINKING PRESS & SOFTWARE • P.O. Box 448, Pacific Grove, CA 93950

PARTS OF SPEECH

NOTE: This lesson is intended to review an instructional unit on these parts of speech. It presents too much information to be used as an introductory lesson.

THINKING SKILL: Hierarchical classification

CONTENT OBJECTIVE: Students will use the branching diagram to identify types of nouns, verbs, and adjectives.

DISCUSSION: TECHNIQUE—Use a transparency of the branching diagram to record student responses as the class reviews three parts of speech. In this lesson the branching diagram is used to illustrate classes and subclasses of three parts of speech. Encourage your students to use the diagram as a memory tool to review for a test.

Extend this lesson by creating a poster, flannel board, easel, or bulletin board display. Draw the diagram of the title and first row (nouns, adjectives, and verbs). Use a different color for labeling each part of speech. As the various parts of speech are explained over several sessions, add the appropriate label to the diagram, forming a visual summary of the unit. Add common words to each category.

DIALOGUE—Encourage students to describe the significant characteristic by which each category is subdivided.

How do we describe different kinds of nouns? (Common nouns describe general categories; proper nouns describe names of specific people, places, or things.) **What characteristic is being described by "common" or "proper"?** (Whether the noun describes a group or an individual.)

RESULT— Parts of speech have different functions and forms. Clarifying functions and forms is the key to understanding, identifying, and remembering parts of speech.

WRITING EXTENSION
• **Describe nouns, verbs, and adjectives and explain their use.**

THINKING ABOUT THINKING
• **How did using the diagram help you understand nouns, verbs, and adjectives clearly? How did using it help you remember the information more accurately?**
• **Suggest another lesson in which using a diagram like this would help you understand what you are learning.**
• **Design another diagram that would help you understand and remember the parts of speech.**

SIMILAR LANGUAGE ARTS LESSONS
• To illustrate class/subclass relationships: parts of speech, types of literature, types of books or reference sources.
• To illustrate headings and subheadings in an outline.
• To depict the family relationships of kings, mythological characters, or characters in books or plays.

PARTS OF SPEECH

DIRECTIONS: Read the passage carefully to identify parts of speech. Record the information on the diagram.

Our English language has different kinds of words. These are called parts of speech. We find three **parts of speech** in most sentences—nouns, verbs, and adjectives. **Nouns** are words which name people, places, or things. There are two types of nouns: **common** nouns and **proper** nouns. For example, "dog" is a common noun, "Rover" is a proper noun. Common nouns name types of objects and are not capitalized. Proper nouns name a specific item and are always capitalized.

Verbs are words which describe action or link words in the predicate back to the subject. There are two types of verbs—**action** verbs and **passive** verbs. Action verbs describe something that the subject of the sentence does, such as, "I told the story." Passive verbs describe something that is done to the subject of the sentence, "I was told the story."

Adjectives are words used to describe nouns or to make them more definite. There are several kinds of adjectives:

Descriptive adjectives tell the color, size of shape of nouns. For example, a "dish" can be described as a "red" dish, a "round" dish, a "large" dish, or a "large, red, round" dish.

Article adjectives call attention to the noun. For example, "bike" refers to any bike, but "the" bike describes only one particular bike. "The" is an article adjective.

Demonstrative adjectives tell which one or ones, such as "that" bike, "these" bikes, "this" bike, and "those" bikes.

Number adjectives tell how many, such as a "few" bikes, "lots" of bikes, or "twenty" bikes.

Possessive adjectives tell whose, for example, "my" bike, "your" bike, "his" bike, or "their" bike.

© 1992 CRITICAL THINKING PRESS & SOFTWARE • P.O. Box 448, Pacific Grove, CA 93950

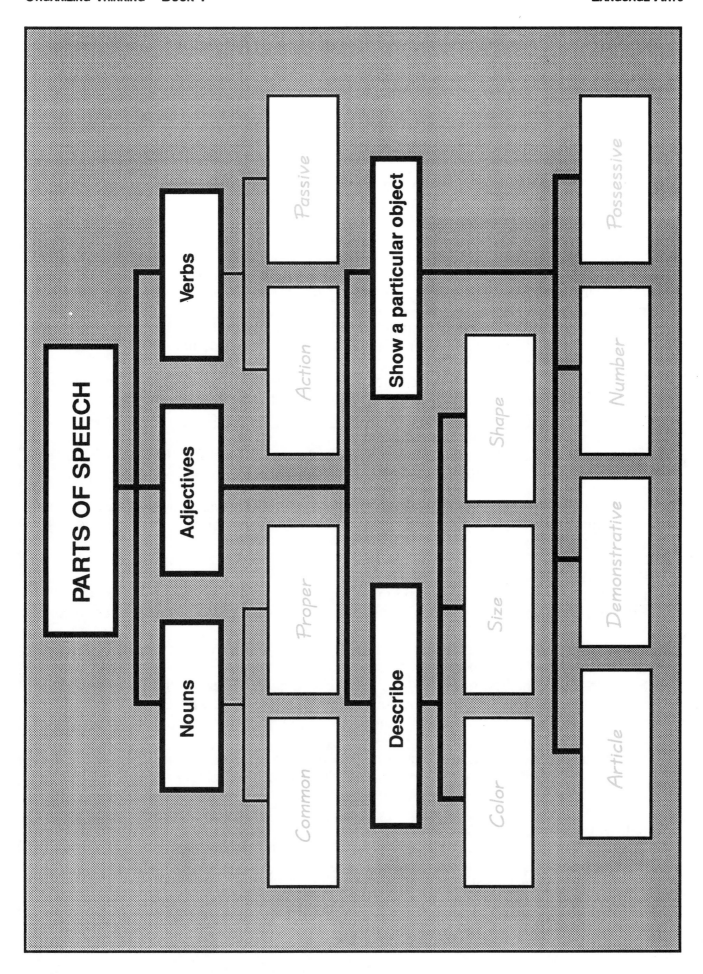

NEWSPAPERS AND MAGAZINES

THINKING SKILL: Compare and contrast

CONTENT OBJECTIVE: Students will use the compare and contrast diagram to differentiate between newspapers and magazines.

DISCUSSION: TECHNIQUE—Use the transparency of the diagram to record student responses regarding newspapers and magazines. Encourage your students to identify additional similarities or differences.

What are some other similarities and differences between magazines and newspapers? (Both newspapers and magazines are less expensive than books. Both can be delivered to homes. Magazines usually contain more colored pictures than newspapers. Magazines often appeal to one interest; newspapers contain different sections for different interests. Newspapers report the news and some general information. Most magazines provide information; only a few report news. Newspapers contain comic strips; some magazines contain cartoons.)

DIALOGUE—As students report differences between newspapers and magazines, discuss those differences by naming the quality that is different. Establish this pattern: **"With regard to** (quality), (item one and its distinction), **but** (item two and its distinction)." For example,

"With regard to size, newspapers are usually printed on large sheets of paper, but magazines are usually printer on smaller sheets of paper."

RESULT—The purpose of newspapers is to report the news. They cost less and are printed often. The purpose of magazines is to provide information about special interests. They cost more and are printed less often.

WRITING EXTENSION
- **Describe how newspapers and magazines are alike and how they are different.**
- **How do you decide whether a newspaper or a magazine will give you better information?**

THINKING ABOUT THINKING
- **How did using the diagram help you understand newspapers and magazines? How did it help you organize your thoughts before you began to write?**
- **Suggest another lesson in which comparing and contrasting would help you understand what you are learning.**
- **Design another diagram that would help you distinguish between newspapers and magazines.** (Students may find that the overlapping classes diagram easily depicts the differences between newspapers and magazines.)

SIMILAR LANGUAGE ARTS LESSONS
- To compare reality and fantasy, types of nonfiction, types of periodicals, types of media.
- To compare types of sentences or parts of speech.
- To compare characters or plots between stories.

NEWSPAPERS AND MAGAZINES

DIRECTIONS: Use the diagram to show how newspapers and magazines are alike and how they are different.

People read both newspapers and magazines to get information. Both contain advertisements which help pay for the cost of making them. Both are sold at newsstands and are printed at regular times—every day, every week, every month, or every few months.

Newspapers are printed on large sheets; magazines are usually printed on smaller sheets. Newspapers cost less than magazines. Newspapers are usually printed every day or every week; magazines are usually printed once a week or once a month.

NEWSPAPERS AND MAGAZINES

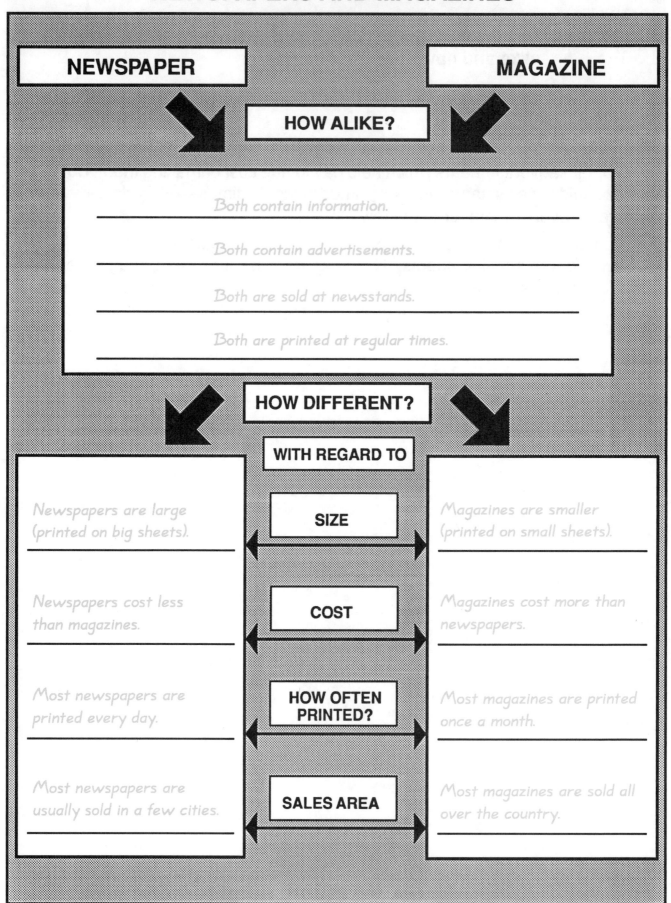

NEWSPAPER

MAGAZINE

HOW ALIKE?

Both contain information.

Both contain advertisements.

Both are sold at newsstands.

Both are printed at regular times.

HOW DIFFERENT?

WITH REGARD TO

SIZE

Newspapers are large (printed on big sheets).

Magazines are smaller (printed on small sheets).

COST

Newspapers cost less than magazines.

Magazines cost more than newspapers.

HOW OFTEN PRINTED?

Most newspapers are printed every day.

Most magazines are printed once a month.

SALES AREA

Most newspapers are usually sold in a few cities.

Most magazines are sold all over the country.

HISTORY OR FICTION?

THINKING SKILL: Class relationships

CONTENT OBJECTIVE: Students will use a class relationship graph to classify types of books as history, fiction, or both.

DISCUSSION: TECHNIQUE—Use a transparency of the class relationship graph to record responses as students discuss each type of book.
DIALOGUE—Encourage your students to describe these relationships using "some," "all," "and," and "not." Sample translations of the diagram using logic quantifiers include:

All comic books are fictional. (Except for instructional comic books.) **All diaries are historical, and not fictional. All fairy tales are fictional, and not historical. All history textbooks are historical, and not fictional. All legends are somewhat historical and somewhat fictional. All myths are fictional, and not historical.**

Discuss how a legend and a myth are alike and how they are different. The Funk and Wagnall's *Standard Dictionary* describes a legend as "an unauthenticated story from earlier times, preserved by tradition and popularly thought to be historical." A myth is "a traditional story focusing on the deeds of gods or heroes, often in explanation of some natural phenomenon." A myth makes no claim to be an historical account; a legend, though embellished, is believed to represent some historical occurrence. For example, legends about Johnny Appleseed are rooted in history, but myths, such as "Pandora's Box," are fictional. Identify examples of each type of story from reading assignments.
Examine the value and appeal of historical novels, such as *Johnny Appleseed, Ben and Me,* or *Little House on the Prairie.*

How does their historical setting add to the story? How does the appeal of the story encourage us to know more about the historical event? How are our purposes in reading history, historical novels, and general fiction different? Why is the information in history books more reliable than information in fiction?

RESULTS—Some types of stories do not fit neatly into history or fiction. The information in history books is more reliable than information in fiction, legends, or historical novels.

WRITING EXTENSION
• **How does a reader decide whether a book is history or fiction?**
• **What are some stories that don't fit clearly in either history or fiction?**

THINKING ABOUT THINKING
• **Why does it matter to the reader whether a story is history or fiction?**
• **Design another graphic organizer to distinguish between history and fiction.** (The compare and contrast graph depicts the difference between history and fiction.)
• **How does the graph help you understand how to use "some," "all," "and," and "no"? Identify another example in which it is important to use these terms correctly.**

SIMILAR LANGUAGE ARTS LESSONS
• To compare characters within or between novels, short stories, or plays.
• To illustrate class relationships in an article, report, or presentation.

HISTORY OR FICTION?

DIRECTIONS: Use the diagram to classify the following kinds of stories.

comic book, diary of a president, fairy tale, historical novel, history textbook, legend, myth

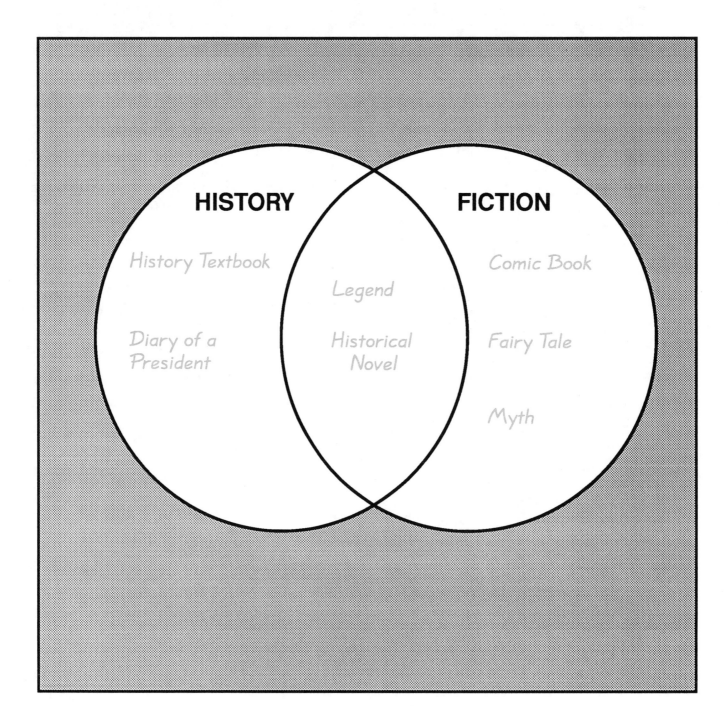

TYPES OF BOOKS

THINKING SKILL: Classification

CONTENT OBJECTIVE: Students will use a branching diagram to identify types of books by their distinguishing characteristics.

DISCUSSION: TECHNIQUE—Use a transparency of the branching diagram to record responses as students sort types of books. To simulate the process in the library, ask students to write the titles they might like to read for each type of book. Students may use their selections as a guide for future reading.

DIALOGUE—This lesson clarifies the significant characteristics of different types of books. Discussion of the answers should model the process on the flowchart.

If you need short facts about a real topic, which types of books on our list provide that? (dictionaries, encyclopedias) **If you need a broader background about real people's lives, what kinds of books do you need?** (biographies) **What real things other than people might you need information about?** (places, objects, systems, organisms, or ideas)

You may take this opportunity to introduce additional language terms which are featured in this lesson. (fiction, nonfiction)

Discuss nonfiction books that are about neither people nor places; e.g., sports, personal appearance and development, hobbies, computers, or social sciences.

RESULTS—By knowing characteristics of books we like to read and other kinds of books that are similar, we can broaden our book selections by reading new kinds of books.

WRITING EXTENSION
• **Describe the reasons that people use for selecting books.**

THINKING ABOUT THINKING
• **Why is it important to read many kinds of books?**
• **What other decisions can be pictured this way?**
• **How did using the flowchart help you find different types of books in the library?**

SIMILAR LANGUAGE ARTS LESSONS
• To depict the steps in independent study or the preparation of a writing assignment.
• To depict rules of punctuation, spelling, grammar, or capitalization.

TYPES OF BOOKS

DIRECTIONS: In each rectangle of the branching diagram, write the type(s) of books which belong in that category. To save space, use the abbreviation if you like.

Adventure (Ad)   Plays (Pl)
Biographies (Bio)   Poetry (Pty)
Encyclopedias (En)   Science (S)
Fantasy (Fa)   Science Fiction (SF)
History (Hi)   Travel (Trv)

© 1992 CRITICAL THINKING PRESS & SOFTWARE • P.O. Box 448, Pacific Grove, CA 93950

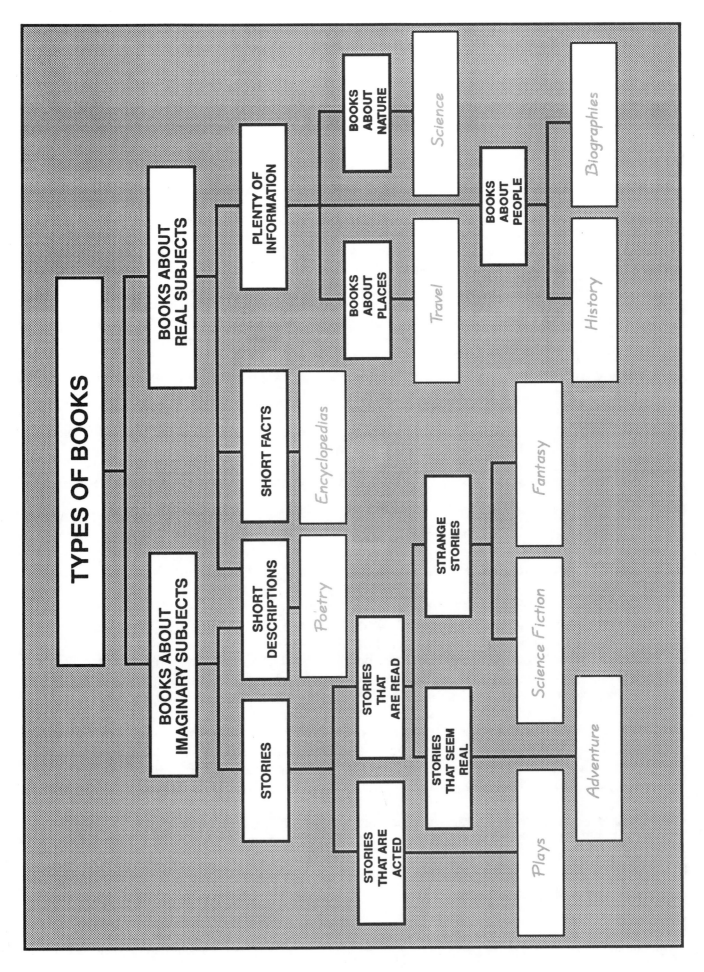

AESOP'S FABLES

THINKING SKILL: Identifying reasons, decisions, results, and conclusions in parallel plots; generalizing a moral.

CONTENT OBJECTIVE: Students will use the parallel flowchart to depict similar themes, reasons, decisions, results, and conclusions in two fables.

DISCUSSION: TECHNIQUE—Use a transparency of the parallel flowchart to record significant features of two Aesop's fables: similar themes, reasons, decisions, results, and conclusions. Because fables are short, simple, interesting to children, and contain significant moral teachings, they are a valuable source for the teaching of critical thinking, moral values, and decision making to elementary students.

This activity demonstrates the comparison of two literary works. By analyzing two stories with similar conflicts and conclusions, students examine two samples, instead of drawing inferences from one story. Students find it interesting that the same themes and conclusions can be present in stories that have different characters and plots. Students may need an explanation of the significance of conflict or theme in a story.

DIALOGUE—Encourage students to identify other *Aesop's Fables* in which greed leads the main character to lose what he has. (Examples: "The Goose That Laid the Golden Egg," "The Lion and the Hare," and "The Tortoise and the Eagle.") Encourage students to find parallel conflicts, plots, and conclusions in other *Aesop's Fables*. Examples of fables which have parallel plots leading to the same moral lesson include:

Honesty is the best policy: "Mercury and the Woodman" and "The Wolf in Sheep's Clothing."

Pride goes before a fall: "Mice and the Weasels," "The Eagles and the Cock," "The Ass Carrying the Image," "The Wolf and His Shadow," "The Gnat and the Lion," "The Horse and the Ass."

Look before you leap: "The Bat and the Weasels," "The Fox and the Goat," "The Frogs and the Well."

Performance is better than appearance: " Mice and the Weasels," "The Peacock and the Crane," "The Horse and the Groom," "The Olive Tree and the Fig Tree," "The Stag at the Pool," " Brother and Sister," "The Rose and the Amaranth."

Don't be fooled by flattery: "The Fox and the Crow," "The Dog , the Cock, and the Fox," "The Grasshopper and the Owl," "The Fox and the Grasshopper," "The Lion and the Bull."

Don't try to be what you're not: "The Ass and the Wolf," "The Monkey and the Camel," "The Eagle, the Jackday, and the Shepherd," "The Crow and the Raven."

If you choose bad companions, others will think that you are bad also: "The Farmer and the Stork," "The Ass and the Purchaser," "The Rivers and the Sea," "Hercules and Plutus."

You can't please everyone: "The Miller, the Son, and the Ass," "Father and Daughter."

Prepare now rather than later: "The Wild Boar and the Fox," "The Grasshopper and the Ants."

There is strength in unity: "The Lion and the Boar," "The Man and His Sons," "The Lion and the Three Bulls," "The Ass and the Mule," "The Belly and the Members."

Deeds count more than words: "The Boasting Traveler," "Two Soldiers and the Robber."

Stay away from danger and treachery: "The Wolf and the Goat," "The Wolf and the Lamb," "The Archer and the Lion."

The parallel flowchart can also be used as a writing tool. List a given story down the left side of the graphic organizer and use the right side to develop an original story having the same conflict or theme and conclusion.

RESULT—Stories which portray different decisions, actions, and results can express the same moral. Moral principles can be expressed effectively in fables.

WRITING EXTENSION
- Select two of *Aesop's Fables* with the same issue and the same moral. How are the decisions, actions, and results different for the main character in each story?
- Write a fable using the parallel flowchart. Outline an existing fable down the left side. Create a story with a similar problem and conclusion. Develop the plot by filling in the right side. Write the story from the flowchart.

THINKING ABOUT THINKING
- Design another graphic organizer to depict the conflict, decisions, actions, results, and moral of a story.
- Design another graphic organizer to compare similar conflicts, decisions, actions, results, and morals of two stories.
- How did using the graphic organizer help you understand the conclusions of the two stories?
- Why was it easier to identify the moral in two stories rather than one?
- Suggest another pair of stories that could be understood more clearly if they were compared this way.

SIMILAR LANGUAGE ARTS LESSONS
- To compare complex plots of novels or plays.
- To compare biographical data.
- To record events for writing narratives.
- To organize information for writing letters, biographies, or stories.

AESOP'S FABLES

DIRECTIONS: Read the two fables carefully. Identify the main character in each fable and write its name in the character box. Decide what the problem is in each story. Find the character's reasons and actions and write them in the boxes. Find the conclusion both stories suggest.

"MERCURY AND THE WOODMAN"

A woodman was chopping down a tree on the bank of a river when his ax fell out of his hands and into the water. As he stood by the water's edge, upset over his loss, Mercury appeared, dived into the river and brought up a golden ax. Mercury asked him if that ax was the one that he had lost. The woodman replied that it was not. Mercury dived a second time, brought up a silver ax, and asked if it was his. The woodman replied that it was not. Once more Mercury dived into the river and brought up the missing ax. The woodman was overjoyed at recovering his property and thanked Mercury warmly. Mercury was so pleased with the woodman's honesty that he made him a present of the other two axes.

When the woodman told his story to his companions, one decided to try his luck for himself. He went to the bank of the river, chopped down a tree, and let his ax drop into the water. Mercury appeared as before, dived into the river and brought up a golden ax. Without waiting to be asked whether it was his or not, the excited fellow stretched out his hand crying, "That's mine! That's mine!" Mercury was so disgusted at his dishonesty that he refused to give him the golden ax or to recover the one that he had let fall into the stream.

"THE DOG AND THE SHADOW"

A dog was walking on a log over a stream with a piece of meat in his mouth when he saw his own reflection in the water. He thought it was another dog with a piece of meat twice as big. He let go of his own meat and charged at the other dog to get the larger piece. The meat which the dog had held in his mouth fell into the water. Of course, all that happened was that he got neither. One was only a reflection and the other was carried away by the current.

COMPARING PLOTS IN TWO STORIES

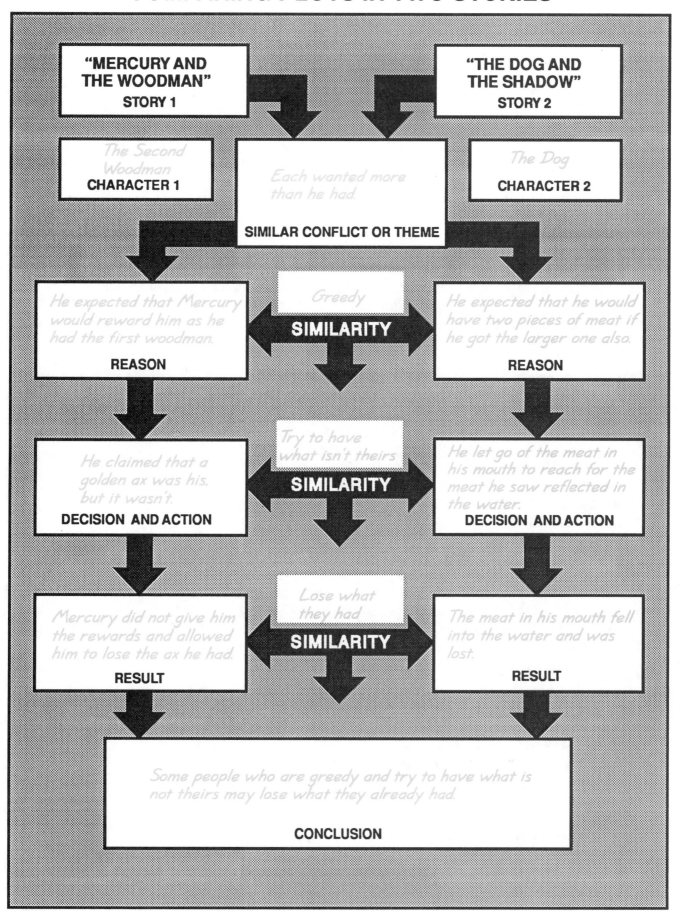

"MERCURY AND THE WOODMAN"
STORY 1

"THE DOG AND THE SHADOW"
STORY 2

The Second Woodman
CHARACTER 1

Each wanted more than he had.

The Dog
CHARACTER 2

SIMILAR CONFLICT OR THEME

He expected that Mercury would reward him as he had the first woodman.
REASON

Greedy
SIMILARITY

He expected that he would have two pieces of meat if he got the larger one also.
REASON

He claimed that a golden ax was his, but it wasn't.
DECISION AND ACTION

Try to have what isn't theirs
SIMILARITY

He let go of the meat in his mouth to reach for the meat he saw reflected in the water.
DECISION AND ACTION

Mercury did not give him the rewards and allowed him to lose the ax he had.
RESULT

Lose what they had
SIMILARITY

The meat in his mouth fell into the water and was lost.
RESULT

Some people who are greedy and try to have what is not theirs may lose what they already had.

CONCLUSION

CHARLOTTE'S WEB: DESCRIBING A CHARACTER

*Note: The following lessons are developed from the first chapter of **Charlotte's Web**. (See page 77.) Since the lessons are substantial and lengthy, one lesson per class session is recommended. Each involves critical reading, class discussion, and a writing application.*

THINKING SKILL: Describing attributes; drawing characterizations from examples

CONTENT OBJECTIVE: Students will use a central idea diagram to identify characteristics and give examples of words, actions, or situations to illustrate each characteristic.

DISCUSSION: TECHNIQUE—As students identify Fern's characteristics, record their ideas on a transparency of the graph. Write an example or quotation which illustrates each characteristic on each "arm" of the diagram. "Think/Pair/Share" discussion allows students to clarify their inferences before answering.

DIALOGUE—To arrive at an informed understanding of a character, we must base our interpretations on specific examples and quotations. Students may follow two approaches as they examine characteristics and examples: they may identify an incident and suggest a characteristic reflected in the incident, or they may identify a characteristic and look for an incident that illustrates it. Using either process, ask for a characteristic and an example.

Why it is important to support our character interpretations by citing examples? How might our understanding of Fern be different if we didn't use examples?

Students may find additional characteristics to describe Fern.
• Persuasive: Convinced her father not to kill the pig.
• Emotional: Got very upset, "out of control."
• Impulsive: She ran out in the wet grass, got her shoes wet, and grabbed her father's ax.
• Asks many questions: "Where's papa going with that ax?"
• Speaks honestly: "Do away with it? You mean kill it?"
• Puts fairness before courtesy: "It's a matter of life and death and you talk about controlling myself."
• Thinks for herself: Has confidence in her own reasons for not killing the pig.

Examples of character analysis for other principal characters in *Charlotte's Web* are explained in the lesson extension activities on pages 75 and 76.

RESULT—When you describe the characteristics of a person or thing, give an example of each characteristic so everyone knows what you are talking about.

WRITING EXTENSION
• **Describe Fern. In each sentence state one characteristic and an example of it.**
• **Use the same diagram to write a description of Mr. Arable.**

THINKING ABOUT THINKING
• **How did using the diagram help you describe a character?**
• **Suggest another lesson where using the central idea diagram would help you understand a character.**

SIMILAR LANGUAGE ARTS LESSONS
• To illustrate factors leading to or resulting from a turning point in a story or biography.
• To illustrate a topic sentence and its supporting statements.
• To illustrate headings and subheadings in an outline.

CHARLOTTE'S WEB: DESCRIBING A CHARACTER

ADDITIONAL CHARACTERIZATION LESSONS FROM *CHARLOTTE'S WEB*
The lessons in this series are taken from the first chapter of the story. If you read the rest of the novel, you may extend this lesson to repeat character analysis with other characters in the novel. Students may use the blank graphic organizer to write interpretations of the principal characters. Students answers may include, but are not limited to, the comments shown on the following completed central idea graphs.

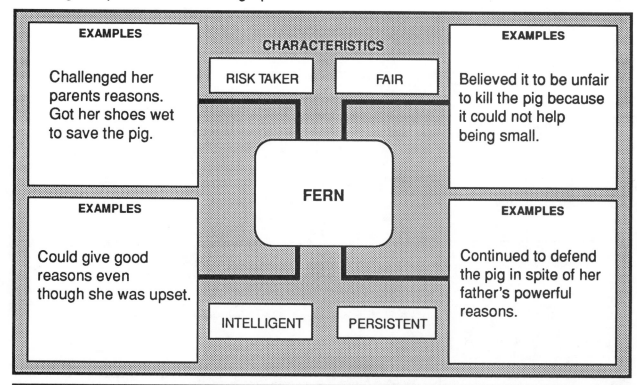

CHARACTERISTICS

RISK TAKER   FAIR

EXAMPLES
Challenged her parents reasons. Got her shoes wet to save the pig.

EXAMPLES
Believed it to be unfair to kill the pig because it could not help being small.

FERN

EXAMPLES
Could give good reasons even though she was upset.

EXAMPLES
Continued to defend the pig in spite of her father's powerful reasons.

INTELLIGENT   PERSISTENT

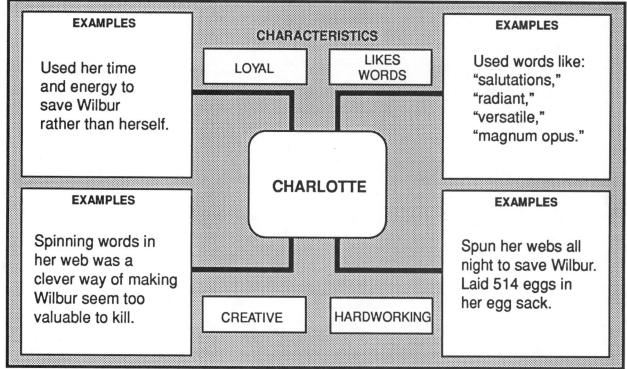

CHARACTERISTICS

LOYAL   LIKES WORDS

EXAMPLES
Used her time and energy to save Wilbur rather than herself.

EXAMPLES
Used words like: "salutations," "radiant," "versatile," "magnum opus."

CHARLOTTE

EXAMPLES
Spinning words in her web was a clever way of making Wilbur seem too valuable to kill.

EXAMPLES
Spun her webs all night to save Wilbur. Laid 514 eggs in her egg sack.

CREATIVE   HARDWORKING

CHARLOTTE'S WEB: DESCRIBING A CHARACTER

ADDITIONAL CHARACTERIZATION LESSONS FROM *CHARLOTTE'S WEB*

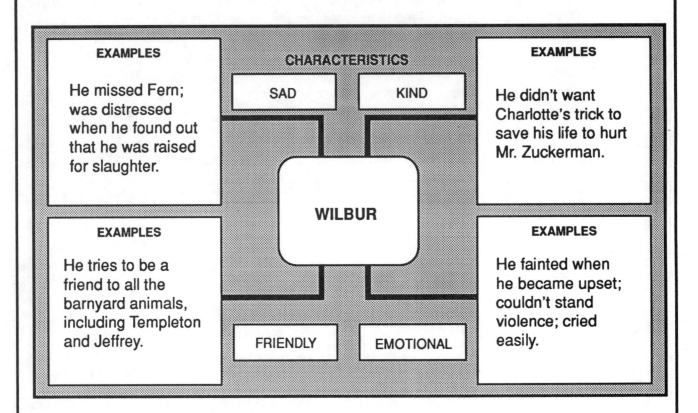

EXAMPLES

He missed Fern; was distressed when he found out that he was raised for slaughter.

EXAMPLES

He tries to be a friend to all the barnyard animals, including Templeton and Jeffrey.

CHARACTERISTICS

SAD   KIND

WILBUR

FRIENDLY   EMOTIONAL

EXAMPLES

He didn't want Charlotte's trick to save his life to hurt Mr. Zuckerman.

EXAMPLES

He fainted when he became upset; couldn't stand violence; cried easily.

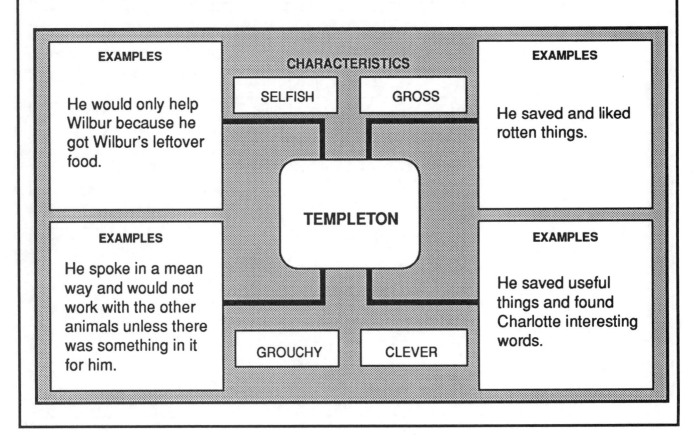

EXAMPLES

He would only help Wilbur because he got Wilbur's leftover food.

EXAMPLES

He spoke in a mean way and would not work with the other animals unless there was something in it for him.

CHARACTERISTICS

SELFISH   GROSS

TEMPLETON

GROUCHY   CLEVER

EXAMPLES

He saved and liked rotten things.

EXAMPLES

He saved useful things and found Charlotte interesting words.

CHARLOTTE'S WEB

"Where is Papa going with that ax?" said Fern to her mother as they were setting the table for breakfast.

"Out to the hog house," replied Mrs. Arable. "Some pigs were born last night."

"I don't see why he needs an ax," continued Fern, who was only eight.

"Well," said her mother, "one of the pigs is a runt. It's very small and weak, and it will never amount to anything. So your father has decided to do away with it."

"Do *away* with it?" shrieked Fern. "You mean *kill* it? Just because it's smaller than the others?"

Mrs. Arable put a pitcher of cream on the table. "Don't yell, Fern!" she said. "Your father is right. The pig would probably die anyway."

Fern pushed a chair out of the way and ran outdoors. The grass was wet and the earth smelled of springtime. Fern's sneakers were sopping by the time she caught up with her father.

"Please don't kill it," she sobbed. "It's unfair."

Mr. Arable stopped walking.

"Fern," he said gently, "you will have to learn to control yourself."

"Control myself?" yelled Fern. "This is a matter of life and death, and you talk about *controlling* myself!" Tears ran down her cheeks as she took hold of the ax and tried to pull it out of her father's hand.

"Fern," said Mr. Arable, "I know more about raising a litter of pigs than you do. A weakling makes trouble. Now run along!"

"But it's unfair," cried Fern. "The pig couldn't help being born small, could it? If *I* had been very small at birth, would you have killed *me?*"

Mr. Arable smiled. "Certainly not," he said, looking down at his daughter with love. "But this is different. A little girl is one thing, a runty pig another."

"I see no difference," replied Fern, still hanging onto the ax. "This is the most terrible case of injustice I ever heard of."

A queer look came over John Arable's face. He seemed almost ready to cry himself.

"All right," he said. "You go back in the house and I will bring the runt when I come in. I'll let you start it on a bottle, like a baby. Then you'll see what trouble a pig can be."

E. B. White. *Charlotte's Web.* New York: Harper and Row, 1980.

DESCRIBING A CHARACTER

DIRECTIONS: An author lets us understand a character by words, feelings or actions in a story. Select from the story a character that you think is interesting. Write the name in the circle. What does the character say or do that tells you what kind of a person he or she is? Write one of the things that the character does or says in each box. Think about what that tells you about that person. Write that characteristic in the little box on the "arm" of the diagram.

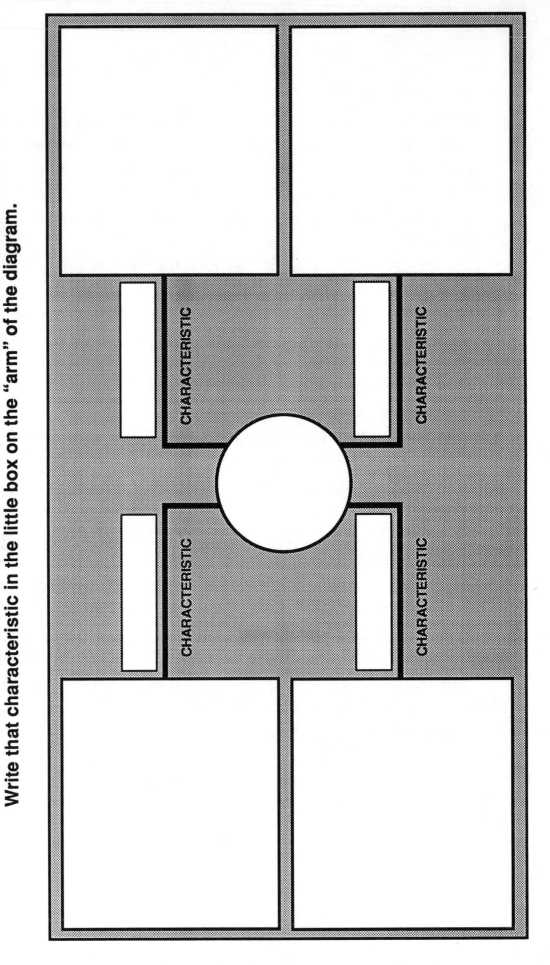

CHARACTERISTIC

CHARACTERISTIC

CHARACTERISTIC

CHARACTERISTIC

DESCRIBING A CHARACTER

DIRECTIONS: An author lets us understand a character by words, feelings or actions in a story. Select from the story a character that you think is interesting. Write the name in the circle. What does the character say or do that tells you what kind of a person he or she is? Write one of the things that the character does or says in each box. Think about what that tells you about that person. Write that characteristic in the little box on the "arm" of the diagram.

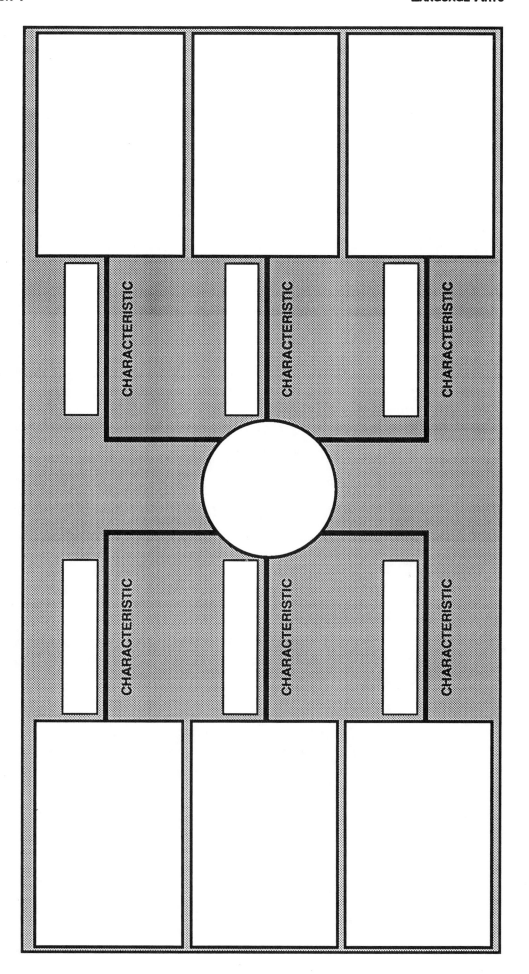

CHARLOTTE'S WEB: DRAWING INFERENCES

NOTE: The second lesson in the series is based on the same excerpt from the first chapter of **Charlotte's Web**. *(See page 77.) The three lessons should be taught sequentially.*

THINKING SKILL: Drawing inferences

CONTENT OBJECTIVE: Students will use a matrix diagram to record inferences drawn from specific actions and quotations from the text.

DISCUSSION: TECHNIQUE—Use a transparency of the matrix diagram to record inferences students identify from specific actions or comments in the story.
   DIALOGUE—Students should work in pairs to discuss what is implied in quotations by the Arables or Fern regarding the life of the pig. For each quotation, use terms like *purposes*, *needs*, *values*, or *beliefs*, to clarify underlying inferences which the characters suggest.
   A more abstract and valuable form of inference involves examining all of the statements and inferences given by a character about an issue and, taking them as a whole, inferring the character's unstated assumptions. The key concept in this chapter is the difference between the Arables' and Fern's assumptions regarding the value of the pig's life. The Arables view the pig as a commodity, an organism that does not express the characteristics that we attribute to humans: intelligence, emotion, personality, spirit, motive, humor, compassion, planning, oral and written language, and problem solving abilities. Fern attributes these human-like characteristics to the pig. For the rest of the novel, pigs, spiders, and other barnyard animals exhibit these characteristics in a funny and poignant fable of compassion and self-sacrifice. Read aloud and discuss the entire novel—a masterpiece of humor, allegory, creative and critical thinking.
   RESULT—To understand the meaning of what is said, one must look at the speaker's underlying purposes, needs, values, or beliefs about an issue.

WRITING EXTENSION
• Describe what Fern believes about the value of the life of the pig.

THINKING ABOUT THINKING
• How did using the diagram help you understand what the characters really meant?
• Suggest another lesson where using the diagram would help you understand the character better.

SIMILAR LANGUAGE ARTS LESSONS
• To record characteristics or actions of characters.
• To record examples of figures of speech, types of writing or books.

© 1992 CRITICAL THINKING PRESS & SOFTWARE • P.O. Box 448, Pacific Grove, CA 93950

CHARLOTTE'S WEB: DRAWING INFERENCES

DIRECTIONS: In each box write what the speaker may believe in making each statement.

MR. AND MRS. ARABLE'S REASONS AND INFERENCES

"The runt pig is small and weak, and it will never amount to anything."	Only large pigs are valuable to the farmer since he sells pigs by weight.
"The pig would probably die anyway."	It can't fight for food. It will be sickly, need extra care, or die from starvation.
"A weakling makes trouble."	It takes the farmer's time and money, causes distress when it dies, takes food from others who need it.
"I know more about raising a litter of pigs than you do."	He has more experience and authority in deciding what should be done with the pig.
"A little girl is one thing; a runty little pig is another."	The pig's life is not as valuable as a human life.

FERN'S REASONS AND INFERENCES

"It's unfair."	The pig doesn't deserve to die.
"The pig couldn't help being born small."	It should not be punished for something that it could not control.
"If I had been very small at birth, would you have killed me?"	The pig's life is as important to it as Fern's life is to her.
"This is the most terrible case of injustice I ever heard of."	The value of the pig's life is not held to the same standard as human life.

CHARLOTTE'S WEB: REASONS AND CONCLUSIONS

NOTE: This third lesson is based on the same excerpt from the first chapter of Charlotte's Web (See page 77.) The lessons should be taught sequentially.

THINKING SKILL: Identifying reasons and conclusions.

CONTENT OBJECTIVE: Students will use the argument diagram to identify reasons and conclusions for and against killing the runt pig in *Charlotte's Web*.

DISCUSSION: TECHNIQUE—Students will use the argument diagram to describe the reasons and conclusions which the Arables and Fern believe regarding the life of the pig. Direct students to write the conclusion in the arch of each diagram. While we commonly look first for reasons and then the conclusion, in this case the Arables' and Fern's conclusions are stated first. Direct students to turn the paper sideways and write the exact reasons that each character gives for his or her conclusions about the life of the pig. As students record quotations from the passage in each "reason" column, encourage them to write in parentheses what the reason infers about the value of the pig's life.

DIALOGUE—In introducing this lesson, it is important to familiarize students with the "structure" of an argument represented by the diagram.

Our reasons "hold up" our conclusions, in much the same way that columns or walls hold up a roof. Without good reasons our conclusions "fall" down because they are not "supported" by good explanations or sufficient evidence.

This passage provides one of the most eloquent examples of persuasive argument in children's literature. The argument represents a transition from an adult, pragmatic view of a pig to a child-like, personified view of a pig, which is the point of view the author maintains through the rest of the book.

The following questions will encourage students to examine and identify reasons and conclusions.

What is the person trying to convince us to believe? How do we know what a person's conclusions are? (actions, statements, or attitudes) **What words signal a person's conclusions?** ("decided," "so," "therefore") **How does a person explain his thinking?** (appeal to authority, practical considerations, humanitarian considerations, appeal for justice, analogous reasons, appeal to emotion) **Describe different types of reasons that people may give for their thinking?**

Students may find additional reasons why the Arables believe that killing the pig is the more reasonable choice:

Mrs. Arable: "The pig will probably die anyway." (It is humane to end the long-term suffering of the pig.)

Mr. Arable: "I know more about raising a litter of pigs than you do." (He has more experience and authority in deciding what is best.)

Mr. Arable: "A little girl is one thing, a runty little pig is another." (The pig's life is not as valuable as human life.)

Students may also find additional reasons why Fern believes that killing the pig is unjust:

Fern: "It's unfair." (One should not punish the pig by killing it.)

Fern: "Just because it's smaller than the others?" (Comparing the runt to other pigs should not be sufficient reason for its death.)

RESULT—To understand an individual's point of view, be sure you know his/her conclusion and reasons.

WRITING EXTENSION
- Give reasons from the story to explain why you think Mr. Arable changed his mind about killing the pig.
- Choose a story that you have recently read or write a short story that has a difference of opinion. Use the two diagrams to show a difference of opinion (reasons and conclusions) that one person might have with someone else.

THINKING ABOUT THINKING
- Suggest another lesson in which using the arch diagram would help you understand an issue.
- How did the diagram help you understand the structure of an argument (reasons and conclusions)?
- Why is it important to identify the reasons and conclusions in an argument?

SIMILAR LANGUAGE ARTS LESSONS
- To describe arguments in news reports, speeches, or in the plots of stories and plays.

CHARLOTTE'S WEB: REASONS AND CONCLUSIONS

DIRECTIONS: In the "arch" of the diagram, write what Mr. and Mrs. Arable think should be done with the pig. Turn the page sideways and write their exact words in each "reason" column.

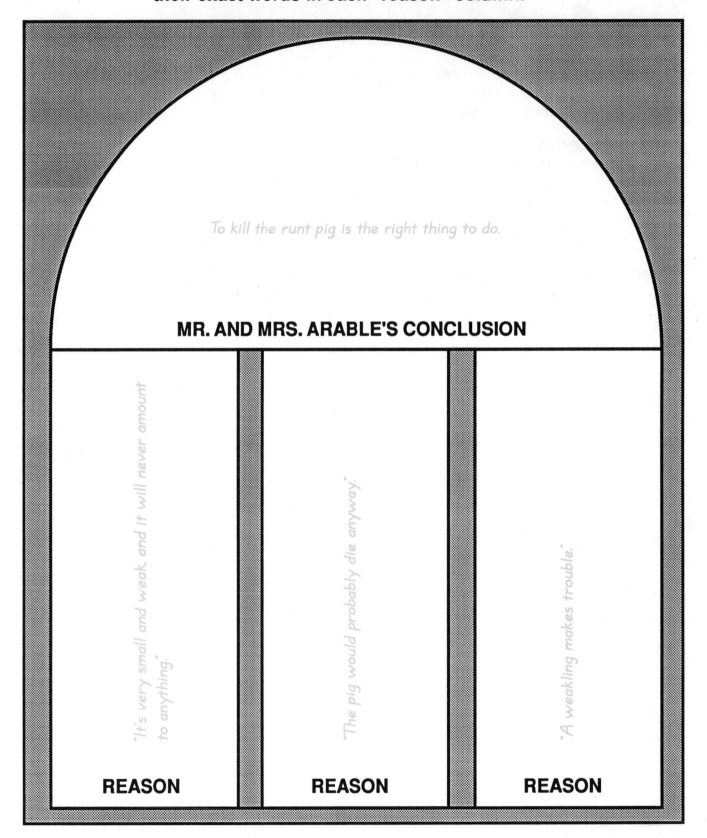

To kill the runt pig is the right thing to do.

MR. AND MRS. ARABLE'S CONCLUSION

"It's very small and weak, and it will never amount to anything."

"The pig would probably die anyway."

"A weakling makes trouble."

REASON   **REASON**   **REASON**

CHARLOTTE'S WEB: REASONS AND CONCLUSIONS

DIRECTIONS: In the "arch" of the diagram, write what Fern thinks should be done with the pig. Turn the page sideways and write her exact words in each "reason" column.

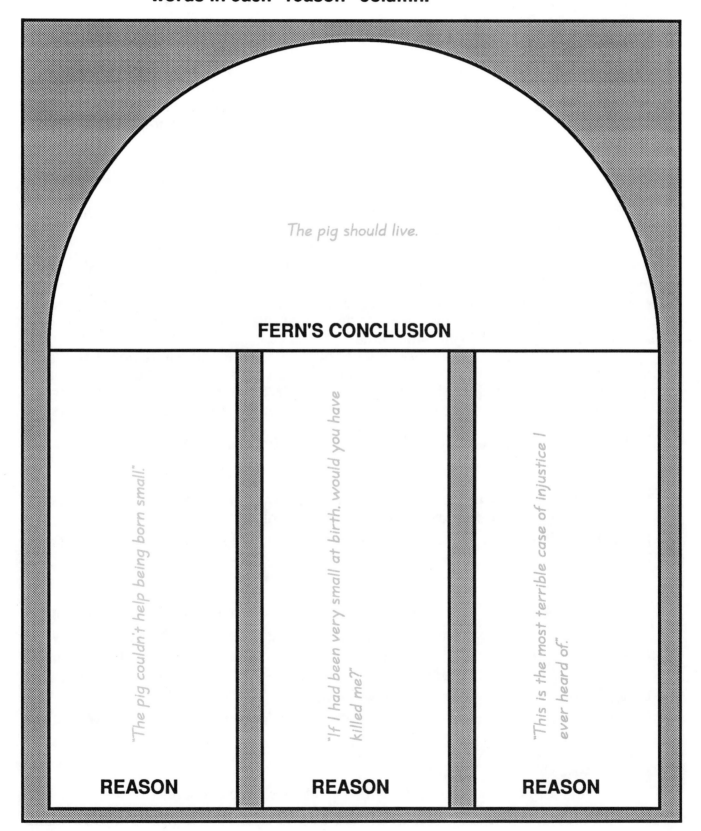

The pig should live.

FERN'S CONCLUSION

"The pig couldn't help being born small."

"If I had been very small at birth, would you have killed me?"

"This is the most terrible case of injustice I ever heard of."

REASON   **REASON**   **REASON**

CHARLOTTE'S WEB: DESCRIBING THE PLOT

THINKING SKILL: Sequencing

CONTENT OBJECTIVE: Students will use a transitive order graph to record, in order, the events happening in *Charlotte's Web*.

DISCUSSION: TECHNIQUE—Use a transparency of the transitive order graph to record students' responses as they report events from *Charlotte's Web* in the order in which they happen. Reproduce the matrix which contains the events in the story in random order. Students should cut apart the boxes on their copy and rearrange them in the appropriate order. Students should then write events in proper order on their copy of the transitive order graph labeled "Plot of *Charlotte's Web*" to show how the plot developed.

DIALOGUE— Encourage students to identify clues they used which show the order. Clues may include their memory of the plot, the quotations which Charlotte wove into the web, Wilbur's growth, etc.

Discuss with students why it is important to remember the events of the story in the right order when we tell a story to someone else.

When we describe the events in a story, we are describing its plot. Why is remembering things in the right order important in telling the story to someone else? (Answers will vary: getting the order confused may change the significance or outcomes of events; the story may not make sense to the listener; events which are reasonable and orderly may seem silly or disconnected if we tell them in the wrong order.)
When we describe the plot of a story, what should we keep in mind in telling it so that the listener understands what happened? (Answers will vary, e.g.: only discuss events that are important; don't get caught up in so many details that the listener becomes confused; when you use "he," "she, " or "they," be sure that the listener knows to whom that pronoun refers.)

RESULT—In telling the plot of a story, describe only important events in the right order.

WRITING EXTENSION
- **Choose a story that you have recently read. List the events in the order in which they happen. Write the plot the way you would tell the story to someone else.**
- **Use the transitive order graph to list events in a story that you make up. Use the list to write your story.**

THINKING ABOUT THINKING
- **What clues/patterns help you recall the order of events that describe the story's plot?**
- **What did you consider important about the events you chose to tell the plot of a story?**
- **How did arranging the events on small pieces of paper help you organize them before you wrote the plot on the graph?**
- **Design another graph to help you show a plot.**
- **Suggest another lesson in which arranging the events in order would help you remember how things happened.**

SIMILAR LANGUAGE ARTS LESSONS
- To depict the steps in instructions, library use, or study-skills procedures.

CHARLOTTE'S WEB: DESCRIBING THE PLOT

DIRECTIONS: Cut apart the boxes. Use what you remember about *Charlotte's Web* to arrange the events in order. Paste the events onto the transitive order graph on the next page

Charlotte died.	Charlotte wrote "HUMBLE" in a web.
Charlotte wrote "RADIANT" in a web.	Charlotte wrote "SOME PIG" in a web to make Mr. Zuckerman think that Wilbur is special.
Charlotte wrote "TERRIFIC" in a web.	Fern saved Wilbur.
Judges awarded Mr. Zuckerman a special prize for Wilbur.	Wilbur took care of Charlotte's egg sack until her babies hatched.
Wilbur was sold to Mr. Zuckerman.	Mr. Zuckerman took his famous pig Wilbur to the fair.

CHARLOTTE'S WEB: DESCRIBING THE PLOT

DIRECTIONS: Use the events that you cut apart. Paste the events in the order they happened to describe the plot of *Charlotte's Web*.

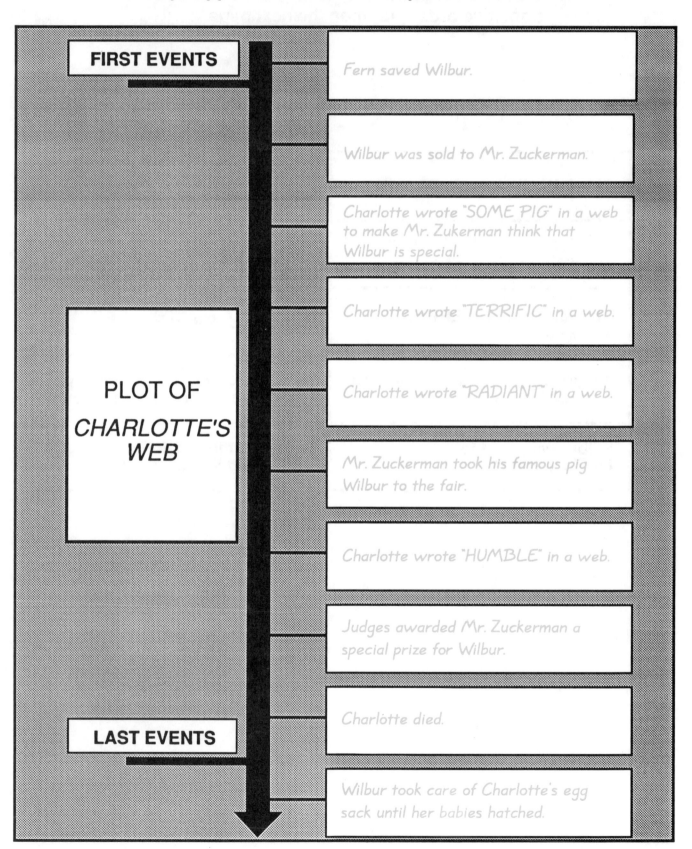

FIRST EVENTS

Fern saved Wilbur.

Wilbur was sold to Mr. Zuckerman.

Charlotte wrote "SOME PIG" in a web to make Mr. Zukerman think that Wilbur is special.

Charlotte wrote "TERRIFIC" in a web.

Charlotte wrote "RADIANT" in a web.

Mr. Zuckerman took his famous pig Wilbur to the fair.

PLOT OF *CHARLOTTE'S WEB*

Charlotte wrote "HUMBLE" in a web.

Judges awarded Mr. Zuckerman a special prize for Wilbur.

Charlotte died.

LAST EVENTS

Wilbur took care of Charlotte's egg sack until her babies hatched.

DESCRIBING A STORY

THINKING SKILL: Describing attributes

CONTENT OBJECTIVE: Students will describe the characteristics of a work of fiction. This process can be used with any story. *Charlotte's Web* and *Horton Hatches the Egg* are used as examples of applying this technique with young children. Some students may be able to fill in the diagram independently; most primary students should use this technique only for discussion.

Previous lessons from *Charlotte's Web* have been based on reading a portion of the first chapter only. Use this lesson after reading the whole novel.

DISCUSSION: TECHNIQUE—Young students may not know how to identify the important characteristics of a story. This lesson features the letters in the word "fiction" as a mnemonic device for describing a narrative. Use a transparency of a blank diagram to record comments which describe a story that you have recently read as a class.

DIALOGUE—You may describe a story by applying the following general principles to any specific novel or short story .

"F"— Friction (conflict). Resolving a conflict or problem makes a story interesting and worthwhile. If there is no conflict, there is no reason for a story. Young students may need an explanation of the term "friction" as conflict.

Is a conflict or problem necessary in a story? Can you think of an interesting story that contains no conflict or problem?

"I"— Ideal or idea (message). The ideal or message is the point or purpose of a story. If there is no ideal, there is no point to a story.

Why is an ideal or message important in a story? Can you think of an interesting story that contains no ideal or message?

"C"— Characters. Students' discussion of characters is often limited to statements of taste—whether they like a character or not. Use the suggestions for describing a character in the *Charlotte's Web* lessons on pages 75–76 to expand the discussion of characters that you have recently read about in your language arts program.

Think about the main character in this story. What characteristics did the character show? Did the character seem real? Did you admire that character? Why or why not? How did he or she relate to others in the story? How does that character give meaning or purpose to the story?

"T"— Title. Students should look at the title in relation to the main idea of the story. Emphasize the necessity of selecting a few words that will convey the sense of the book.

How does the title fit the story? How does it relate to the characters, actions, or ideals of the story? Can you think of any other title that might have been better suited to the events and characters?

"I"— Imitate. It is much easier for elementary students to describe "who" (characters) or "what" (plot), than it is to describe "how" (style). Expand the discussion of style presented in these lessons to include aspects that you have discussed in your language arts program, for example: humor, dialogue, kind of language, use of detail, or imagery.

If you were going to write a book like this one, what would it be like? What kind of characters or actions would you select? How would the characters talk? If you read the story out loud, how would the story sound? (scary, funny, rhyming, told like a child, an animal, or a special character)

"O"— Order of Events. Most children's stories are written in simple chronological order and told from a single point of view. When describing the plot of a story, elementary students often tell the story in much more detail than a simple statement of the plot requires. They may give more attention to one event than it warrants. Many elementary students believe that telling the plot is all that is entailed in describing a story. Encourage students to state the plot in ten to twelve sentences.

Identify any stories which you have read in class that feature different organizational patterns, such as stories within a story, stories told from different viewpoints, stories told in flashbacks, etc.

"N"— Newness (novelty). Discuss why novelty (uniqueness) is important in a story?

What makes this book different from other books? How does the appeal of a unique and interesting book encourage you to expand the kinds of books you read? Identify a book that was so different that it encouraged you to read a kind of book that you don't usually select. Why is it important that we read many kinds of books?

Sample student responses for three popular children's stories (*Charlotte's Web, Horton Hatches the Egg, and Stone Soup*) are illustrated on pages 91–93. *Horton Hatches the Egg* is a useful story for teaching the characteristics of **F.I.C.T.I.O.N.** Students like it, consider it an easy story to understand, and can therefore give their attention to the features of the story. Use **F.I.C.T.I.O.N.** in book reports, library displays, bulletin boards, and descriptive speeches.

RESULT—One can understand and describe a story better by discussing important characteristics.

WRITING EXTENSION
• **Use the F.I.C.T.I.O.N. to describe a story, television show, or play.**

THINKING ABOUT THINKING
• **How did using the graph help you describe a story?**
• **Suggest another lesson where using the graph would help you understand a story.**

SIMILAR LANGUAGE ARTS LESSONS
• To record examples of figures of speech, types of literature, types of writing, or types of books.

DESCRIBING A STORY

Notes to teachers: Encourage students to give these kinds of answers to describe *Charlotte's Web.* Add any characteristics that have been introduced in your reading/language arts instruction. For most primary students, this lesson should be conducted by discussion only.

DESCRIBING A STORY

Charlotte's Web

FRICTION OR CONFLICT
- Although Wilbur knew he was raised for slaughter, he didn't want to die.
- People think that animals do not have human characteristics (personality, problem solving, emotions, written language, compassion), animals in the story do.

IDEAL
- All life is valuable.
- The care one gives comes back.
- Although one may face limitations, creativity, attitude, and caring can overcome them.

CHARACTERS
- Wilbur: kind, sensitive, emotional, sometimes depressed or whining, trusting, wishy-washy.
- Charlotte: kind, loving, wise, practical, doesn't tolerate immaturity or defeat.
- Templeton: practical, cunning, sarcastic, loyal, clever.

SIGNIFICANCE OF TITLE
- Charlotte's web saved Wilbur's life. It represents the creativity, intelligence, and self-sacrifice of an animal that is normally feared or underestimated.

IMITATE IT? (STYLE)
- Animals show human traits.
- Use dialog to tell the story.
- Unexpected action and use of words "splendid pig" and "humble."
- Animals speak with humor and sarcasm.

ORDER OF EVENTS
- Although the story is told sequentially, each chapter is almost a story unto itself (problem and resolution).

NOVELTY (WHY IS IT DIFFERENT?)
- Beings which we usually think are less intelligent or undesirable sometimes demonstrate characteristics that we think of as the best human traits.

DESCRIBING A STORY

Notes to teachers: Encourage students to give these kinds of answers to describe *Horton Hatches the Egg.* Add any characteristics that have been introduced in your reading/language arts instruction. For most primary students, this lesson should be conducted by discussion only.

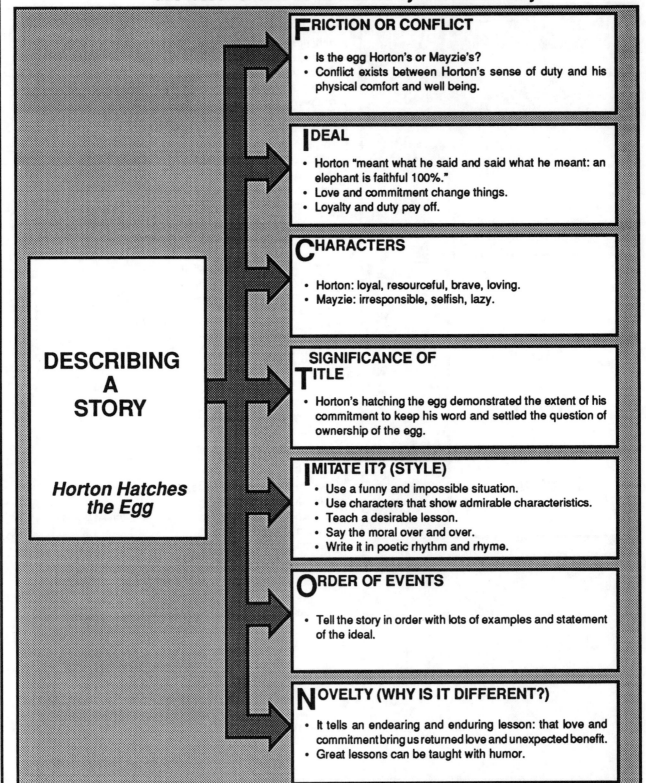

DESCRIBING A STORY

Horton Hatches the Egg

FRICTION OR CONFLICT

- Is the egg Horton's or Mayzie's?
- Conflict exists between Horton's sense of duty and his physical comfort and well being.

IDEAL

- Horton "meant what he said and said what he meant: an elephant is faithful 100%."
- Love and commitment change things.
- Loyalty and duty pay off.

CHARACTERS

- Horton: loyal, resourceful, brave, loving.
- Mayzie: irresponsible, selfish, lazy.

SIGNIFICANCE OF TITLE

- Horton's hatching the egg demonstrated the extent of his commitment to keep his word and settled the question of ownership of the egg.

IMITATE IT? (STYLE)

- Use a funny and impossible situation.
- Use characters that show admirable characteristics.
- Teach a desirable lesson.
- Say the moral over and over.
- Write it in poetic rhythm and rhyme.

ORDER OF EVENTS

- Tell the story in order with lots of examples and statement of the ideal.

NOVELTY (WHY IS IT DIFFERENT?)

- It tells an endearing and enduring lesson: that love and commitment bring us returned love and unexpected benefit.
- Great lessons can be taught with humor.

DESCRIBING A STORY

Notes to teachers: Encourage students to give these kinds of answers to describe *Stone Soup.* **Add any characteristics that have been introduced in your reading/language arts instruction. For most primary students, this lesson should be conducted by discussion only.**

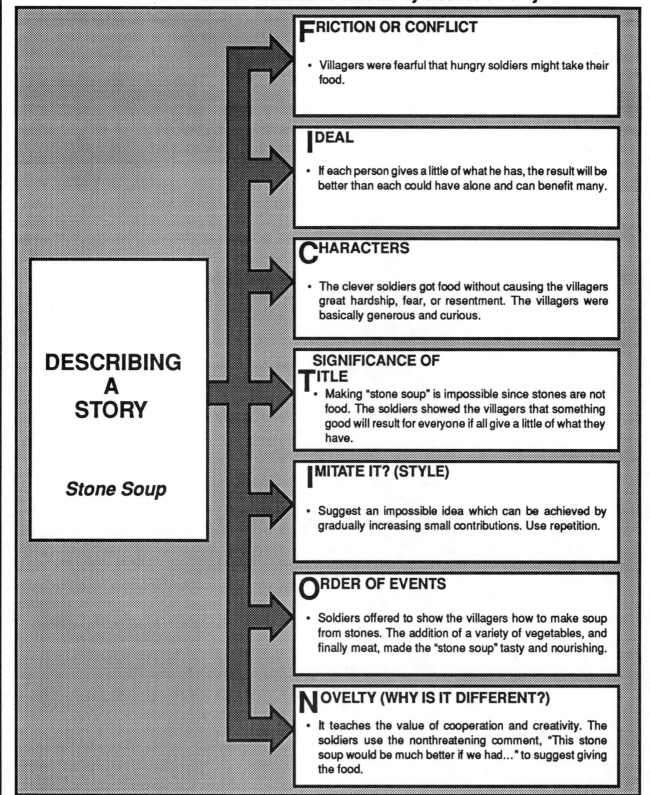

DESCRIBING A STORY

Stone Soup

FRICTION OR CONFLICT

- Villagers were fearful that hungry soldiers might take their food.

IDEAL

- If each person gives a little of what he has, the result will be better than each could have alone and can benefit many.

CHARACTERS

- The clever soldiers got food without causing the villagers great hardship, fear, or resentment. The villagers were basically generous and curious.

SIGNIFICANCE OF TITLE

- Making "stone soup" is impossible since stones are not food. The soldiers showed the villagers that something good will result for everyone if all give a little of what they have.

IMITATE IT? (STYLE)

- Suggest an impossible idea which can be achieved by gradually increasing small contributions. Use repetition.

ORDER OF EVENTS

- Soldiers offered to show the villagers how to make soup from stones. The addition of a variety of vegetables, and finally meat, made the "stone soup" tasty and nourishing.

NOVELTY (WHY IS IT DIFFERENT?)

- It teaches the value of cooperation and creativity. The soldiers use the nonthreatening comment, "This stone soup would be much better if we had..." to suggest giving the food.

DESCRIBING A STORY

DIRECTIONS: Use this diagram to describe a story that you have read.

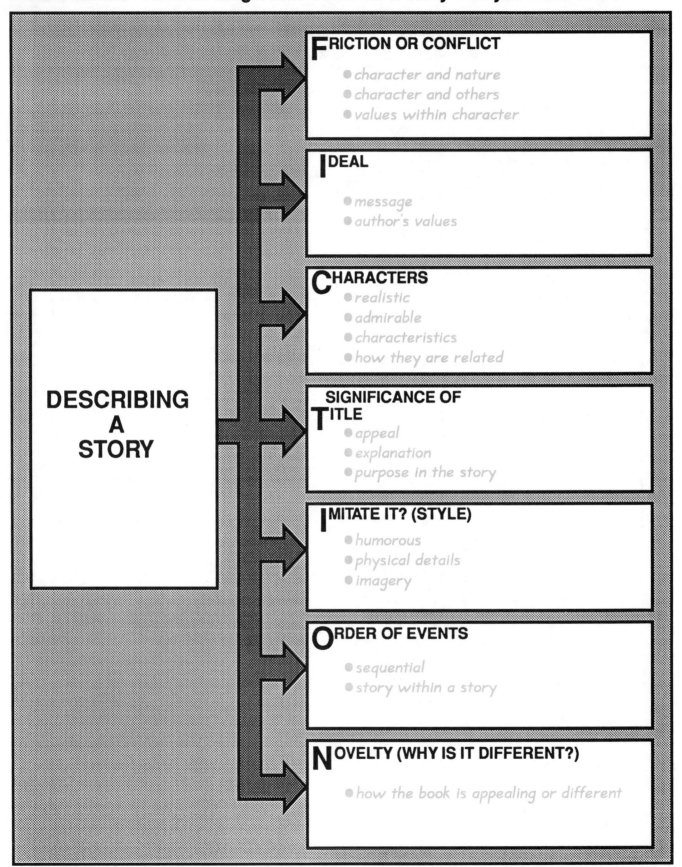

FRICTION OR CONFLICT
- *character and nature*
- *character and others*
- *values within character*

IDEAL
- *message*
- *author's values*

CHARACTERS
- *realistic*
- *admirable*
- *characteristics*
- *how they are related*

SIGNIFICANCE OF **T**ITLE
- *appeal*
- *explanation*
- *purpose in the story*

IMITATE IT? (STYLE)
- *humorous*
- *physical details*
- *imagery*

ORDER OF EVENTS
- *sequential*
- *story within a story*

NOVELTY (WHY IS IT DIFFERENT?)
- *how the book is appealing or different*

DESCRIBING A STORY

"THE STEAM SHOVEL"

THINKING SKILL: Verbal analogies; interpreting figurative language; comparison

CONTENT OBJECTIVE: Students will use the compare or contrast graph to identify analogous characteristics of a steam shovel and a dinosaur. Students will perceive that using a simple metaphor in a poem conveys many images, characteristics, and connections.

DISCUSSION: TECHNIQUE—Confirm that students understand the characteristics and operation of a steam shovel by discussing a picture or film of one. Confirm that students understand the characteristics of dinosaurs, in this case a brontosaurus, by discussing a picture or film of one.

Use the transparency of the compare or contrast graph to record responses as students examine the similarities between a steam shovel and a dinosaur. Ask students to think about how the characteristic on the arrow applies to a steam shovel and a dinosaur. Prompt students to identify many adjectives, nouns, and verbs that describe each characteristic of both. Record the class's combined descriptors of a steam shovel on the left side of the graph and the descriptors of a dinosaur on the right. Encourage students to identify additional characteristics that a steam shovel and a dinosaur have in common and list descriptors for each.

After students have generated a long list of comparisons, read aloud and discuss Lynn Skapyak's "The Steam Shovel." Circle all the comparisons which students have generated that apply to the image of a steam shovel as a dinosaur in the Skapyak poem.

The poem blanks in the exercise follow the same pattern as "The Steam Shovel." Encourage students to compare their poems to "The Steam Shovel" and to identify the many connections between a steam shovel and a dinosaur suggested in their poems and in Skapyak's. Additional poems containing similar metaphors have been provided. For each poem use a compare or contrast diagram to generate characteristics that both things share and words they can associate with both.

DIALOGUE—Encourage students to generate as many words as possible about a steam shovel and a dinosaur. (If the students do not know how to describe a steam shovel, Mike Mulligan and His Steam Shovel by Virginia Lee Burton [Houghton Mifflin: Boston, 1967] contains a labeled diagram of the parts of a steam shovel on the inside front and back covers.) Describe the comparison as an analogy. For example:

The digging action of a steam shovel seems like the eating action of a dinosaur. (Emphasize the analogy by pointing to the descriptor, the characteristic, and the object on the transparency.)

This lesson provides a rich opportunity to define **metaphor: describing one object, person, condition, or idea by its similarity to another**. Use the same examination process for other figures of speech: simile, personification, and hyperbole. Discuss how similarities and differences make puns funny.

The process of making correlations is a rigorous form of comparison and is the primary thinking skill goal of the lesson. Metaphors are a natural and dramatic context to help students do this kind of thinking. Using the process to interpret the dinosaur metaphor in "The Steam Shovel" is the content goal. Teaching students to interpret the poem by using the thinking process of comparison allows them to understand the meaning of the poem more fully.

Encourage students to identify other objects that might be like a dinosaur and other animals that might be like a steam shovel. Identify other poems that the class has read that describe an object as a living thing or a living thing as an object.

RESULTS—Metaphors express ideas richly because they are analogies. They help us perceive something better by its similarity to something else. Metaphors are useful in poems because they can be used to describe two things in very few words.

WRITING EXTENSION
- **How are a steam shovel and a dinosaur alike?**
- **Poems are expressive because the poet conveys so much meaning in so few words. In Skapyak's "The Steam Shovel," how does the image of a dinosaur describe a steam shovel to you?** (Students may express their responses by writing a similar poem, an extended description, or by giving an oral description of the student's emotional response.)
- **If a dinosaur is a good way of describing a steam shovel, then a steam shovel may also be a good image for describing a dinosaur. Use the information on your graph to write a dinosaur poem using steam shovel words or write a third verse to "The Steam Shovel."**
- **Why would you use a metaphor rather than describing something directly? Suggest other reasons for using metaphors.**

THINKING ABOUT THINKING
- **How does listing the characteristics of a steam shovel and a dinosaur on the graph help you "see" the many ways that a steam shovel seems to act like a dinosaur?**
- **Describe the steps in your thinking as you compared a steam shovel with a dinosaur.**
- **How did your idea of a steam shovel change after you examined how it was like a dinosaur?**
- **Suggest another poem in which using this diagram would help you understand its meaning.**
- **Identify an experience in which someone taught you concepts about something that you could not see by comparing it with something that you could see. How did the comparison help you "picture" the new idea?**
- **Why do people enjoy "playing with words" by using metaphors to explain their thoughts?**

SIMILAR LANGUAGE ARTS LESSONS
- To interpret figurative language.
- To compare or contrast characters within or between stories, plays, novels, etc.
- To compare or contrast two parts of speech or kinds of stories.

"THE STEAM SHOVEL"

by Lynn Marie Skapyak

Dinosaurs are not all in books
with necks that do not swing,
flat, monster beast, who merely looks
like he could eat up anything.

I saw a hungry one, just yesterday,
loudly chomping his steel jaws
as he ate, downtown by the bay,
huffing as he moved, on rubber claws.

He threw dirt and rocks to the side
scooping earth loads in his iron head,
leaving an empty hole, oh so wide.
Chugging white smoke puffs as he fed.

DIRECTIONS: On the comparison graph on the next page, write words about the steam shovel and the dinosaur. In each box on the left, write words which relate that characteristic of a steam shovel. In the box on the right, write words which relate that characteristic to a dinosaur.

Use the words on the graph to write a poem that describes a steam shovel using dinosaur words or a poem about a dinosaur using steam shovel words. Each line represents a syllable or beat.

_____

_____ _____ _____ _____ _____ _____

_____ _____ _____ _____ _____ _____

_____ _____ _____ _____ _____ _____

_____ _____ _____ _____ _____ _____

Lynn Marie Skapyak. "The Steam Shovel." Reprinted by permission of the author.

"THE STEAM SHOVEL"

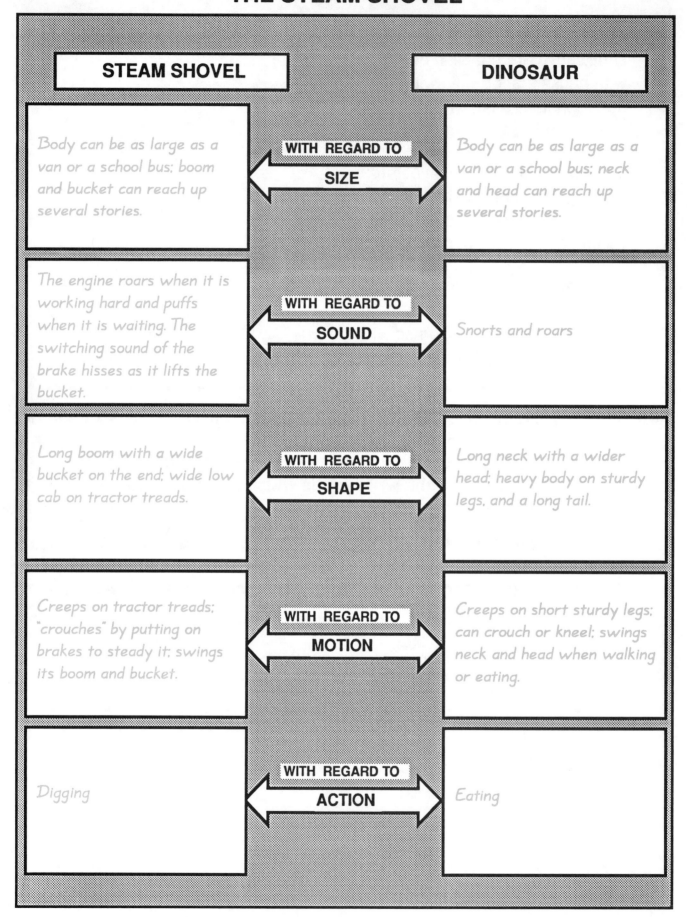

STEAM SHOVEL

DINOSAUR

Body can be as large as a van or a school bus; boom and bucket can reach up several stories.

WITH REGARD TO SIZE

Body can be as large as a van or a school bus; neck and head can reach up several stories.

The engine roars when it is working hard and puffs when it is waiting. The switching sound of the brake hisses as it lifts the bucket.

WITH REGARD TO SOUND

Snorts and roars

Long boom with a wide bucket on the end; wide low cab on tractor treads.

WITH REGARD TO SHAPE

Long neck with a wider head; heavy body on sturdy legs, and a long tail.

Creeps on tractor treads; "crouches" by putting on brakes to steady it; swings its boom and bucket.

WITH REGARD TO MOTION

Creeps on short sturdy legs; can crouch or kneel; swings neck and head when walking or eating.

Digging

WITH REGARD TO ACTION

Eating

POEMS WITH SIMILAR METAPHORS

"STEAM SHOVEL"
by Charles Malam

The dinosaurs are not all dead.
I saw one raise its iron head
To watch me walking down the road
Beyond our house today.
Its jaws were dripping with a load
Of earth and grass that it had cropped.
It must have heard me where I stopped,
Snorted white steam my way,
And stretched its long neck out to see,
And chewed, and grinned quite amiably.

"THE TOASTER"
by Lynn Marie Skapyak

A silver-sided dragon on the table sits
gobbling our white bread.
Two pieces slip down the slits,
CLICK turns the black belly to red.
Up pops warm toast ready to zip away,
Lucky for me the beast is not hungry today.

"THE GARDEN HOSE"
by Lynn Marie Skapyak

A snake slid in the grass *swishing*,
hissing, *slithering*, as it goes.
Until Daddy grabs the long black thing
squirting water on his toes.

Charles Malam. "Steam Shovel." In *Upper Pasture: Poems by Charles Malam.* © 1930, 1958 Charles Malam. Reprinted by permission of Holt, Rinehart and Winston, Inc.
Lynn Marie Skapyak. "The Toaster" and "The Garden Hose." Reprinted by permission of the author.

DESCRIBING A GOOD SPEECH

THINKING SKILL: Describing attributes, class/subclass

CONTENT OBJECTIVE: Students will use the branching diagram to identify characteristics of a good speech.

DISCUSSION: TECHNIQUE—Use a transparency of the branching diagram to record the characteristics of a good speech as students discuss information from the passage. Discuss why each characteristic is important.

DIALOGUE—Discuss examples of good speaking. Show a videotape of an effective speech or ask a good student speaker to present a speech. 4-H clubs often hold elementary grade speech tournaments. Invite winners to speak to your class.

According to what we have read, what made this a good speech? Is there anything that the speaker might have done to make it better?

Use the branching diagram for a bulletin board design as you develop your speech unit. Add each characteristic to your bulletin board as it is discussed in class.

RESULT—Understanding the characteristics of a good speech can improve your speaking skills and your appreciation of good speeches.

WRITING EXTENSION
• **Describe the characteristics of a good speech.**
• **Select one characteristic of a good speech. Describe how you have used it well.**

THINKING ABOUT THINKING
• **How can using the diagram help you understand characteristics of a good speech?**
• **How did using the diagram help you organize your thoughts before you wrote?**
• **Suggest another lesson where using a diagram would help you understand what you are learning.**
• **Which characteristics of a good speech do you already use well? Which do you expect to improve?**
• **Design another diagram that will help you organize a speech.**
• **How does knowing what makes a good speech change how you listen to one?**

SIMILAR LANGUAGE ARTS LESSONS
• To illustrate part/whole relationships: parts of a book, parts of a letter.
• To illustrate class/subclass relationships: parts of speech, types of books, or reference sources.
• To illustrate headings and subheadings in an outline.
• To show the family relationships of kings, mythological characters, or characters in books or plays.

DESCRIBING A GOOD SPEECH

DIRECTIONS: Read the passage carefully to find out how to give a good speech. Write the information on the diagram as you read.

A good speech should be about something you know. It should be well planned and spoken in a pleasant way.

Use your own knowledge to select your speech topic. Your speech may be about some special person or event. It may be about something you know how to do. Talk about something that you like, such as your hobbies. Give facts and interesting examples that fit your topic.

Planning your speech well allows the listeners to understand your ideas easily. A good speech begins and ends well. Start with a good example or a joke to interest the audience in your ideas. For a good ending, repeat the main idea of the speech to remind your audience of what is important.

How you speak may be as important as what you are saying. Your voice should be loud enough to be heard easily, but you should not shout. Speak clearly and not too slowly or too fast.

Your appearance is also important. Look at different people in the audience so they know that you are interested in them. Stand up straight. Don't slouch to one side, lean on a chair, or rock back and forth. Move your hands naturally; do not clench your fist or wave your hands often.

Listen to and watch good speakers to see how these ideas work together in a good speech. Keep these tips in mind when you give a speech.

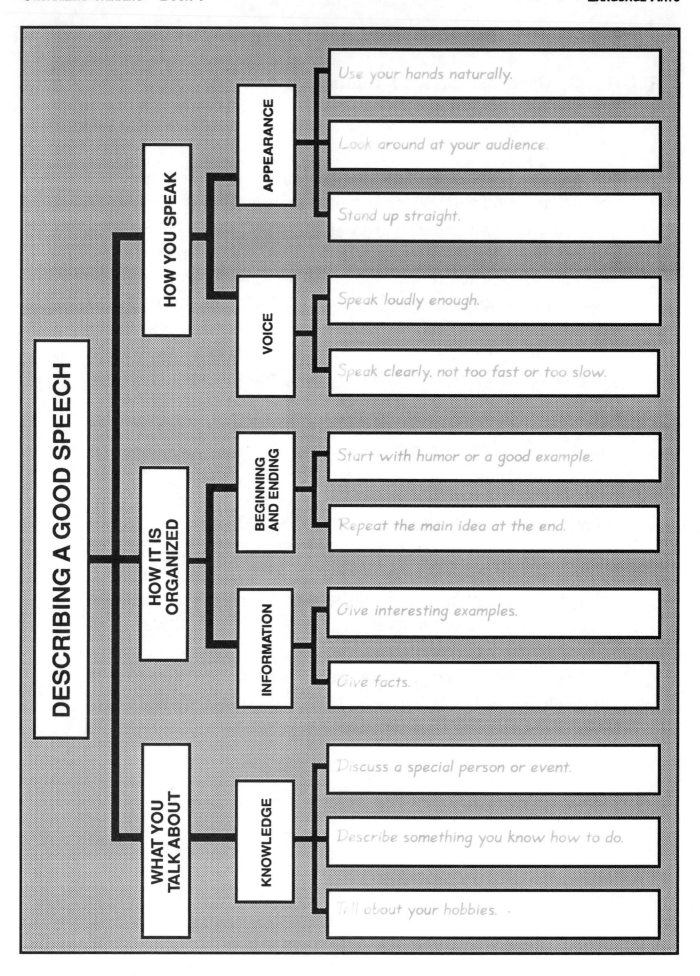

DESCRIBING A GOOD SPEECH

HOW YOU SPEAK

APPEARANCE

Use your hands naturally.

Look around at your audience.

Stand up straight.

VOICE

Speak loudly enough.

Speak clearly, not too fast or too slow.

HOW IT IS ORGANIZED

BEGINNING AND ENDING

Start with humor or a good example.

Repeat the main idea at the end.

INFORMATION

Give interesting examples.

Give facts.

WHAT YOU TALK ABOUT

KNOWLEDGE

Discuss a special person or event.

Describe something you know how to do.

Tell about your hobbies.

SPEECH ANALYSIS MATRIX

CHARACTERISTIC	APPLICATION	RATING

Subject
KNOWLEDGE
  hobbies
  something you know
    how to do
  special person or event		

INFORMATION
  facts
  examples		

Logical Organization
SUPPORTING MATERIALS
  main idea
  facts
  interesting examples		

PLANNING
  good start
  effective ending		

Presentation
VOICE
  speak clearly
  loud enough		

APPEARANCE
  look at the audience
  stand up straight
  use your hands naturally		

I'M LISTENING

THINKING SKILL: Evaluation

CONTENT OBJECTIVE: Students will use a matrix graph to evaluate their listening skills.

DISCUSSION: TECHNIQUE—This lesson uses a graphic organizer primarily for personal insight. Reproduce a class set of the matrix. After students have rated their current listening skills, collect and tally their responses. Use a transparency of the matrix to summarize the class's evaluation of their strong and weak listening skills.

DIALOGUE—Examine each listening habit. Discuss why it is important and what might prevent people from listening carefully. Write each skill on the board. As students identify what interferes with listening, ask them to identify what they can do to listen better. Write a second column of "Listening Tips." Create a poster of students own listening tips.

LISTENING HABIT	LISTENING TIPS
I concentrate on what is being said.	
I ask about what I don't understand.	
I keep my mind from wandering.	
I think about what I am hearing.	
I listen to directions carefully.	
I think about the words and feelings.	
I try to think about the speaker's ideas fairly.	
I listen for main ideas.	
I pay attention to ideas that are new to me.	
I recall what I heard to check my understanding.	

Good listening habits are necessary for learning, and learning is a big part of growing. Why is it important to concentrate on what is being said and to keep your mind from wandering? (I can't go back later and look at the material again as I can when reading something.) **What might keep you from listening this way?** (My seat might be uncomfortable. I may not be interested in the subject or there is something about the speaker that distracts me. I may be trying to do something else while I am listening to the speaker and that takes my attention away. I may be hungry, tired, or upset. Someone else is trying to get my attention.)

How can you think about what you are hearing? (I need to compare the new information I am hearing with what I already know. If it fits with what I know, I can add it to my "storybuilding" about the subject. If not, I need to decide whether to change my mind about old information or to question the new information.) **Why is it important to think about whether or not you believe what you are hearing?** (I need to know if it is reasonable or true before I store the information in memory. I do not want to store wrong information.)

Why is it important to ask about anything you do not understand? (I may get confused about an important part and then miss or not understand the rest of what is being said. What I am hearing may not agree with what I already know. I need more answers so I can evaluate what I am hearing. I need to understand what the speaker means.) **What might keep you from asking questions?** (I might feel shy about letting others know I do not understand, or scared because others seem to understand and I do not. I may not know what kind of questions to ask.)

Why is it important to listen carefully to directions? (Usually directions give an order or organization for doing things. Directions sometimes tell me how to do my assignment. Directions often tell me how much time I have to do the work.) **What might keep you from listening this way?** (I might be working on something else and trying to finish it. I might not know what important things to listen for and listen instead to the information that doesn't matter.)

Why is it important to think about the words being used and the feelings behind them? (The way the speaker says the words can change the meaning of them. I need to know whether the speaker is being funny or serious. The speaker's tone of voice and manner can create a special feeling or mood.) **What might keep you from listening this way?** (The speaker may not give any clues as to how serious s/he is. I may not know enough about the subject to know if the speaker is saying something funny or not.)

Why is it important to think fairly about the speaker's ideas? (If I do not keep an open mind, I may not be willing to reconsider my own ideas, attitudes, and understanding. The speaker may present some exciting new ideas. New ideas help me understand many other ideas I already have. The speaker may give me ideas that will lead to new ideas of my own.) **What might keep you from listening this way?** (Something is bothering me. Something about the speaker distracts my attention. I have disagreed with the speaker before. I do not like the topic or am not interested in learning more about it. Other people do not listen fairly to me.)

Why is it important to listen for main ideas? (The main idea describes what the person is really talking about. Sometimes the speaker uses more than one main idea. The main idea gives me the connection to the details. I need to be able to tell which details belong to which idea when the speaker goes from one idea to another. I need to know why the speaker is giving the details s/he does about the idea and why they are important.) **What might keep you from listening this way?** (The speaker may not present the main idea clearly. I may not know what to listen for. The ideas and details may not be presented in good order and get all mixed up in my head. I don't ask questions when I am confused.)

Why is it important to recall what you heard so you can check your understanding of it? (I want to understand the whole idea not just part of it. Replaying my memory of the whole idea may help me understand it better and see how all the parts fit together. I need to remember what was said because I do not have anything I can go back to and read.) **What might keep you from recalling and reflecting on what you heard?** (I didn't listen carefully all the time. I didn't understand one part so I stopped listening. I couldn't hear what the speaker was saying some of the time. I wanted to do something else. I did not think about what was being said.)

RESULT—If we understand what makes good listening and know what to do to listen well, we can better understand and use what we hear. We are in charge of our own understanding.

WRITING EXTENSION
• **Describe what you do now to be a good listener.**

THINKING ABOUT THINKING
• **How did using the diagram help you understand listening?**
• **Suggest another lesson in which depicting information on a matrix graph would help you understand what you are learning.**
• **Design another graph that would help you describe listening.**

SIMILAR LANGUAGE ARTS LESSONS:
• To organize information from texts, films, or speeches.
• To describe books, stories, or characters by two characteristics.

© 1992 CRITICAL THINKING PRESS & SOFTWARE • P.O. Box 448, Pacific Grove, CA 93950

I'M LISTENING

DIRECTIONS: Think about each listening habit. Recall an example when you listened like that. Write a few words to remind yourself how you did it. Decide how often you listen well and put a check mark in the appropriate box.

LISTENING HABIT	EXAMPLE	USUALLY	SOMETIMES	SELDOM
I concentrate on what is being said.				
I ask about what I don't understand.				
I keep my mind from wandering.				
I think about whether I should believe what I am hearing.				
I listen to directions carefully.				
I think about the words and feelings.				
I try to think about the speaker's ideas fairly.				
I listen for main ideas.				
I pay attention to ideas that are new to me.				
I recall what I heard to check my understanding.				

DESCRIBING CLASS RELATIONSHIPS

NOTE: The following three lessons introduce elementary students to class logic. One or two examples per class session is recommended to allow sufficient class discussion.

THINKING SKILL: Verbal classifications

CONTENT OBJECTIVE: Students will represent class relationships between words using a number of diagrams.

DISCUSSION: TECHNIQUE—Encourage students to state the relationships shown in the various diagrams. Draw the diagram on the chalkboard or use a transparency of the blank diagram and write in the terms as they are discussed. As each relationship is stated, point to the position of each term to emphasize how its position on the diagram is related to the meaning of the statement. After each example, encourage students to state and draw similar relationships.

DIALOGUE—(FAMILY RELATIONSHIPS) Use the terms "all," "no," "not," and "some," to express the class relationships shown in the first diagram. This exercise refers only to human mothers; if students refer to animal mothers, accept that comment.

All fathers are parents. All mothers are parents. Not all parents are mothers. Not all parents are fathers. No mothers are fathers. No fathers are mothers. All mothers are women. All female teachers are women. Some female teachers are mothers. Some mothers are teachers. Some female teachers are not mothers. Some mothers are not teachers. All women are people. All mothers are people. All mothers are women. Not all women are mothers. Not all people are women.

In the second exercise use sentences like the following:

Some living things are plants. Some living things are animals. Some living things are not plants. Some living things are not animals. Some plants are vegetables. Some plants are trees. Some plants are not vegetables. Some plants are not trees. No plants are animals. No animals are plants. Some animals are birds. Some animals are not birds. Some animals are fish. Some animals are not fish. No bird is a fish. No fish is a bird.

(VEHICLES) Use the terms "all," "no," "not," and "some," to describe class relationships.

All planes are vehicles. Some vehicles are planes. Some vehicles are not planes. All jets are planes. Some planes are not jets. Some planes are jets. All cars are vehicles. Some vehicles are cars. Some vehicles are not cars. All station wagons are cars. Some cars are station wagons. Some cars are not station wagons.

(STUDENTS, SOCCER PLAYERS, AND SCOUTS) Use the terms "and" and "not" to describe the following relationships. In common English usage, "but" is used in place of "and."

Anita is a girl who plays soccer and is a scout.
Hannah is a girl who does not play soccer and is not a scout.
Jessica is a girl who plays soccer, but is not a scout.
Justo is a boy who plays soccer and is a scout.
Lorenzo is boy who is a scout, but does not play soccer.

Marco is a boy who does not play soccer and is not a scout.
Yolanda is a girl who is a scout, but does not play soccer.

RESULT—One can understand the meaning of statements containing "some," "all," and "no" by picturing their classes.

WRITING EXTENSION
• Select some people or things that are related. Draw their relationships using the circles like we did in the lesson. Use *"all," "no," " not,"* and *"some"* to describe the relationships.

THINKING ABOUT THINKING
• Why is it important to understand what *"some," "all,"* and *"no"* mean in a sentence?
• How do the circles help you understand how things are related?
• Identify other objects or ideas that would be easier to understand if they were described this way?

SIMILAR LANGUAGE ARTS LESSONS
• To illustrate class relationships in an article, report, or presentation.

DESCRIBING PEOPLE

DIRECTIONS: Draw a line from the group of words to the diagram which pictures the correct relationship. Use the abbreviations in the parentheses to label the diagrams correctly. One example is shown.

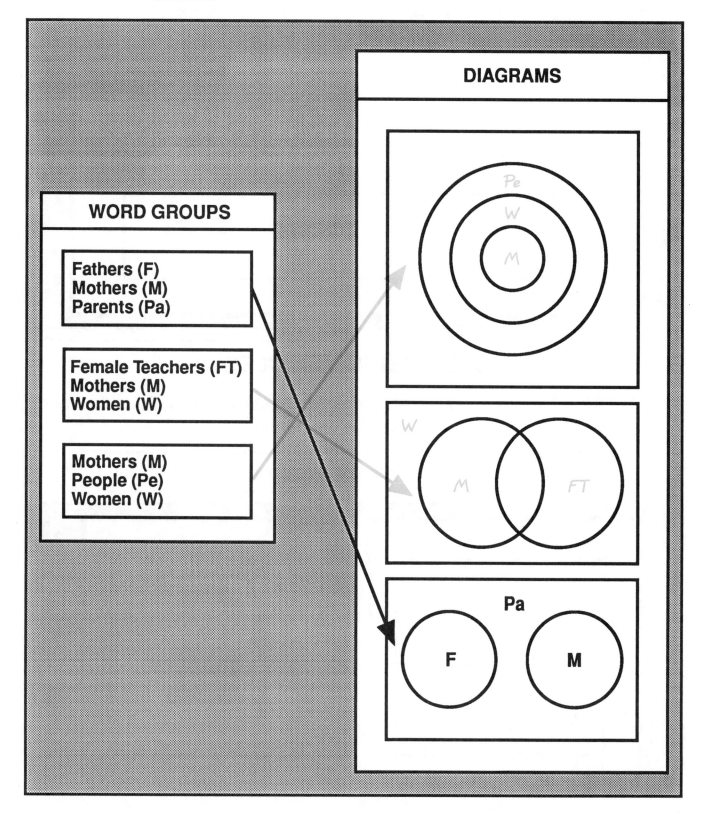

DESCRIBING LIVING THINGS

DIRECTIONS: Label the classification diagram to show the relationship among the following words.

animals, ferns, fish, insects, living things, plants, trees

living things

plants

ferns | trees

animals

insects | fish

DESCRIBING VEHICLES

DIRECTIONS: Label the classification diagram to show the relationship among the following words.

cars, convertibles, jets, planes, station wagons, vehicles

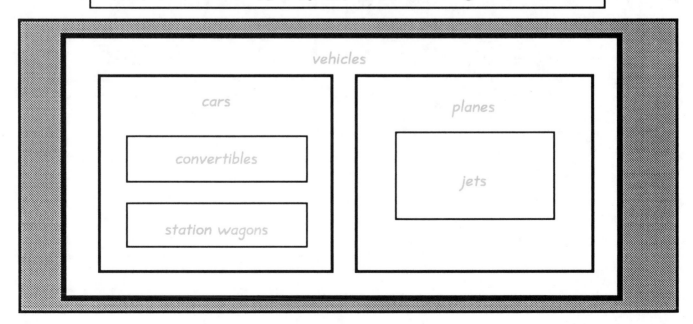

vehicles

cars

convertibles

station wagons

planes

jets

DESCRIBING ACTIVITIES OF STUDENTS

DIRECTIONS: Label the graph below to describe each of the following individuals:

Anita plays soccer and is in scouts.
Hannah does not play soccer and is not in scouts.
Jessica plays soccer, but is not in scouts.
Justo plays soccer and is in scouts.
Lorenzo does not play soccer, but is in scouts.
Marco plays soccer, but is not in scouts.
Yolanda does not play soccer, but is in scouts.

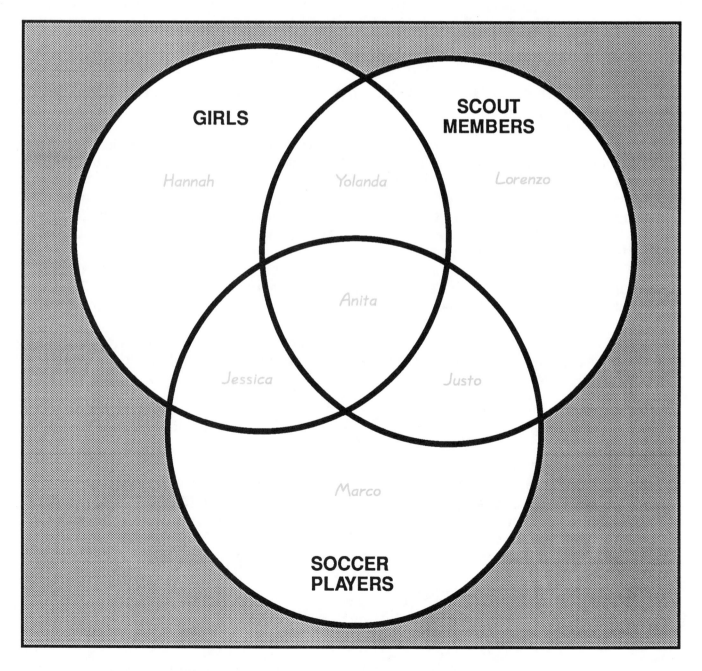

MAIN IDEA AND SUPPORTING DETAILS

THINKING SKILL: Identifying main idea and supporting details

CONTENT OBJECTIVE: Students will identify main idea and supporting details in a given passage.

DISCUSSION: TECHNIQUE—Select an appropriate paragraph from a science or social studies text. Use a transparency of the arch diagram to record students' responses regarding the main idea and supporting details. To introduce this lesson, explain the structure of an expository paragraph. The main idea is the overarching theme connecting the details together. It is a statement of the effect of the many details. The main idea "grows out of" and "rests upon" adequate details to support it. Supporting details clarify, illustrate, or provide examples of the main idea.

Direct students to identify which sentence in the paragraph is the general statement to which the other sentences are examples or reasons. Students will write the main idea in the arch of the diagram, turn the paper sideways, and write the sentences providing details and examples in each column.

DIALOGUE—Explain the key characteristics of a main idea.

A main idea is a single thought that states a point of view. The details in the paragraph support that single thought.

To illustrate the structure of a paragraph with main idea and supporting details, direct students to highlight the main idea with a pink pen and supporting details with a yellow pen. Use the same process as students review each other's expository writing. If a student's writing contains few pink marks, then the student is writing facts with little, if any, interpretation or organization. If a student's writing contains few yellow marks, then the student is expressing generalizations without adequate supporting information. The color coding alerts students to omissions or superfluous sentences in their writing.

To design a bulletin board which illustrates this principle, assemble three passages from children's magazines or *Weekly Readers*. Photo-enlarge them to an appropriate size. Display the passages containing main ideas and supporting details on a bulletin board using the same color coding.

RESULT—To read a paragraph critically, identify the main idea and the details that support it. The main idea should interpret or summarize what the details mean and should not express more than the details support.

WRITING EXTENSION
• Describe how to distinguish the main idea from supporting details.

THINKING ABOUT THINKING
• How did using the arch diagram help you picture the main idea in this passage?
• Why is it important to recognize the main idea and supporting details in a passage?
• How can recognizing the main idea and supporting details help you understand more clearly what you read?
• Design another diagram to illustrate a main idea and supporting details.

SIMILAR LANGUAGE ARTS LESSONS
• To illustrate headings and subheadings in an outline.
• To illustrate reasons and conclusion.

MAIN IDEA AND SUPPORTING DETAILS

DIRECTIONS: **Read the passage carefully. In the "arch" of the diagram write the main idea in a statement which tells what the sentences in the paragraph mean. The main idea sentence "grows out of" and "rests upon" the other details in the paragraph. It should state a point of view. It should say only what the supporting details mean. It should be limited to a single idea.**

Turn the paper sideways and write a supporting detail sentence in each column. Supporting details explain, illustrate, provide examples for, or justify the main idea.

There are more flowering plants than most people realize. There are about 200,000 different kinds of flowering plants. More than half of all the plants that grow have flowers. All fruits and many vegetables are flowering plants.

MAIN IDEA AND SUPPORTING DETAILS

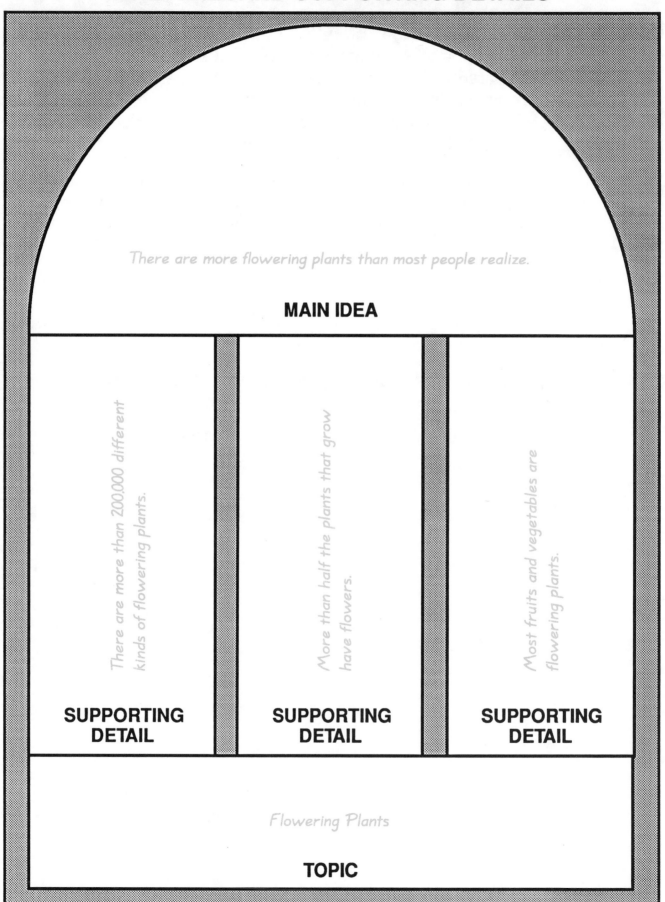

There are more flowering plants than most people realize.

MAIN IDEA

There are more than 200,000 different kinds of flowering plants.

More than half the plants that grow have flowers.

Most fruits and vegetables are flowering plants.

SUPPORTING DETAIL   **SUPPORTING DETAIL**   **SUPPORTING DETAIL**

Flowering Plants

TOPIC

MAIN IDEA AND SUPPORTING DETAILS

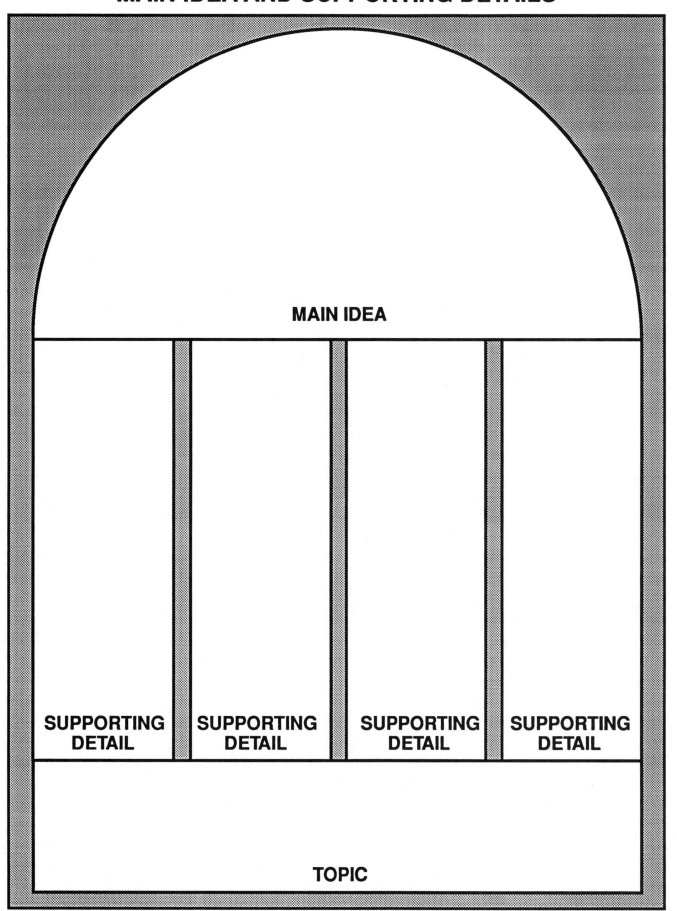

MAIN IDEA

SUPPORTING DETAIL   **SUPPORTING DETAIL**   **SUPPORTING DETAIL**   **SUPPORTING DETAIL**

TOPIC

CHAPTER 3—WRITING LESSONS

WRITING DEFINITIONS
(central idea graph)

WRITING YOUR
AUTOBIOGRAPHY
(interval graph)

WRITING A REPORT
(flowchart)

DESCRIPTIVE WRITING:
A COMMON OBJECT
(central idea graph)

EXPOSITORY WRITING:
A HISTORICAL EVENT
(central idea graph)

CREATIVE WRITING:
DINOSAUR
(web diagram)

WRITING DEFINITIONS

THINKING SKILL: Verbal classification

CONTENT OBJECTIVE: Student will use a central idea diagram to analyze and write clear definitions. They will identify the class to which a term belongs and the characteristics that make it different from others.

DISCUSSION : TECHNIQUE—Use a central idea diagram to record students' suggestions of characteristics that distinguish one term from others in the same class. After students have read the description of an appropriate definition, select a definition from your science or social studies text. Ask students to picture the information on the diagram. Use the diagram to record class discussion of the term.

DIALOGUE—Explain the connection between clear understanding and stating appropriate definitions.

Can you think of a time when you misunderstood what someone was explaining because the idea or thing they were talking about was unclear in your mind? (For example, if a teacher uses the term "sum" and a student does not know which part of the addition process the sum refers to, the student may become confused about addition.)
Why is it important to name the characteristics that make something different from things that are similar to it? Can you think of a time when you couldn't remember clearly what something is because you confused it with other similar things or ideas?

Encourage students to use appropriate oral and written definitions in all academic areas. Prompt them to include the category and the qualifiers for each term you ask them to define. Emphasize the category and the qualifiers in each definition that you give. Model and insist upon appropriate definitions in explanations, class discussion, and examinations. Allow ample time for students to explain significant characteristics and to give examples, especially those statements which include "some," "all," and "no."

RESULT—When defining an object, organism, person, process, or idea , one expresses clearly the category to which the thing belongs and the qualifiers that make it different from other things in that class.

WRITING EXTENSION
• **Apply this model to definition questions on unit tests.**

THINKING ABOUT THINKING
• **How does knowing how to write appropriate definitions help you give clearer answers in class and on tests?**
• **How does using the graphic organizer help you write better definitions?**
• **How does the model definition help you write better definitions?**
• **How does listening for the category and qualifiers help you understand more clearly what is being said?**

SIMILAR LANGUAGE ARTS LESSONS
• To organize and write descriptive paragraphs.
• To describe main ideas and supporting details.
• To describe artifacts, museum displays, performances, and television shows.
• To describe organisms, geographic features, physical science and astronomical terms.

WRITING DEFINITIONS

DIRECTIONS: Read the passage to be sure that you know what a definition should contain. Read the information about a bicycle. Identify the class and the characteristics that describe a bicycle.

A **definition** is a clear statement of the meaning of a word. A good definition lets the reader know exactly what the word means and what makes the word different from similar ones. A complete definition of any noun should contain the **class** to which the person, place, or thing belongs. It should also state the **characteristics** that make it different from others.

Suppose you had never seen a bicycle and someone told you, "A bicycle is something that kids ride to school." The last part of the sentence tells you that a bicycle is a vehicle. The definition doesn't give you enough information to tell the difference between a bicycle and a bus or other vehicles which "kids ride to school."

Suppose someone told you that a bicycle has two wheels, handlebars, and is powered by pedaling with one's feet. This definition gives the characteristics of a bicycle, but you may not know what a bicycle really is. It could be a game or sports equipment.

Your definition of a bicycle must include:

1. the **class** to which it belongs.

2. the **characteristics** that make it different from others.

WRITING DEFINITIONS

DIRECTIONS: Read the passage to be sure that you know what a definition should contain. Read the information about a bicycle. Identify the class and the characteristics that describe a bicycle.

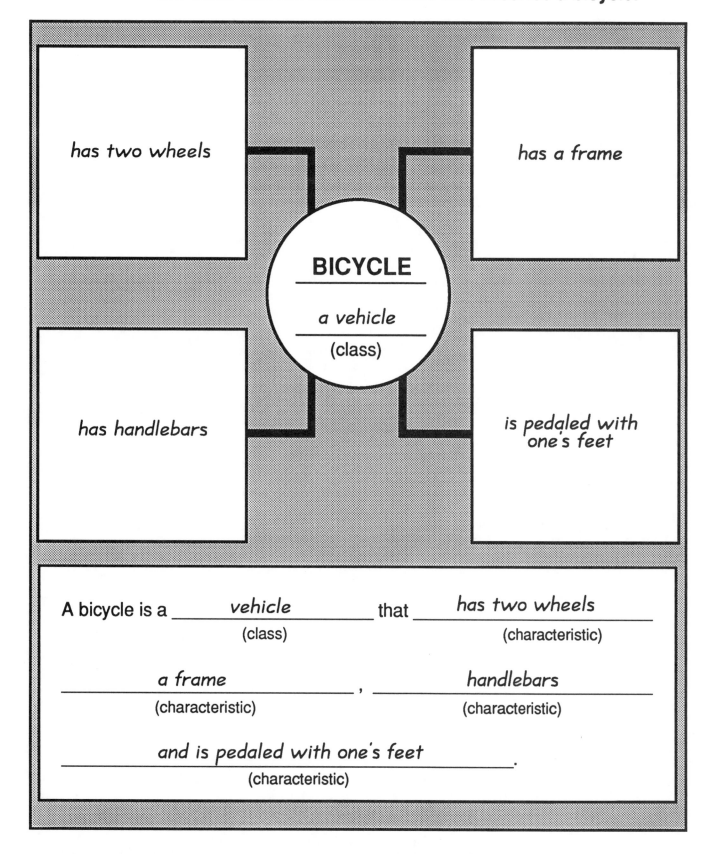

has two wheels

has a frame

BICYCLE

a vehicle

(class)

has handlebars

is pedaled with one's feet

A bicycle is a _____*vehicle*_____ that _____*has two wheels*_____
(class)   (characteristic)

_____*a frame*_____ , _____*handlebars*_____
(characteristic)   (characteristic)

_____*and is pedaled with one's feet*_____.
(characteristic)

WRITING DEFINITIONS

DIRECTIONS: **Select a word from a science or a social studies lesson. Write one characteristic in each box. Use the model sentence to write your definition.**

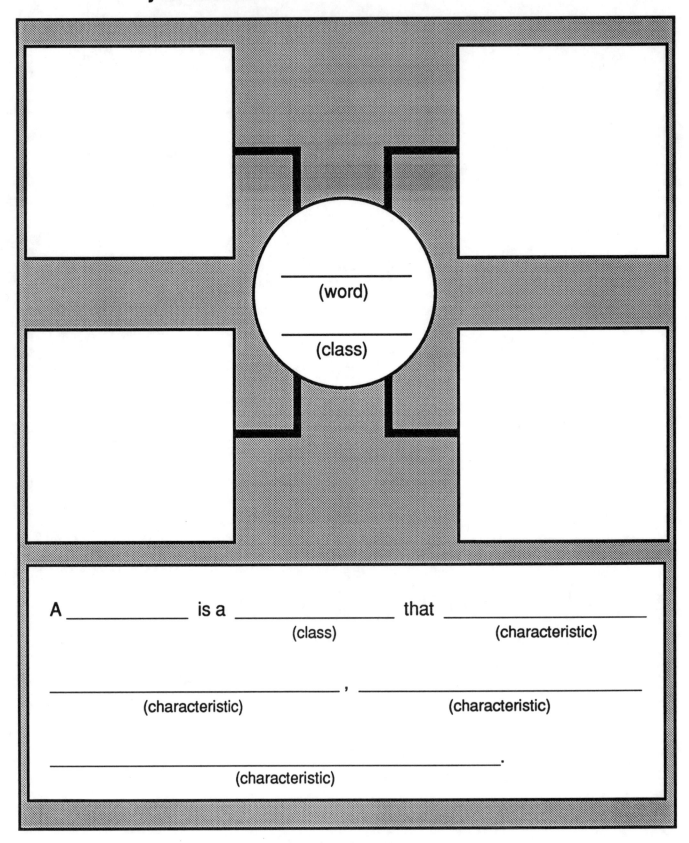

_____ (word)

_____ (class)

A _____ is a _____ that _____
                               (class)   (characteristic)

_____ , _____
       (characteristic)   (characteristic)

_____.
               (characteristic)

WRITING YOUR AUTOBIOGRAPHY

THINKING SKILL: Verbal sequences, recognizing chronological order

CONTENT OBJECTIVE: Students will use a time line to write an autobiography.

DISCUSSION: TECHNIQUE—Explain the use of the time line. Students use the time line to record their memories in chronological order. Each student must decide the range of months or years about which s/he is going to write and label each mark on the time line. (See the directions on page 15.) Define autobiography.

DIALOGUE—Since few youngsters routinely keep journals or diaries, writing an autobiography can provide a valuable record of each child's experiences. Because writing an autobiography draws on the student's own experiences, it conveys the message that each child's experiences are valuable. Encourage this writing assignment as a family history opportunity by suggesting that students involve older family members in recalling the special events in the life of the child. Help students appreciate the significance of their childhood experiences by sharing special memories from your own childhood.

What do you remember most from when you were a small child? List five experiences that seem important to you. What is it about these experiences that make them stand out in your mind?

Students often identify family milestones that were unusually happy or dramatic. They may also relate incidents that seem ordinary, but are common experiences that all people share and value. These situations may be funny, may illustrate growing up, offer some personal insight about oneself or others, or may demonstrate healthy solutions to problems we all face.

Encourage students to read biographies, autobiographies, and autobiographical novels and short stories. Laura Ingalls Wilder is an excellent example of an author who used her childhood experiences as a basis for her books.

RESULT—Recording the important events of our lives chronologically produces a valuable record of our growth.

WRITING EXTENSION
* **Describe how a sequence of events in your childhood developed some talent, good habit, or special quality in you or changed your life.**

THINKING ABOUT THINKING
* **How did using the time line help you remember the events in your life?**
* **Suggest another lesson in which a time line would help you understand what you are learning.**
* **How did remembering the time order help you appreciate how far you've come in doing something that is important to you?**

SIMILAR LANGUAGE ARTS LESSONS
* To record the plots of stories or plays.
* To record biographical data.
* To organize information for writing letters, biographies, or stories.

WRITING YOUR AUTOBIOGRAPHY

DIRECTIONS: Use the time line to write important events in your life in the order in which they happened. Decide the length of time you are going to write about. Label each mark on the time line by years, months, or weeks. Write as many details as you can remember.

Talk to your friends, your parents, and your grandparents. Add events which they suggest to your time line. Use your time line to write your autobiography.

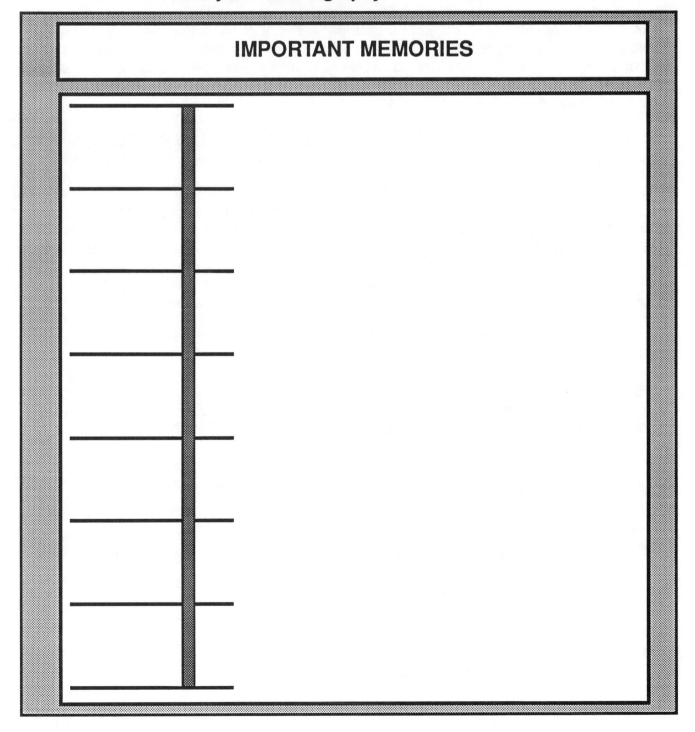

IMPORTANT MEMORIES

WRITING A REPORT

THINKING SKILL: Verbal sequences

CONTENT OBJECTIVE: Students will use a flowchart to identify the steps in writing a report.

DISCUSSION: TECHNIQUE—Use a transparency of the flowchart to record responses as students report the steps for writing a report. Use the steps to check on students' progress.

Reproduce the matrix which contains the steps in random order. Direct students to cut apart the boxes and to rearrange them in the appropriate order. Students should then record the order on the flowchart to illustrate the process.

Other graphics may be useful in helping students to organize their reports. See the lessons on descriptive writing, expository writing, narrowing a topic, main idea and supporting details, and assumptions, reasons, and conclusions.

DIALOGUE—Encourage students to identify clues they used which show order.

RESULT—Preparing a report is more efficient and effective if it is carried out according to a sequential plan. The plan follows a logical sequence of decision making and research.

WRITING EXTENSION
• Why is it important to follow given steps in preparing a report?

THINKING ABOUT THINKING
• What clues or patterns did you see that suggest an order in preparing a report?
• What should you consider important when selecting a topic?
• Design another graphic organizer to help you prepare a report.
• Suggest another lesson in which using a flowchart would help you understand what you are learning.

SIMILAR LANGUAGE ARTS LESSONS
• To depict the steps in instructions, library use, or study-skills procedures.
• To depict the plot of a story.
• To depict the rules of punctuation, spelling, grammar, or capitalization.

WRITING A REPORT

DIRECTIONS: Cut the boxes apart. Use the following information to put the steps in order. Write the steps for writing a report on the flowchart.

When you need to write a report, pick a topic that you like. Decide what you want to find out about that topic. Go to the library and locate books which give you more information about it.

As you read, write the important facts and ideas on small cards. Arrange your cards in the order in which the facts and ideas should appear in your paper. You can rearrange the cards easily if you change your mind.

Write your first paper as carefully as you can. Leave an extra space between each line of writing so that there will be room to make changes. Discuss your report with your teacher, your parents, or your study partner. Make any changes which will make your paper better.

Now you are ready to write your final report.

DISCUSS FIRST WRITING	GO TO THE LIBRARY
MAKE CHANGES IN FIRST WRITING	ORGANIZE NOTES
PICK A TOPIC	TAKE NOTES
WRITE REPORT THE FIRST TIME	WRITE REPORT THE SECOND TIME

WRITING A REPORT

DIRECTIONS: Write the steps for writing a report on the flowchart. Use the information you cut apart.

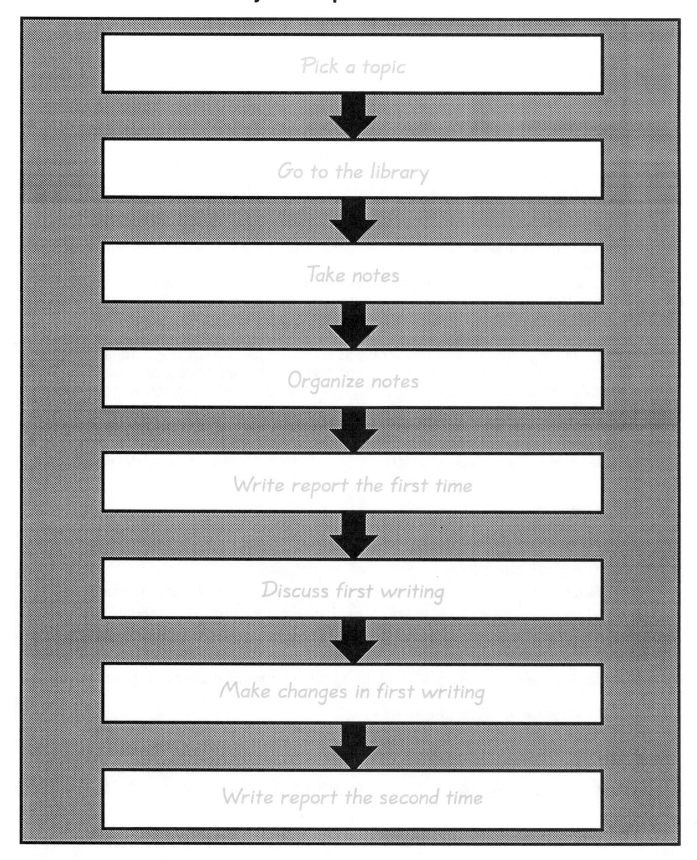

DESCRIPTIVE WRITING: A COMMON OBJECT

NOTE: For more "branches," use the diagram in the creative writing lesson. To modify this exercise as a social studies lesson, select a common object from other periods of history and encourage students to describe it thoroughly.

THINKING SKILL: Verbal classification; identifying attributes; identifying main idea and supporting details

CONTENT OBJECTIVE: Students will organize information on a central idea graph to describe a common object thoroughly.

DISCUSSION: TECHNIQUE—Use a transparency of the central idea graph to record details as students describe a common object.

DIALOGUE—Most objects are described by general categories: how an object looks, what it is made of, what it is used for, and its value. Describing the object gives the reader the richest possible image of its appearance. Encourage students to see the object "with new eyes" and to use precise language when describing even the smallest details. Characteristics may include color, shape, size, texture, condition, similes, and metaphors.

Describing the **parts** of the object gives the reader an impression of what it looks like and how it is manufactured. Encourage students to use precise language to describe the components. Characteristics may include shape, function, assembly, operation, and manufacture.

Describing the **kind** of object gives the reader associations with other similar objects. Encourage your students to notice similar objects and to use precise language in describing the category to which the object belongs, other objects in that same class, and qualifiers that differentiate it from similar items. The object may be in the center of the diagram and subclasses of it on the "arms."

RESULT—The purpose for describing an object, person, organism, idea, or institution determines which of its characteristics is emphasized:

Description – significant characteristics	How it looks – several details
What are its parts – components	Other kinds – name them

WRITING EXTENSION

- Select a common object and describe it thoroughly.

THINKING ABOUT THINKING

- How did using the diagram help you "see" and describe the object differently?
- How did using the diagram help you organize your thoughts about the object?
- Design another diagram that would help you observe or describe an object.
- How does knowing how to describe something help you understand what you see?
- How has your understanding of describing things changed after doing this lesson?

SIMILAR LANGUAGE ARTS LESSONS

- To organize main ideas and supporting details when preparing speeches or papers.
- To illustrate classes and subclasses, such as parts of speech or types of books.
- To describe artifacts, museum displays, performances, or television shows.
- To describe organisms, geographic features, physical science or astronomical terms.

DESCRIPTIVE WRITING: A COMMON OBJECT

DIRECTIONS: Select an interesting and important object in your house, your school, or your neighborhood. Use each of the diagrams to record all the details and information about the object that would help you to explain it to someone who has never seen one.

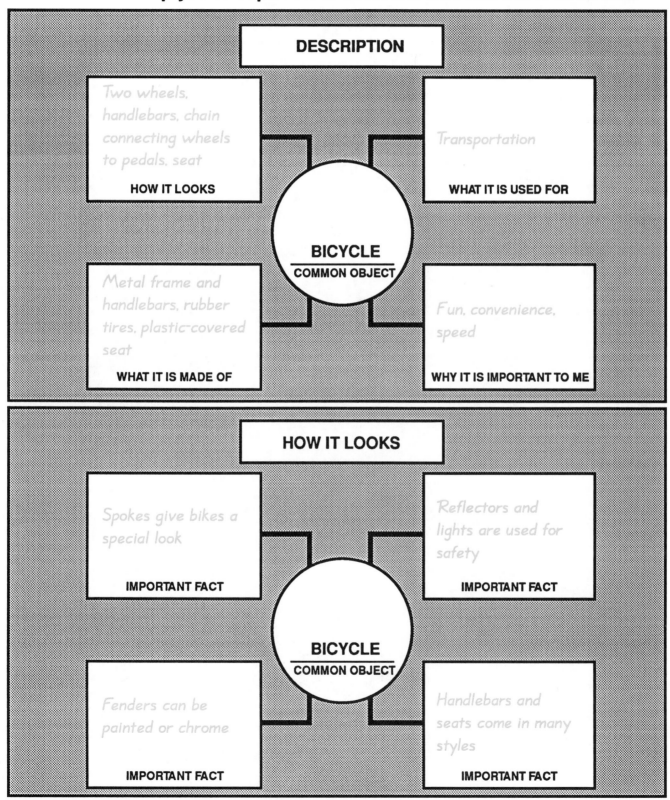

DESCRIPTION

Two wheels, handlebars, chain connecting wheels to pedals, seat
HOW IT LOOKS

Transportation
WHAT IT IS USED FOR

Metal frame and handlebars, rubber tires, plastic-covered seat
WHAT IT IS MADE OF

Fun, convenience, speed
WHY IT IS IMPORTANT TO ME

BICYCLE
COMMON OBJECT

HOW IT LOOKS

Spokes give bikes a special look
IMPORTANT FACT

Reflectors and lights are used for safety
IMPORTANT FACT

BICYCLE
COMMON OBJECT

Fenders can be painted or chrome
IMPORTANT FACT

Handlebars and seats come in many styles
IMPORTANT FACT

DESCRIPTIVE WRITING: A COMMON OBJECT

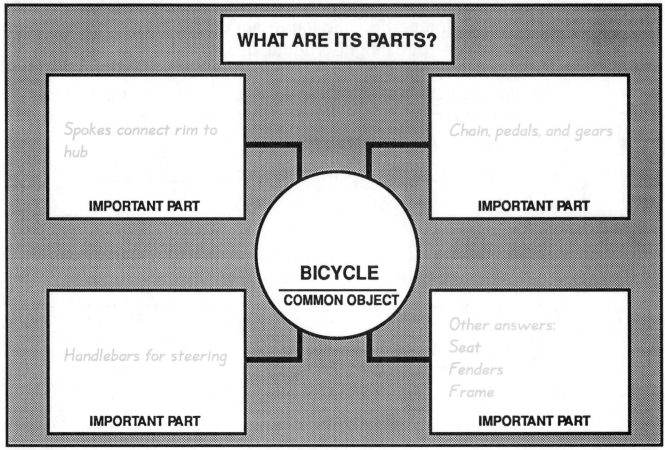

WHAT ARE ITS PARTS?

Spokes connect rim to hub

IMPORTANT PART

Chain, pedals, and gears

IMPORTANT PART

BICYCLE
COMMON OBJECT

Handlebars for steering

IMPORTANT PART

Other answers:
Seat
Fenders
Frame

IMPORTANT PART

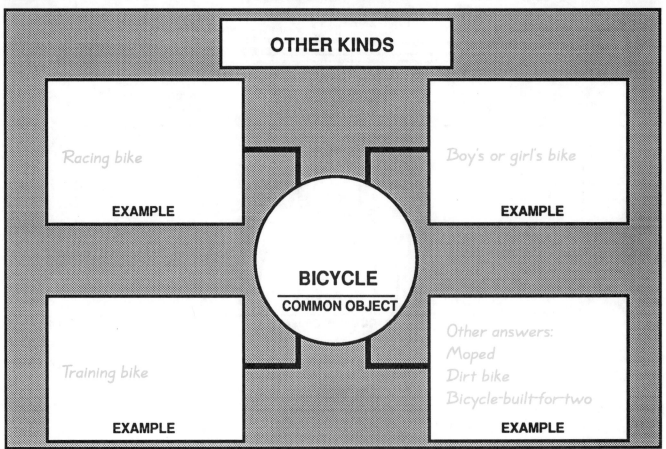

OTHER KINDS

Racing bike

EXAMPLE

Boy's or girl's bike

EXAMPLE

BICYCLE
COMMON OBJECT

Training bike

EXAMPLE

Other answers:
Moped
Dirt bike
Bicycle-built-for-two

EXAMPLE

EXPOSITORY WRITING: A HISTORICAL EVENT

THINKING SKILL: Verbal classification, identifying attributes

CONTENT OBJECTIVE: Students will use the central idea graph to organize information to describe a significant event thoroughly.

DISCUSSION: TECHNIQUE—Use a transparency of the central idea graph to help students describe an historical event. Show your students that discussing the significant features of an event helps them understand current or past events meaningfully. To introduce this lesson, reproduce a class set of a news article from your *Weekly Reader* or student news magazine. Direct students to use a colored pen to highlight significant features of the event. Confirm that each element of a journalistic description (*who, what, when, where,* and *why*) has been identified by the class.

You may apply the diagram to any historical event. In this lesson Columbus's discovery of the New World is examined like a news story.

To extend this lesson, encourage students to fill in the diagram as a critical viewing exercise. This process may also be used to examine the plot of a story which the class has recently read.

DIALOGUE—Discuss why each element of a journalistic description (*who, what, when, where,* and *why*) is important in our understanding of an event.

Discuss why it is important to recognize the background situations which contribute to events.

RESULT—To understand the significance of an event, we must know its key elements, the factors leading to it, and the consequences of it.

WRITING EXTENSION

• **Select an event (an historical event) and describe it carefully. Identify the factors leading to it and its possible consequences.**
• **Describe something special that happened in your family or a sports event.**

THINKING ABOUT THINKING

• **How did using the diagram help you write more clearly?**
• **Design another diagram to describe an event.**
• **Suggest another lesson in which describing the key features, the background, and the consequences of an event would help you understand it more fully.**

SIMILAR LANGUAGE ARTS LESSONS

• To describe the climax or turning point in a story.
• To describe performances, television shows, or current events.

DESCRIBING A HISTORICAL EVENT

At the time of Columbus, people in Europe bought cotton, silk, spices, and other needed products from China and India. In the 1400s the trade routes were closed. Europeans would have to sail around Africa or reach China by crossing the ocean.

By 1450 mapmakers knew that the earth was not flat. Many sailors still feared sailing off the end of a flat ocean. Columbus believed that the earth was round like a ball. He thought he could get to India and China by crossing the Atlantic Ocean. Like other sailors of his time, Columbus thought that the earth was much smaller than it is. He had no idea that the Atlantic Ocean and the Pacific Ocean were not the same body of water. He did not know that another continent stood between Europe and China.

With three small ships, the *Santa Maria*, the *Pinta*, and the *Niña* Columbus set sail with a crew of convicts, criminals, and inexperienced sailors. The sailors did not share Columbus's great dream. They were worried about sailing in unknown waters. They wanted to turn back and even plotted to kill Columbus. On October 12, 1492, after 33 days on the open sea, they sighted an island in the Bahamas which Columbus called San Salvador.

Believing that he had reached an island near India, Columbus called the native people "Indians." He explored the nearby islands looking for a continent. The little *Niña* headed home to Spain carrying Columbus and the news of his discoveries.

Columbus made three more trips across the Atlantic Ocean. Disappointed and disgraced at failing to find the mainland of Asia, Columbus died in 1506.

          © 1992 CRITICAL THINKING PRESS & SOFTWARE • P.O. Box 448, Pacific Grove, CA 93950

DESCRIBING A HISTORICAL EVENT

DIRECTIONS: Select an historical event. Use the diagram to describe the event.

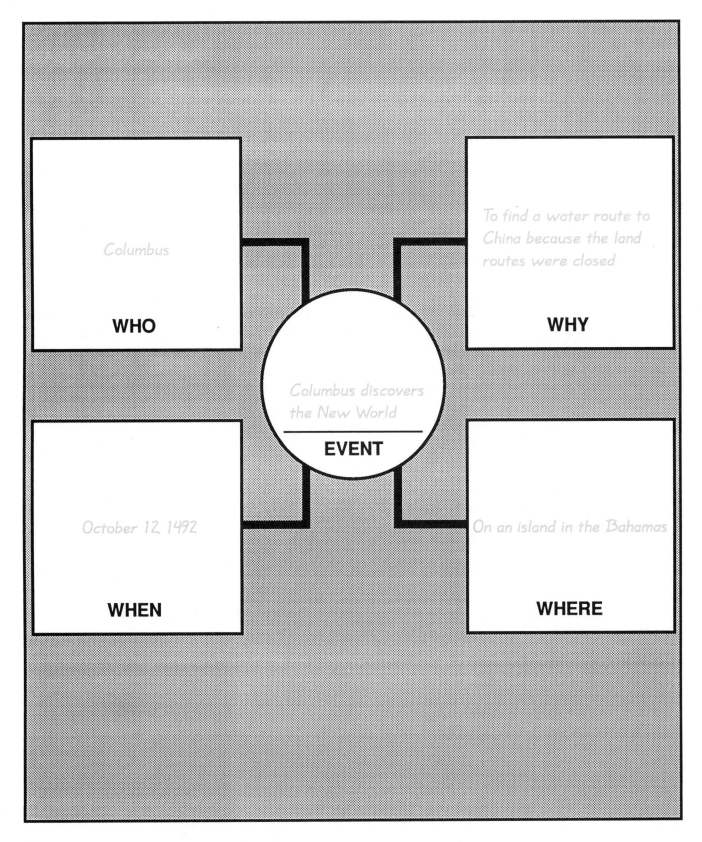

CREATIVE WRITING: DINOSAUR

NOTE: This lesson extends the concept of metaphor from the lesson on "The Steam Shovel."

THINKING SKILL: Verbal classification and analogy, identifying attributes and metaphors

CONTENT OBJECTIVE: Students will use the web diagram to form metaphors or similes in creative writing.

DISCUSSION: TECHNIQUE—To demonstrate the process, write a word associated with "dinosaur" in the box on one of the diagram's "arms." In the box on each branch, write a word that you associate with the word in the box. Ask students to continue adding words to "arms" or branches to produce as many connections as possible. Students may add additional "arms" and branches to the diagram to generate more ideas.

After students have completed the diagram individually, compile a class composite "web" of words associated with dinosaurs. Because students' ideas will probably exceed the number of branches on the worksheet, a transparency of the diagram will not be adequate for class discussion. Draw a web diagram on the chalkboard and continue to add "arms." For the writing exercise, students may use their own diagrams or the class composite "web" for ideas. Ask each student to select words on "arms" and branches and use those associations to write a story about dinosaurs.

Extend this lesson by asking students to find stories, poems, advertisements, and cartoons about dinosaurs. Use the web diagram to organize the metaphors and descriptions of dinosaurs. Produce the class composite as a story, a poem, a bulletin board, or a mobile.

DIALOGUE—Encourage each student who suggests a primary connection to suggest several branches. Allow other students to add branches. Encourage as many students as time and student interest will allow to contribute connections. Not all the associations will result in metaphors.

RESULT—Generating connections provides a pool of ideas for creating metaphors or descriptions. Generating many connections produces numerous, interesting descriptions.

WRITING EXTENSION

* **Use the web diagram to organize your ideas about another object or animal. Then write a story or poem about that object or animal.**

THINKING ABOUT THINKING

* **How did using the web diagram help you write about a dinosaur?**
* **Design another diagram to help you picture connections.**
* **How did using the web diagram help you realize that you know more connections than you thought?**
* **Suggest another lesson in which using a web diagram would help you understand and write about something that you are learning.**

SIMILAR LANGUAGE ARTS LESSONS

* To organize students' creative thinking about images or metaphors to write speeches, poems, or humor.
* To organize students' creative thinking to find creative alternatives or solutions to problems.

CREATIVE WRITING: DINOSAUR

DIRECTIONS: In the box on each "arm" of the circle, write a word connected with a dinosaur. In the box on each branch, write another word connected with the word on the "arm." Choose the most interesting "dinosaur connections" and use them to write a poem,.

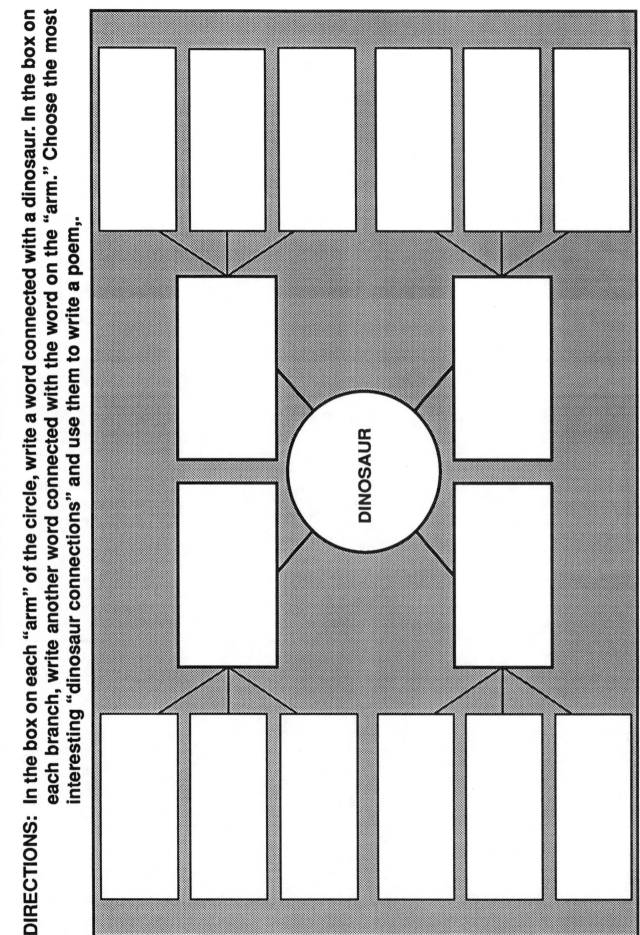

DINOSAUR

CHAPTER 4—SOCIAL STUDIES LESSONS

DRAW YOUR FAMILY TREE (branching diagram)		NEIGHBORHOODS AND CITIES (overlapping classes diagram)
	NEW ENGLAND AND THE SOUTHWEST (compare and contrast)	
LAND FORMS AND BODIES OF WATER (branching diagram)		EXPLORERS AND DISCOVERERS (time line)
	GOODS AND SERVICES (compare and contrast)	
PRODUCERS AND CONSUMERS (matrix and cycle diagrams)		TAXES AND THE COMMUNITY (cycle diagram)
	CHECKS AND MONEY (compare and contrast)	
CASHING A CHECK (flowchart and cycle diagram)		PRODUCTS FROM OIL (branching diagram)
	NEEDS AND RESOURCES: THE BUFFALO AS A SOURCE OF SUPPLY (branching diagram)	
WHAT GOVERNMENT DOES (branching diagram)		CITY, STATE, AND NATIONAL GOVERNMENTS (matrix)

DRAW YOUR FAMILY TREE

THINKING SKILL: Verbal sequencing and classification

CONTENT OBJECTIVE: Students will use a branching diagram to record how members of their family are related.

DISCUSSION: TECHNIQUE—Unlike most *Organizing Thinking* lessons, this activity involves individual products, not class discussion of a given passage. Students use one of the three branching diagrams to illustrate how members of their family are related.

Second grade students may need to use a large sheet of paper to draw pictures of family members, rather than writing names on the diagram. Use the diagram as a model.

Third or fourth grade students may use the second diagram to research the birth dates and birthplaces of their family members. The third diagram asks students to draw aunts and uncles. Students may write the names of cousins, great-aunts, or great-uncles in the margins. Students from large families may need to extend the diagram with another sheet of paper.

DIALOGUE—Each row on the diagram represents a generation. Young children may use the terms "grandparents," "cousins," "aunts," and "uncles," but they may not be able to conceptualize family relationships. Unless there is great difference in age between siblings, the children in a specific generation of a family will grow up, marry, and have children of their own at about the same time. Use the branching diagram to confirm family relationships.

Discuss the interest that people demonstrate in knowing their family background. Encourage students to discuss relatives they do not know and family history with older members of their family. Encourage students to identify how their grandparents' experiences while growing up were different from theirs.

Because so many children in school today have extended families of stepparents, it is important that the diagram should include as many members of the larger family as children feel comfortable with. To illustrate stepparents, divide another copy of the diagram in half and staple the appropriate half onto the diagram. For some children, this may be the first time that they "see" how all the members of their family are related. No distinction should be made between natural and extended family members.

Children sometimes believe that members of a family all have the same last name. This does not take into account maiden names, remarried mothers, women who retain the name of their family of origin, or cultures in which the family name is listed first.

RESULT—Everyone's family tree is different. Our family tree gives us a record of how the many members of our family are related.

WRITING EXTENSION
- **Use your family tree to describe your family's generations.**

THINKING ABOUT THINKING
- **How did using the diagram help you understand and research the relationships within your family?**
- **Suggest another lesson in which using a branching diagram would help you understand what you are learning.**
- **Design another diagram that would help you picture your family.**

SIMILAR SOCIAL STUDIES LESSONS
- To depict branches or divisions of government.
- To describe types of buildings, artifacts, or institutions belonging to various cultures.

DRAW YOUR FAMILY

DIRECTIONS: In this lesson you will draw your family using some symbols.

Family tree diagrams are used to show relationships between generations in a family. By using symbols you can show relationships between:

> mother and father
> parents and children
> sisters and brothers

Here are the symbols that are used.

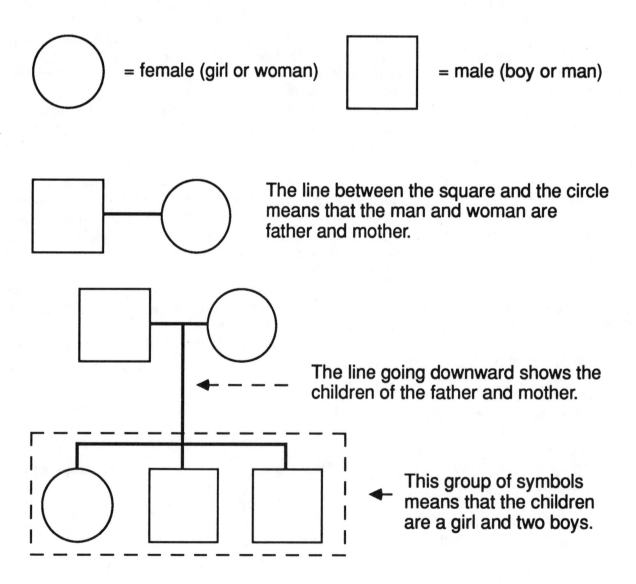

○ = female (girl or woman)   □ = male (boy or man)

The line between the square and the circle means that the man and woman are father and mother.

The line going downward shows the children of the father and mother.

This group of symbols means that the children are a girl and two boys.

DRAW YOUR FAMILY

DIRECTIONS: Write the first and last names of a member of your family in each square or circle. Draw your symbol and the circles and squares for your sisters and brothers. If you have stepparents, add them to your diagram by drawing more squares or circles.

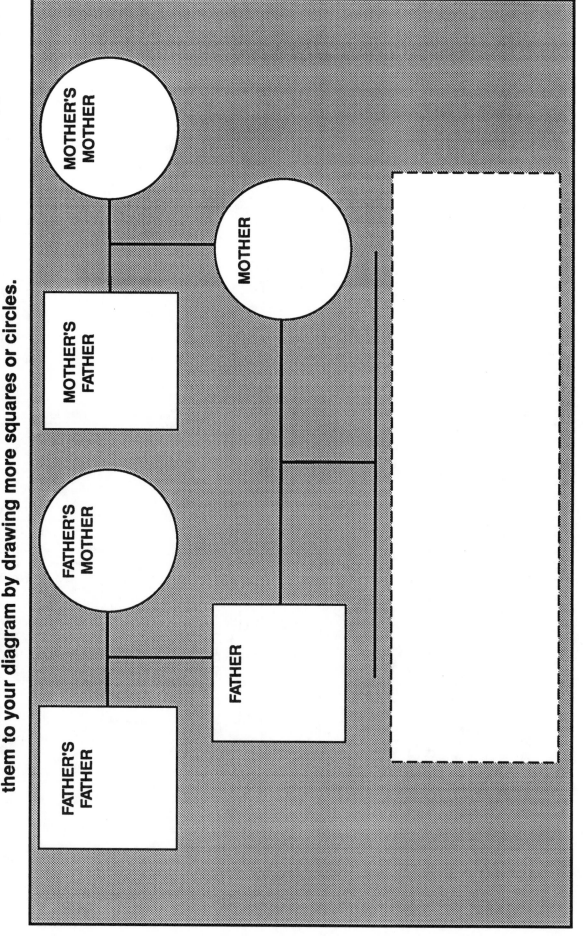

DRAW YOUR FAMILY

DIRECTIONS: Write the first and last names of a member of your family in each square or circle. Draw your symbol and the circles and squares for your sisters and brothers. If you have stepparents, add them to your diagram. Find out when and where each person was born and write it on the line.

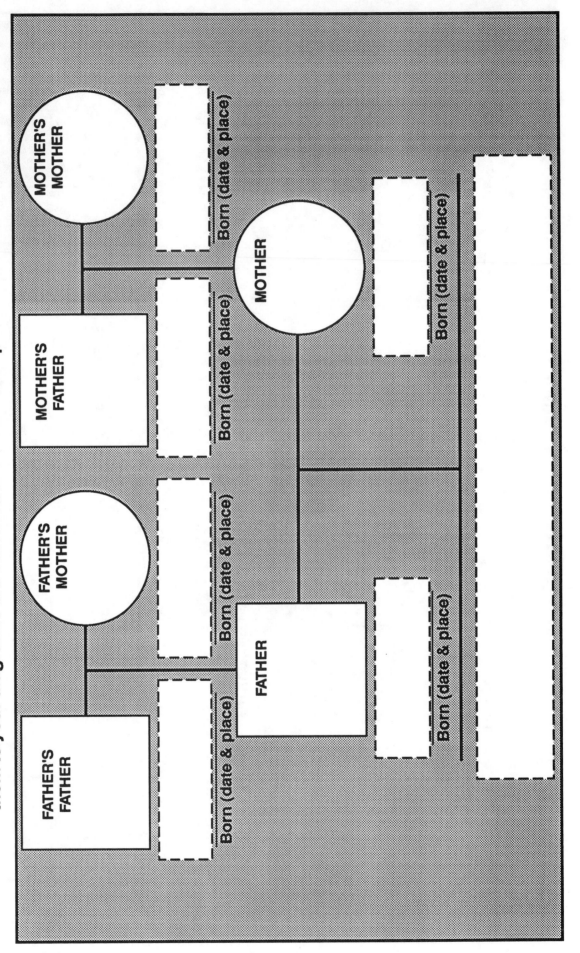

MOTHER'S MOTHER

Born (date & place)

MOTHER'S FATHER

Born (date & place)

MOTHER

Born (date & place)

FATHER'S MOTHER

Born (date & place)

FATHER'S FATHER

Born (date & place)

FATHER

Born (date & place)

Born (date & place)

DRAW YOUR FAMILY

DIRECTIONS: Write the first and last names of a member of your family in each square or circle. Draw your symbol and the circles and squares for your sisters and brothers. Draw your aunts and uncles in the boxes next to your parents.

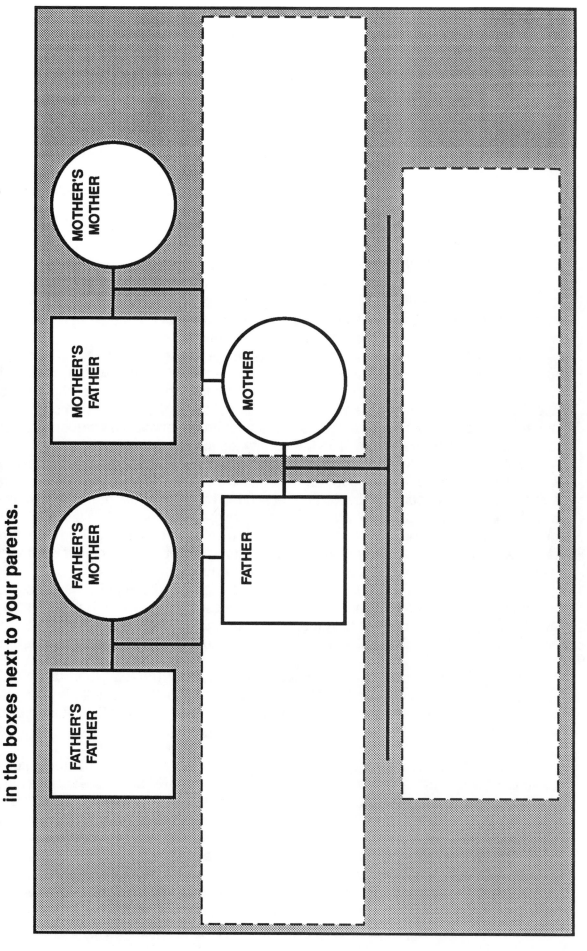

NEIGHBORHOODS AND CITIES

NOTE: In the first two diagrams the term "neighborhood" refers to the area in which the school is located. This lesson may be varied to describe students' home neighborhoods, which in some communities would help students understand the variety of ethnic neighborhoods which their school serves.

THINKING SKILL: Verbal classifications

CONTENT OBJECTIVE: Students will use an overlapping classes diagram to identify their state, city, and neighborhood. They will use a matrix to write the names of places in their neighborhoods.

DISCUSSION: TECHNIQUE—Use a transparency of the overlapping classes diagram to record responses as students discuss locations in their state, city, and neighborhood. Select four students or groups of students from different parts of your school's neighborhood to list the number of places to live, buy things, learn, or have fun in each of their neighborhoods. Use a transparency of the matrix to record student responses.

DIALOGUE—Some elementary students do not distinguish between a neighborhood and a city. In small towns or rural areas the neighborhood may refer to the whole the city. Since giving directions and identifying city buses may require knowing the name of the neighborhood or subdivision, young children should know the name of their neighborhood and adjoining neighborhoods. If the neighborhood has no proper name, encourage students to describe it as local people do. In rural areas, give the county location of the school.

To understand a neighborhood, students should identify its people, businesses, agencies, and institutions, as well as its geographical limits. For second grade classes the first diagram contains simple concepts of divisions. The second diagram offers more detail in map reading and directions. It may be used with third and fourth grade social studies lessons or with second graders who have good map reading skills and knowledge of the neighborhood. If your school is located in a neighborhood with curved or irregular streets, enlarge your city map on a copy machine and follow the given directions with your neighborhood map.

The third diagram (a matrix) prompts students to identify community resources, businesses, and buildings. The names of neighborhood businesses, streets, and buildings may reflect the ethnic representation of their neighborhood. The matrix may be used with any grade level. Students should complete this diagram with their study group or cooperative learning team.

Why is it helpful to know the names of streets and businesses in your neighborhood? (giving directions, finding an address, and understanding what is available) **Why is it helpful to know the location of your neighborhood compared to others?** (If students go shopping with their parents or to residences outside their neighborhood, they learn to orient themselves.)

Encourage students to use prepositions accurately to describe their neighborhood. Example: "I live in the Little River neighborhood in the city of Miami in the state of Florida." Third and fourth graders may also identify the county they live in. An optional diagram is provided to illustrate the relationship between city, county, and state divisions. Elementary students sometimes confuse "county" with "country," an understandable misunderstanding in areas in which the land outside the city is an open, rural area.

Two bulletin board designs are provided to illustrate these relationships.

RESULT—To locate and describe a neighborhood, we discuss its people, businesses, agencies, and institutions, as well as its geographical limits.

WRITING EXTENSION
- Describe your neighborhood (its location, businesses, and special places).
- Pretend that you are describing where you live to someone from another country who is not very familiar with the United States. Write what you would say to help that person understand what your neighborhood and city are like.

THINKING ABOUT THINKING
- How did using the diagram help you understand how to describe your neighborhood?
- Suggest another lesson in which you think that recording information this way would help you understand what you are learning.

SIMILAR SOCIAL STUDIES LESSONS
- To describe cultures, governments, economic systems, historical trends, or characteristics of any two cultures, historical figures, discoveries or technological change, historical events, geographical features or natural resources.
- To depict statistics and survey results.

BULLETIN BOARD DESIGNS

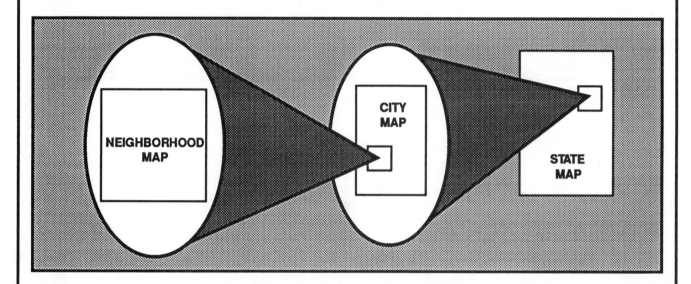

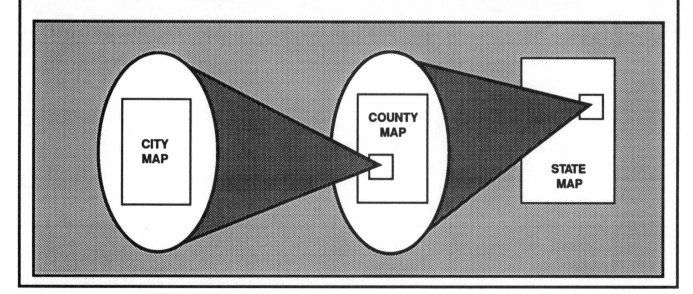

NEIGHBORHOODS AND CITIES

DIRECTIONS: If this is a map of your school neighborhood, draw your school on the correct side of the middle box. Label the streets on each side of it. Draw and label the buildings in each block. Draw a small circle in the street intersection for each traffic light.

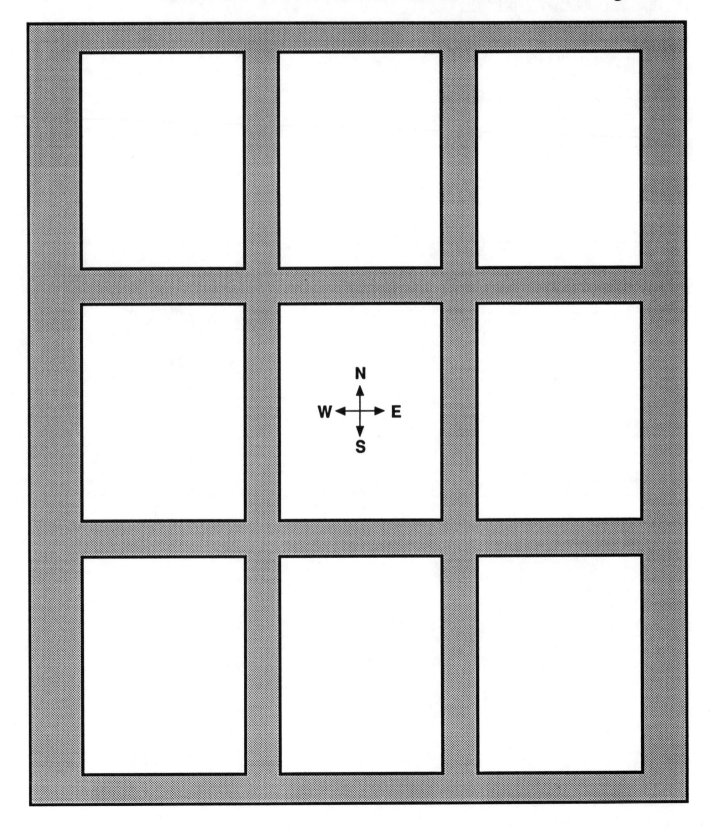

© 1992 Critical Thinking Press & Software • P.O. Box 448, Pacific Grove, CA 93950

NEIGHBORHOODS AND CITIES

DIRECTIONS: Write examples of places to live, places to buy things, places to learn, and places to have fun in the neighborhood of each student in your study group.

PLACES IN YOUR NEIGHBORHOOD

KINDS OF PLACES	Student	Student	Student	Student
Places to Live				
Places to Buy Things				
Places to Learn				
Places to Have Fun				

NEIGHBORHOODS AND CITIES

DIRECTIONS: **Your neighborhood is made up of the streets, buildings, homes, stores, and parks near your home. In the neighborhood square, write the names of streets and buildings in your neighborhood. If your neighborhood has a name, write it on the line in the neighborhood square.**

Write the name of your city on the line in the city square. If there are other neighborhoods in your city, write their names in the city square.

Write your state on the line in the state square. Write the names of other cities in your state in the large square.

MY STATE IS _____
Some cities in my state are:

MY CITY IS _____
Some neighborhoods in my city are:

MY NEIGHBORHOOD IS _____
Some streets, and buildings in my neighborhood are:

NEIGHBORHOODS AND CITIES

DIRECTIONS: Your neighborhood is made up of the streets, homes, buildings, and parks near your home. In the neighborhood square, write the names of streets and buildings in your neighborhood. If your neighborhood has a name, write it on the neighborhood line.

Write your city on the line in the city square. If there are other neighborhoods in your city, write their names in the city square.

Write your county on the line in the county square. Write the names of other cities in your county in the same square.

Write the name of your state on the line in the state square. Write the names of other counties in your state in the same square.

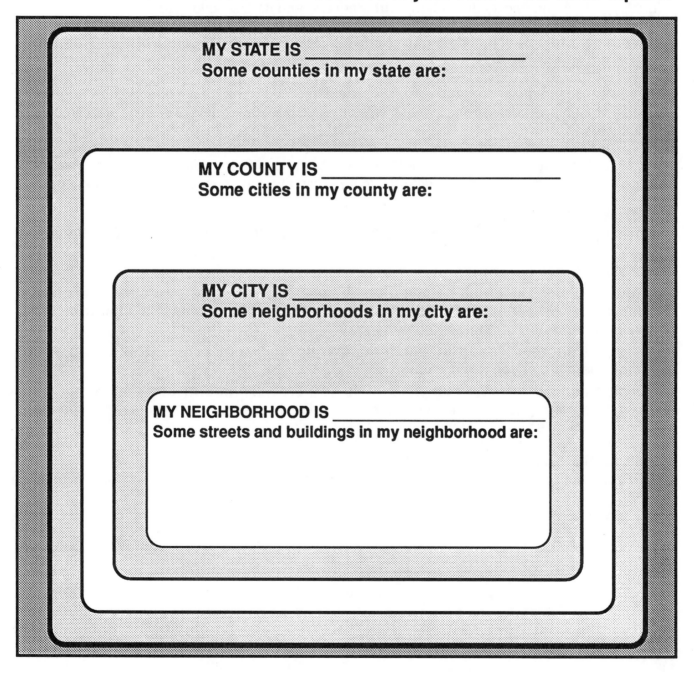

MY STATE IS _____
Some counties in my state are:

MY COUNTY IS _____
Some cities in my county are:

MY CITY IS _____
Some neighborhoods in my city are:

MY NEIGHBORHOOD IS _____
Some streets and buildings in my neighborhood are:

NEW ENGLAND AND THE SOUTHWEST

THINKING SKILL: Verbal similarities and differences

CONTENT OBJECTIVE: Students will use a compare and contrast graph to record the similarities and differences between New England and the Southwest with regard to geography and climate.

DISCUSSION: TECHNIQUE—Use a transparency of the compare and contrast graph to record student responses as the class discusses characteristics of New England and the Southwest. Encourage students to identify additional similarities and differences.

DIALOGUE—Show the location of New England and the Southwest on a map of the United States. As students report differences between New England and the Southwest, discuss those differences by naming the quality that is different. Establish this pattern: **"With regard to** (quality), (item one and its distinction), **but** (item two and its distinction).

"With regard to size of the states, the states in New England are small, but the states in the Southwest are very large.

Characteristics of these areas are usually considered appropriate for general knowledge of primary students. Students living in these areas may discuss the variety of terrains and climates in local areas.

RESULT—New England and the Southwest both have farms, cities, and many kinds of people. The two regions are very different in size, climate, seasons, and kinds of farming.

WRITING EXTENSION
• **Describe how New England and the Southwest are alike and how they are different.**

THINKING ABOUT THINKING
• **How did using the graph help you understand and remember the similarities and differences between New England and the Southwest? How does this differ from the way you understood the written passage?**
• **Suggest another lesson in which comparing and contrasting would help you understand what you are learning.**
• **Design another diagram that would help you organize information that compares two countries.** (Students may find that the overlapping classes diagram can be used to depict similarities and differences between two regions.)

SIMILAR SOCIAL STUDIES LESSONS
• To compare any two cultures, forms of government, historical figures, or historical events.

NEW ENGLAND AND THE SOUTHWEST

DIRECTIONS: **Read the passage carefully to determine how New England and the Southwest are alike and how they are different. Use the compare and contrast graph on the next page to record their similarities and differences.**

Both New England and the Southwest have large cities and small towns. Both have people who have come from other countries. Since many of the early settlers came from England, the states in the northeast are called "New England." The New England states are generally small in area. Many early settlers of the Southwest came from Mexico or Spain. Many southwestern towns and cities have Spanish names.

The states in the hot, dry southwest are large. Large areas in the southwest are too dry for growing crops. In flat areas where water is available, farms are large. Because it does not rain much, it is necessary for southwestern farmers to water their crops. Since the winters are mostly mild in the Southwest, crops can be grown all year.

It is cool and wet in New England. The farmers on the small farms in New England do not have to water their crops. Crops are planted in the spring, grow in the summer, and are harvested in the fall.

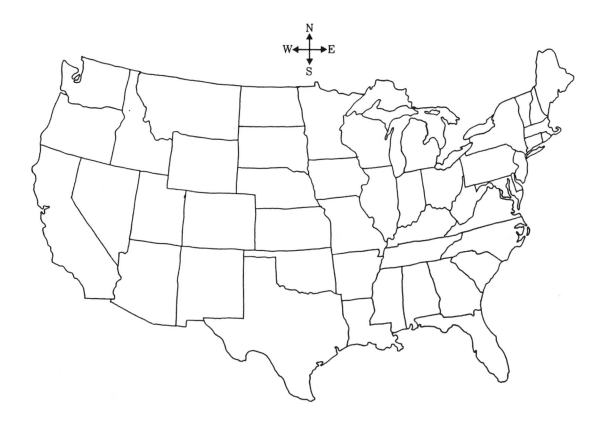

NEW ENGLAND AND THE SOUTHWEST

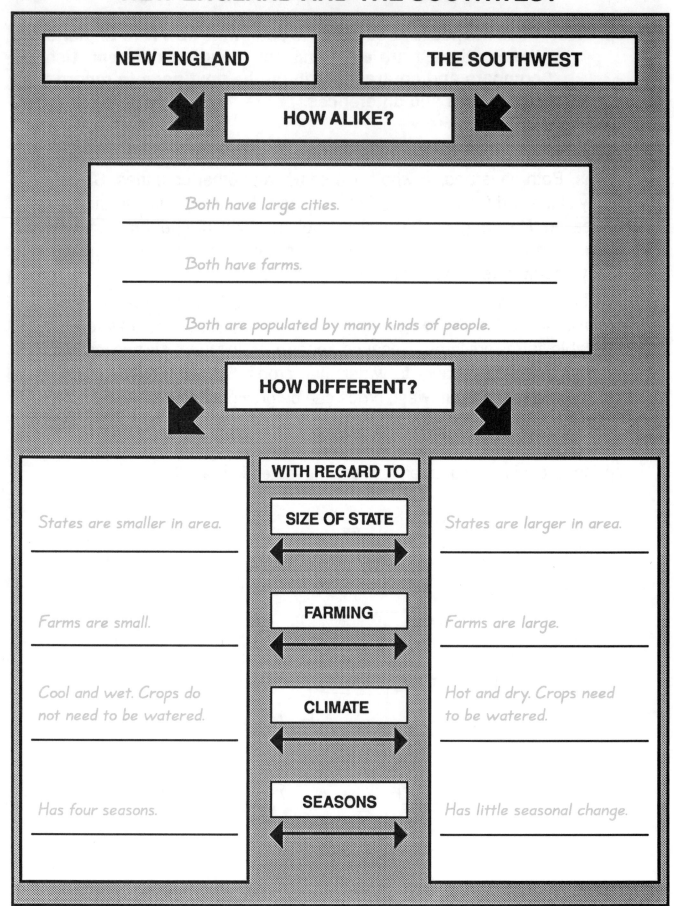

NEW ENGLAND

THE SOUTHWEST

HOW ALIKE?

Both have large cities.

Both have farms.

Both are populated by many kinds of people.

HOW DIFFERENT?

WITH REGARD TO

NEW ENGLAND		THE SOUTHWEST
States are smaller in area.	**SIZE OF STATE**	*States are larger in area.*
Farms are small.	**FARMING**	*Farms are large.*
Cool and wet. Crops do not need to be watered.	**CLIMATE**	*Hot and dry. Crops need to be watered.*
Has four seasons.	**SEASONS**	*Has little seasonal change.*

LAND FORMS AND BODIES OF WATER

THINKING SKILL: Verbal classification

CONTENT OBJECTIVE: Students will use the branching diagram to identify types of land and water forms.

DISCUSSION: TECHNIQUE—Use a transparency of the branching diagram to record student responses about land and water forms as they compare labeled terms on a map to descriptions of a variety of land and water forms. Use the cut-out terms and definitions as "paper manipulatives" to allow students to match descriptions with the location of terms on the map.

DIALOGUE—State the category to which each term belongs and the characteristics that make it different from others in that category. For example:

An <u>ocean</u> is <u>the largest body</u> of water; it <u>separates land masses.</u> A <u>lake</u> is <u>a body of water</u> that is <u>completely surrounded by land.</u> A lake is different from an ocean by size. An ocean surrounds land; a lake is completely surrounded <u>by</u> land.

In discussing land forms and bodies of water, emphasize the importance of sufficient qualifiers to distinguish the given term from similar ones. Encourage students to select the most precise category which fits the term. Generalize the characteristics used to describe land and water forms: location, elevation, surrounding areas, shape, size, purpose, and whether it is natural or man-made.

Use this graphic organizer as a design for a bulletin board.

RESULT—One may clarify geographic terms by defining them carefully and by identifying the categories and characteristics clearly.

WRITING EXTENSION
• **What characteristics are used to distinguish among various types of land forms and bodies of water?**

THINKING ABOUT THINKING
• **How did using the diagram help you understand and remember the types of land forms and bodies of water?**
• **How does using the graph to classify land forms and bodies of water help you understand them more clearly? How does this differ from the way you understood the information from the map?**
• **Design another diagram that would help you distinguish land forms and bodies of water.** (Students may find that the overlapping classes diagram or the compare and contrast diagram can be used to distinguish geography terms.)

SIMILAR SOCIAL STUDIES LESSONS
• To depict branches or divisions of governments or institutions.
• To describe dwellings, weapons, artifacts, household articles, or tools belonging to various eras, cultures, people, events, or groups.
• To describe the functions of buildings, governmental divisions, or community institutions.

LAND FORMS AND BODIES OF WATER

DIRECTIONS: Examine the map carefully to determine the significant characteristics of the land formations and bodies of water which are labeled on the map. Cut apart the terms and definitions and match each term to its definition. Record the information on the branching diagram.

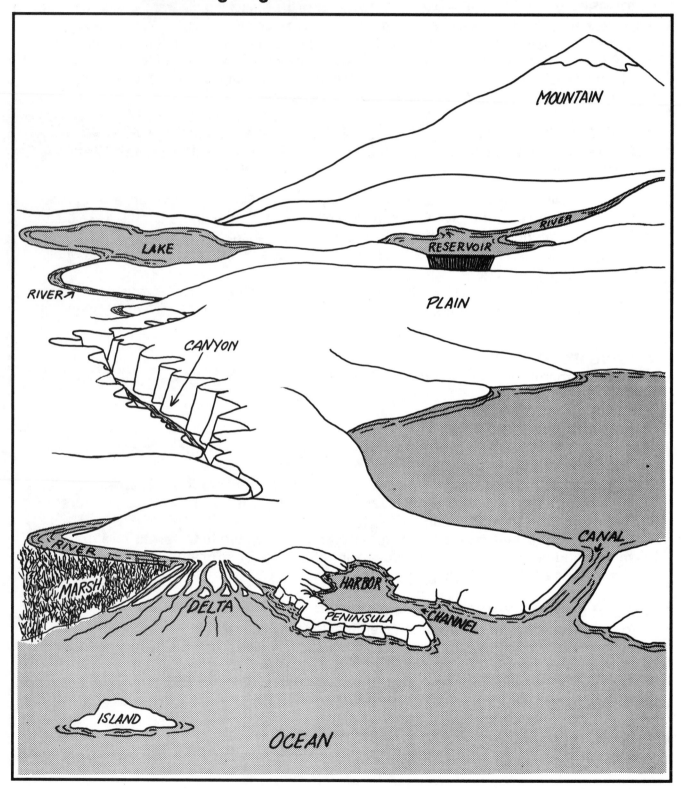

LAND FORMS AND BODIES OF WATER

CANAL	a man-made waterway for transportation or irrigation	**MARSH**	a low wetland
CANYON	a narrow valley with high, steep sides	**MOUNTAIN**	the highest land mass whose peaks rise above its surroundings
CHANNEL	a narrow waterway connecting two bodies of water	**OCEAN**	a large body of salt water that separates land masses
DELTA	a land deposit at a river's mouth	**PENINSULA**	land surrounded by water on three sides
HARBOR	a sheltered area along a seacoast where ships can anchor	**PLAIN**	a large area of flat or gently rolling land
ISLAND	land completely surrounded by water	**RESERVOIR**	a man-made lake for storing water
LAKE	a large body of water completely surrounded by land	**RIVER**	a narrow body of water that flows into a larger one

DEFINITIONS: LAND FORMS AND BODIES OF WATER

the highest land mass whose peaks rise above its surroundings

a low wetland

a land deposit at a river's mouth

a man-made lake for storing water

land completely surrounded by water

a man-made waterway for transportation or irrigation

land surrounded by water on three sides

a narrow body of water that flows into a larger one

a large area of flat or gently rolling land

a narrow valley with high, steep sides

a large body of water completely surrounded by land

a narrow waterway connecting two bodies of water

a large body of salt water that separates land masses

a sheltered area along a seacoast where ships can anchor

© 1992 CRITICAL THINKING PRESS & SOFTWARE • P.O. Box 448, Pacific Grove, CA 93950

LAND FORMS AND BODIES OF WATER

DIRECTIONS: Write each term for land forms or bodies of water in the box that best describes it.

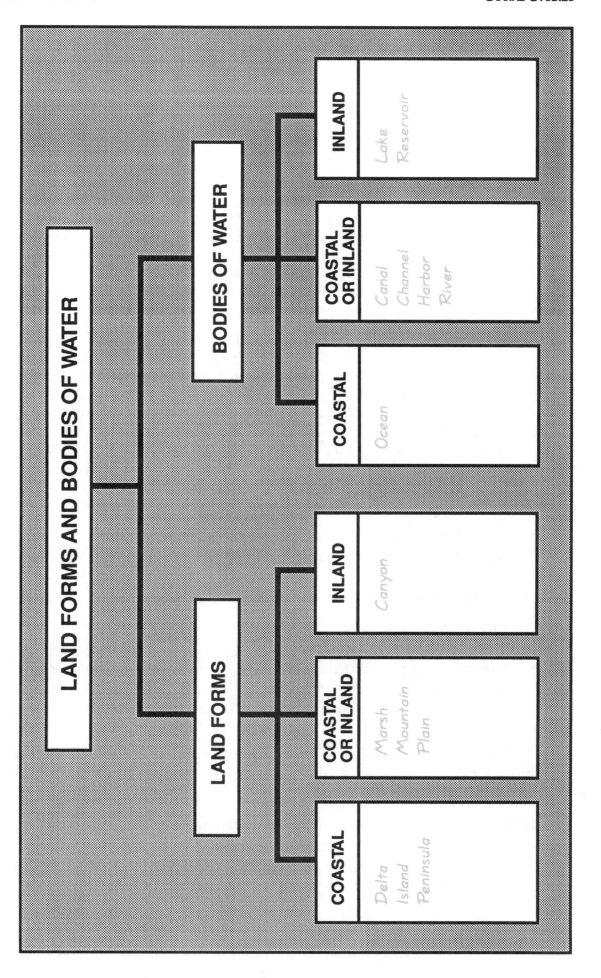

LAND FORMS AND BODIES OF WATER

BODIES OF WATER

INLAND
Lake
Reservoir

COASTAL OR INLAND
Canal
Channel
Harbor
River

COASTAL
Ocean

LAND FORMS

INLAND
Canyon

COASTAL OR INLAND
Marsh
Mountain
Plain

COASTAL
Delta
Island
Peninsula

EXPLORERS AND DISCOVERERS

THINKING SKILL: Verbal sequences

CONTENT OBJECTIVE: Students will use an interval graph to record discoveries in the New World between 1490 and 1570.

DISCUSSION: TECHNIQUE—Use a transparency of the interval graph to record responses as students discuss the order of occurrence of discoveries.

DIALOGUE—Young children have difficulty understanding that Columbus believed he could travel east to Asia by sailing west from Spain. Columbus did not know that North and South America stood between Europe and India. Demonstrate this by taking an expendable world map and cutting out North and South America. (For emphasis do the cutting in front of the class.) Point out that Columbus thought there was a single ocean between Europe and India.

Why did Columbus name the new world natives "Indians"? (Because he thought he had landed near India.) **How long was it from the time Columbus discovered the New World until the first permanent European settlement was established?** (From 1492 to 1565. [1565 – 1492 = 73 years]) **Do you know anyone who is 73 years old?** (Grandparents) **Seventy-three years seems like a long time. What happened during the 73 years from 1492 to 1565?** (The vast New World was discovered, explored, and mapped. This is remarkable since the area of the Americas is so large and so far from Europe.

RESULT— It was 73 years (from 1492 to 1565) from the discovery of the New World until the establishment of the first permanent settlement in the United States.

WRITING EXTENSION

• **Choose one discovery. Write a fictional diary of what you might be doing if you were living during that time.**
• **Compare modern astronauts to early explorers.**

THINKING ABOUT THINKING

• **How did using the diagram help you understand and remember the order in which discoveries were made? How does this differ from the way you understood the information from the written passage.**
• **Suggest another lesson in which using an interval graph would help you understand what you are learning.**
• **Design another diagram that would help you organize information that describes discoveries.**

SIMILAR SOCIAL STUDIES LESSONS

• To compare significant events in the lives of famous leaders.
• To relate historical events to sequential changes in technology, institutions, and theories.
• To correlate historical, sociological, economic, or political events from different cultures or countries during a specific time period.

EXPLORERS AND DISCOVERERS

DIRECTIONS: Read this passage about explorers and discoverers. Write each explorer beside the correct year on the time line.

At the time of Columbus, people in Europe bought cotton, silk, spices, and other needed products from China and India. Merchants used land routes or sea routes through the Indian Ocean to get to China and India. In the 1400s the land routes were closed.

By 1450 mapmakers knew that the earth was not flat. Many sailors still feared sailing off the end of a flat ocean. Columbus believed that the earth was round like a ball. He thought he could get to India and China by crossing the Atlantic Ocean. Columbus thought that the earth was much smaller than it is. He had no idea that the Atlantic Ocean and the Pacific Ocean were not the same body of water. He did not know that another continent stood between Europe and China

With three small ships, the *Santa Maria*, the *Pinta*, and the *Niña,* Columbus set sail from Spain. On October 12, 1492, after 33 days on the open sea, they sighted an island in the Bahamas. Columbus called this island San Salvador. Believing that he had reached an island near India, Columbus called the native people "Indians."

Amerigo Vespucci questioned that the world was as small as Columbus believed. Vespucci reached the islands of the Caribbean in 1494. His careful notes and drawings of the trees, fruit, flowers, birds, and natives did not match travelers' descriptions of China. He reasoned that the large land was an unknown continent and called it the New World. North and South America were named for Amerigo Vespucci.

Other Europeans began exploring the New World. In 1497 John Cabot discovered land near Canada. In 1513 Balboa discovered the Pacific Ocean. In the same year Ponce de Leon, one of Columbus's officers, discovered Florida.

Could Columbus have been right? Was it possible to reach China by sailing west? Was there some way to get around the continent that stood between Spain and Asia? In 1519 Ferdinand Magellan traveled west with five ships across the Atlantic Ocean and south along the coast of South America. He crossed the Pacific Ocean and sailed around India and Africa. In 1521 Magellan was killed in the Philippines, but in 1522 18 of the original 280 men returned to Spain. They had proved Columbus's belief in reaching the East by sailing west.

In 1540 Coronado set out from the Gulf of California and wandered through the American southwest looking for cities of gold. In 1565 St. Augustine, the first permanent settlement in the new world, was settled by the Spaniards.

EXPLORERS AND DISCOVERERS

DIRECTIONS: Read the passage on page 155. On the time line write the explorer, his discovery, and the date of the discovery.

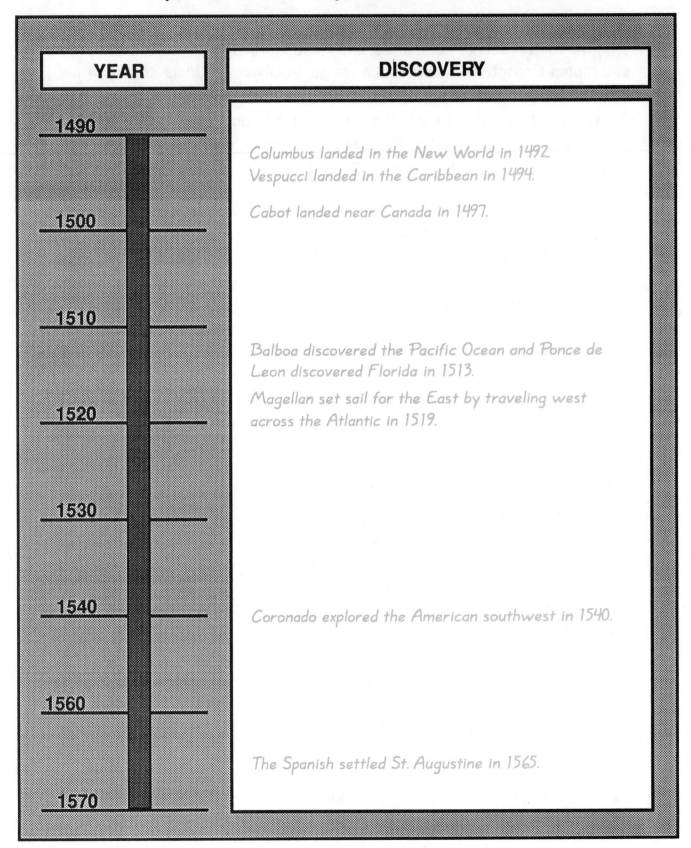

YEAR	DISCOVERY
1490	
	Columbus landed in the New World in 1492. Vespucci landed in the Caribbean in 1494.
1500	Cabot landed near Canada in 1497.
1510	
	Balboa discovered the Pacific Ocean and Ponce de Leon discovered Florida in 1513.
1520	Magellan set sail for the East by traveling west across the Atlantic in 1519.
1530	
1540	Coronado explored the American southwest in 1540.
1560	
	The Spanish settled St. Augustine in 1565.
1570	

GOODS AND SERVICES

THINKING SKILL: Verbal differences

CONTENT OBJECTIVE: Students will use the compare and contrast graph to differentiate between goods and services.

DISCUSSION: TECHNIQUE—Use a transparency of the compare and contrast graph to record responses as students examine the differences between goods and services. Encourage students to give numerous examples of people who produce goods and people who perform services.

DIALOGUE—As students report differences between goods and services, discuss those differences by **naming** the quality that is different. Establish this pattern: **"With regard to** (quality), (item one and its distinction), **but** (item two and its distinction)." For example:

"With regard to what people pay for, goods refer to things that people make or grow, but services refer to what people do."

Why is it helpful to know how goods and services are alike and how they are different? (Students recognize that one pays for things [goods]. They may not realize that services are needed and provide a source of income for workers.)

RESULT—To understand our interdependence, one must think about jobs as sources of income and as suppliers of what is needed by the community.

WRITING EXTENSION
- **Describe how goods may be used by people performing services.**
- **Describe how services may be used by people producing goods.**

THINKING ABOUT THINKING
- **How did using the graph to compare and contrast goods and services help you understand these ideas?**
- **Suggest another lesson in which using this graph to compare and contrast would help you understand what you are learning.**
- **Design another diagram that would help you organize information to compare two social studies terms.**

SIMILAR SOCIAL STUDIES LESSONS
- To compare and contrast historical figures or events.
- To contrast any two historical events, such as battles, revolutions, invasions, cultural blending, formation of institutions, publications, trade developments, or discoveries of unknown land or technological change.
- To contrast the effect of geographical features or natural resources on the development of cultures in various parts of the world

GOODS AND SERVICES

DIRECTIONS: **Read the passage carefully to determine how goods and services are alike and how they are different.**

People need shelter, food, and clothing. They buy goods and services to fill their needs.

Some people make things that are sold to other people. Farmers grow food that people buy. Things that are made or grown to be sold are called **goods.** People buy goods at stores.

Some people help other people by providing **services.** Services are jobs that people do for others. Doctors, nurses, teachers, and repairmen are a few people who provide services. People get services in stores, offices, or from the government.

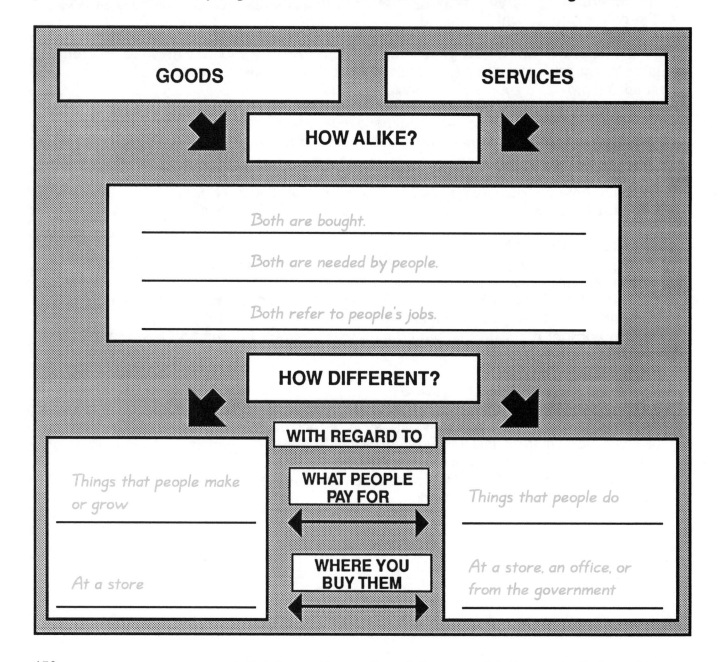

PRODUCERS AND CONSUMERS

THINKING SKILL: Verbal differences

CONTENT OBJECTIVE: Students will use the matrix chart to show the relationship between producers and consumers. Students will use the cycle diagram to show the economic cycle of interdependence between producers and consumers.

DISCUSSION: TECHNIQUE—Use a transparency of the matrix chart and have a student arrange the "cut-out" responses on the chart.

DIALOGUE— When discussing the matrix, clarify when the barber is acting as a producer and when he is acting as a consumer. When discussing the cycle diagram, clarify how each worker needs the goods and services of others. The cycle also illustrates the flow of money within the community.

Emphasize the interdependence between people who make goods and people who provide services. Set up a simulation of jobs in the community with twelve students. Each student should be labeled with a job, some that provide goods and others that provide services. Students should exchange a single dollar of play money to purchase goods and services. With each transaction students should declare the goods or services that the dollar purchases. (Example: When the "grocer" hands the bill to the "doctor," the student playing the grocer may say, "I need to get my eyes checked, and I am purchasing a service.") The object of the game is to circulate the dollar to all the students in the fewest transactions.

Why is it helpful to know that producers are also consumers? (To help you appreciate the contributions of all workers.)

RESULT—People who make goods and people who provide services are also consumers of other goods and services.

WRITING EXTENSION
• **Describe how goods may be used by people performing services.**
• **Describe how services may be used by people producing goods.**

THINKING ABOUT THINKING
• **How did using the chart help you understand these ideas?**
• **Suggest another lesson in which using a chart would help you understand what you are learning.**
• **Design another diagram that would help you organize information to compare two social studies terms.**

SIMILAR SOCIAL STUDIES LESSONS
• To describe two historical figures, discoveries of unknown land, inventions, geographical features, or natural resources.
• To show the results of a survey.
• To record characteristics of people, places, events, nations by two variables.

PRODUCERS AND CONSUMERS

DIRECTIONS: Read the passage carefully to find out how a person can be both a producer and a consumer. Cut out the four answers below and place them in the correct boxes in the chart.

People who make goods are called **producers.** Workers who make things and farmers who grow food produce what is bought. People who provide services are also **producers.** Doctors, teachers, barbers, and city workers produce a service that others pay for.

People who buy goods and services are called **consumers.** When a **producer** uses his money to buy goods or services then he also becomes a **consumer.**

	AS PRODUCER	AS CONSUMER
BARBER		
GROCER		

Buys vegetables with money earned by giving haircuts

Pays the barber for a haircut with money earned by selling vegetables

Gives haircuts

Sells vegetables

PRODUCERS AND CONSUMERS

DIRECTIONS: Use the answers that you cut apart to complete the producer-consumer cycle below.

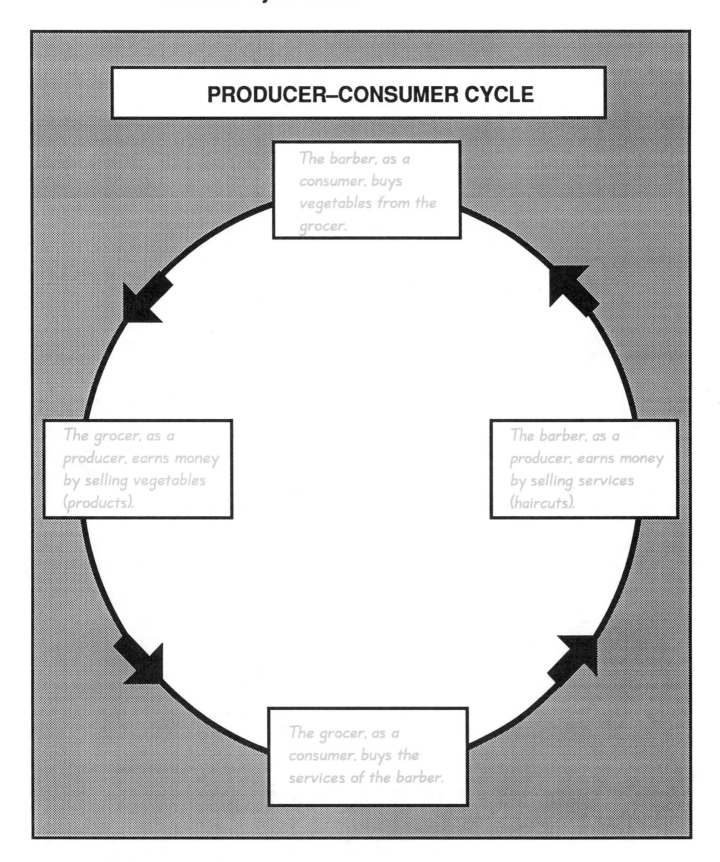

PRODUCER–CONSUMER CYCLE

The barber, as a consumer, buys vegetables from the grocer.

The grocer, as a producer, earns money by selling vegetables (products).

The barber, as a producer, earns money by selling services (haircuts).

The grocer, as a consumer, buys the services of the barber.

PRODUCERS AND CONSUMERS: EXCHANGE OF MONEY

DIRECTIONS: Read the following passage, then fill in the producer cycle below.

A teacher earns money for her work. She uses part of her salary to buy groceries. The grocer uses his earnings to pay for an eye examination. The eye doctor needs gasoline for his car. The gas station owner uses the money he made selling gasoline to get his television set repaired. The TV repairman goes to the druggist to buy medicine. The druggist sends his children to school.

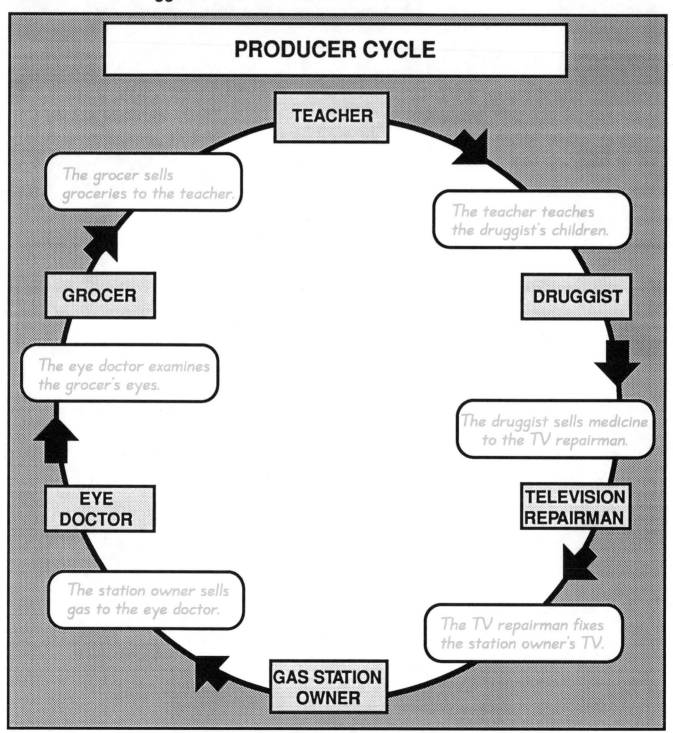

PRODUCER CYCLE

TEACHER

The grocer sells groceries to the teacher.

The teacher teaches the druggist's children.

GROCER

DRUGGIST

The eye doctor examines the grocer's eyes.

The druggist sells medicine to the TV repairman.

EYE DOCTOR

TELEVISION REPAIRMAN

The station owner sells gas to the eye doctor.

The TV repairman fixes the station owner's TV.

GAS STATION OWNER

PRODUCERS AND CONSUMERS: EXCHANGE OF MONEY

DIRECTIONS: Read the passage below, then fill in the consumer cycle below.

A teacher earns money for her work. She uses part of her salary to buy groceries. The grocer uses his earnings to pay for an eye examination. The eye doctor needs gasoline for his car. The gas station owner uses the money he made selling gasoline to get his television set repaired. The TV repairman goes to the druggist to buy medicine. The druggist sends his children to school.

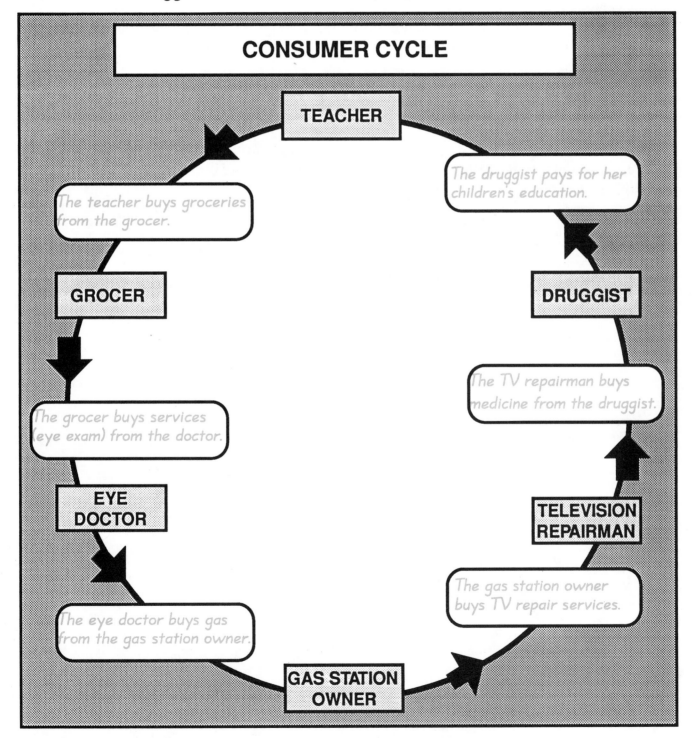

CONSUMER CYCLE

TEACHER

The teacher buys groceries from the grocer.

GROCER

The grocer buys services (eye exam) from the doctor.

EYE DOCTOR

The eye doctor buys gas from the gas station owner.

GAS STATION OWNER

The gas station owner buys TV repair services.

TELEVISION REPAIRMAN

The TV repairman buys medicine from the druggist.

DRUGGIST

The druggist pays for her children's education.

TAXES AND THE COMMUNITY

THINKING SKILL: Verbal classification

CONTENT OBJECTIVE: Students will use a cycle graph to show the flow of tax money through the community.

DISCUSSION: TECHNIQUE—Use a transparency of the cycle graph to record responses as students discuss the flow of tax money through the community.

DIALOGUE—As students identify the steps in the cycle, discuss how they or their families are involved in each of the steps.

RESULT—To understand the flow of tax money through the community, one must look at the steps in the process and how each step affects you as a resident of the community.

WRITING EXTENSION
• Explain the importance of paying taxes.

THINKING ABOUT THINKING
• Why is knowing the steps in tax money cycle important?
• Suggest another lesson in which using a cycle graph would help you understand what you are learning.

SIMILAR SOCIAL STUDIES LESSONS
• To depict trade cycles.
• To depict cycles in governmental actions (passing laws).
• To depict economic cycles (flow of personal income).

TAXES AND THE COMMUNITY

DIRECTIONS: Read the passage below and then fill in the cycle diagram.

People who live in a community pay taxes.

The tax money is used to pay workers who provide services to the community. Policemen, firemen, workers who repair streets and roads, and secretaries who keep city records are paid by money that comes from taxes.

City workers pay businesses for goods and services. Business owners pay taxes for city services.

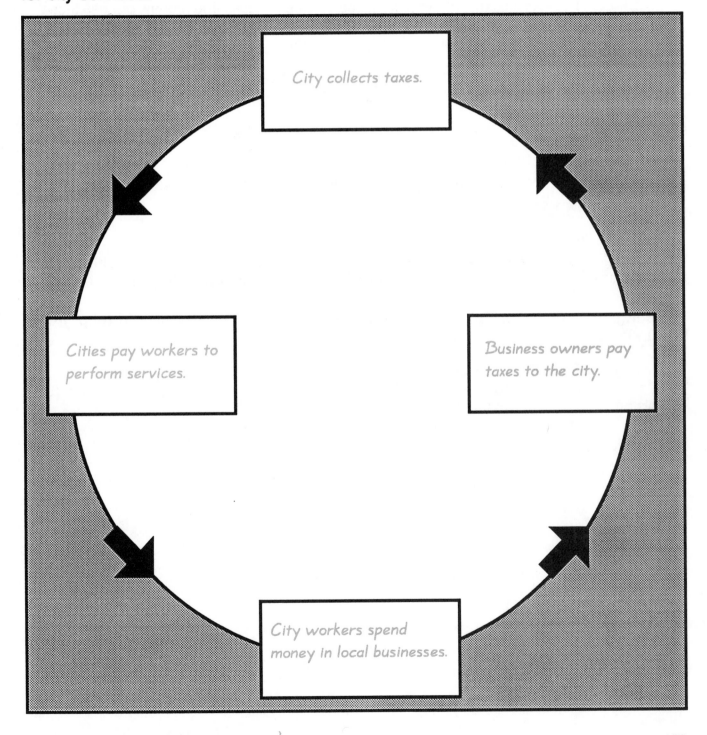

CHECKS AND MONEY

THINKING SKILL: Verbal similarities and differences

CONTENT OBJECTIVE: Students will use a compare and contrast graph to record the similarities and differences between checks and money with regard to what they are and how they are used.

DISCUSSION: TECHNIQUE—Use a transparency of the compare and contrast graph to record student responses as the class discusses characteristics of checks and money. Encourage students to identify additional similarities and differences.

DIALOGUE—As students report differences between checks and money, discuss those differences by naming the quality that is different. Establish this pattern: **"With regard to** (quality), (item one and its distinction), **but** (item two and its distinction).

"With regard to record, a check is a record of payment, but when money is used, a written receipt is necessary for proof of payment.

RESULT—Checks are a convenient way of paying for things.

WRITING EXTENSION
- Describe how checks and money are alike and how they are different.
- Explain how a check can serve as a receipt.

THINKING ABOUT THINKING
- How did using the graph help you understand and remember the similarities and differences between checks and money? How does this differ from the way you understood the written passage?
- Suggest another lesson in which comparing and contrasting would help you understand what you are learning.

SIMILAR SOCIAL STUDIES LESSONS
- To compare any two cultures, forms of government, economic systems, historical trends, historical figures, or two discoveries.

CHECKS AND MONEY

DIRECTIONS: Read the passage carefully to determine how checks and money are alike and how they are different. Use the graphic organizer on the next page to record their similarities and differences.

People receive checks or money for work that they do. Checks and money can be used to buy things. You can put checks and money into the bank. This is called making a **deposit.** You can write a check to get money from a bank. This is called **withdrawing** (you cannot withdraw money or cash checks for more than you deposited).

A check can be written for any amount of money. It usually takes many pieces of money to buy something that is expensive. One check can purchase an expensive thing.

When you pay for something with a check the business person will ask for proof of who you are **(identification)**. When you buy something with money you don't need identification. Checks are always printed on paper while money can be paper or metal.

When you write a check the bank returns your used checks to you. You then have proof that you made a payment or a purchase. When you purchase goods with money, you will need a **receipt** to prove that you purchased the goods.

CHECKS AND MONEY

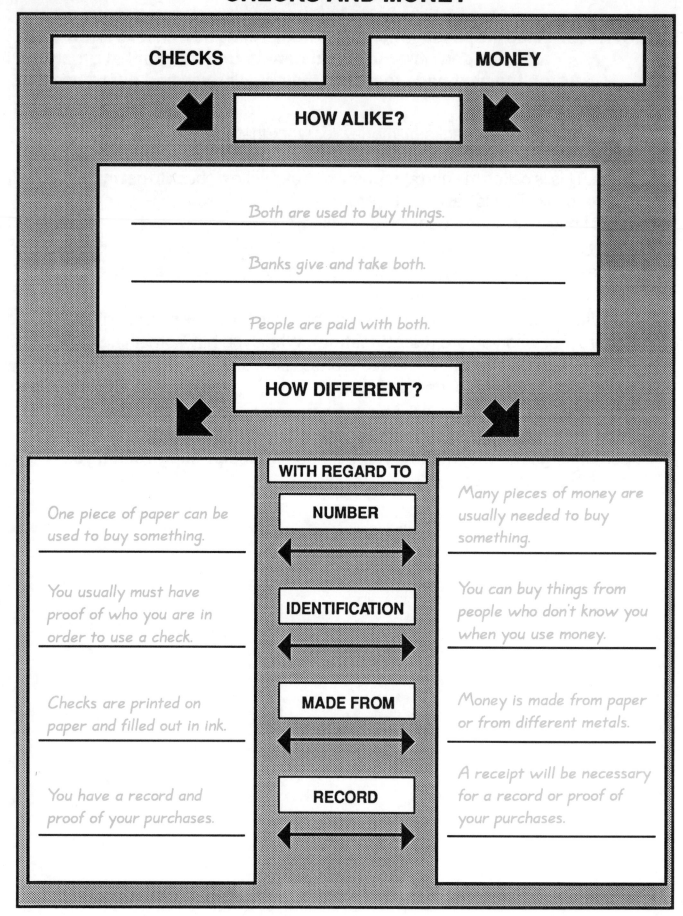

CASHING A CHECK

THINKING SKILL: Verbal sequences

CONTENT OBJECTIVE: Students will use a flowchart and a cycle diagram to depict the process of cashing a check.

DISCUSSION: TECHNIQUE—Use a transparency of the flowchart to record responses as students discuss the steps involved in writing and cashing a check. Use a transparency of the cycle diagram to record responses as students discuss the cycle of events in cashing a check. A model check is provided on this page. Have students practice writing a check.

DIALOGUE—Discuss the process of cashing a check. Discuss the importance of depositing enough money.

RESULT—It is important to deposit money before writing a check.

WRITING EXTENSION

- **Describe the steps in cashing a check.**

THINKING ABOUT THINKING

- **Suggest another lesson in which using a flowchart or a cycle diagram might help you understand or clarify what you are learning?**

SIMILAR SOCIAL STUDIES LESSONS

- To depict trade cycles (e.g., slave trade, raw materials trade, etc.).
- To depict cycles in governmental actions (e.g., legislative processes, election processes, judicial review processes, etc.).
- To depict economic cycles (flow of personal income, taxes, etc.).

John Doe
1532 Maple Drive
Midtown, IN 47803

001

_____ **19** _____

PAY TO THE
ORDER OF _____ **$** _____

_____ **DOLLARS**

**FIRST BANK
OF MIDTOWN**
Midtown, IN 47803

FOR_____   _____
                                                    Signature

00101537 01234 001

CASHING A CHECK

DIRECTIONS: Read the passage below carefully. Determine the cycle of steps in writing and cashing a check. Write in the steps on the flow chart.

In order to write a check, you must first deposit more money in the bank than the amount of the checks you plan to write. After you write a check, you take your check to a person in the bank called a teller. The teller will ask for your identification and then give you your money. You should count your money before leaving the teller's window.

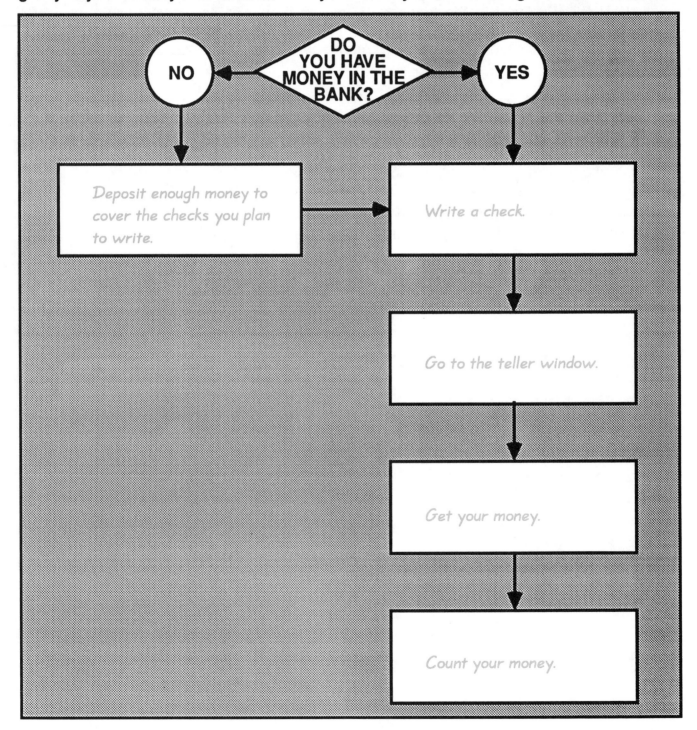

CASHING A CHECK

DIRECTIONS: **Read the passage below carefully. Determine the cycle of steps in writing and cashing a check. Write in the steps on the cycle diagram.**

After a person deposits money in the bank, he can write checks. If a person needs to buy groceries, he can write a check to the grocery store. The manager of the grocery store cashes the check. The bank sends the cancelled check back to the person who wrote the check. The cancelled check is a record showing that person has paid what he owed.

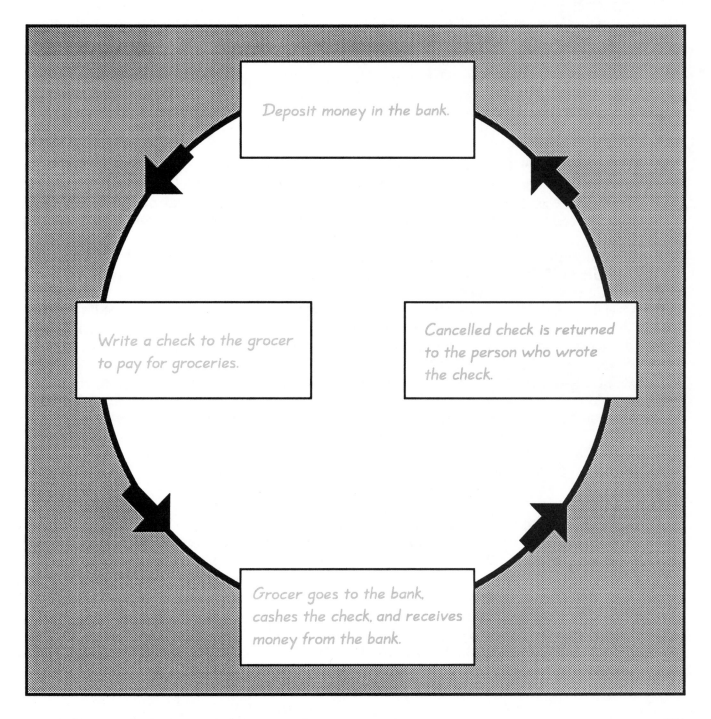

PRODUCTS FROM OIL

NOTE: This lesson may be used alone or extended by the series of lessons on the Indian's use of the buffalo.

THINKING SKILL: Verbal classification

CONTENT OBJECTIVE: Students will use the branching diagram to identify products and materials our families use which are made from petrochemicals.

DISCUSSION: TECHNIQUE—Use a transparency of the branching diagram to record students' identification of needed products which are produced from petrochemicals.

DIALOGUE—Ask students to identify many objects in the classroom that are made from petroleum products. Include clothing and plastics. Identify a natural material from which that object could be made, such as comparing a wool sweater to an acrylic sweater.

Why are petrochemical products cheaper than natural materials? (Natural products require more expensive processing; the source of wool is more limited than the source of petroleum.) **What makes petrochemical products (acrylic, nylon, polyester) so plentiful and versatile?** (Many compounds can be made from petroleum. Synthetic products can be produced with special characteristics [washability, strength, imitation of natural materials, endurance, colorfastness, ease of storage, and ease of manufacture].) **How do petrochemical products affect our jobs and personal habits?** (Petrochemical products are used to manufacture computers, automobiles, television sets, appliances, food packaging, etc. Because petroleum products are less expensive, they are often thrown away.) **Petroleum products are usually less biodegradable than natural materials. How does that affect their disposal?**

Although petrochemical products seem plentiful and cheap, why should we use this resource efficiently? (Petrochemicals are a nonrenewable resource and may ultimately be used up or limited. Petrochemical producing nations may not always choose the United States as a market.) **What would happen if our source of petrochemicals became limited?** (Our technology would have to develop synthetic fibers and fuels from other materials; people would have to change their habits to accommodate the scarcity; recycling would become more important and cost effective.)

RESULT—By understanding the source of materials for the products we use, we can understand its significance on our habits, the costs of goods, and the effect on us if that source should be changed. Petrochemical products are versatile, cheap, and plentiful.

WRITING EXTENSION
• Describe the importance of petrochemicals in the products we use.

THINKING ABOUT THINKING
• How does seeing the many types of petrochemical products we use pictured this way help us understand how important petrochemicals are to us?
• How does understanding the significance of a resource affect the way we use it?

SIMILAR SOCIAL STUDIES LESSONS
• To depict branches or divisions of governments, institutions, or social science disciplines.
• To classify dwellings, weapons, household articles, tools, architectural structures.
• To describe people, events, artifacts, groups, or eras.

PRODUCTS FROM OIL

DIRECTIONS: Identify products we use that are made from oil. Use the branching diagram to record products by their uses.

Chemicals made from oil are called **petrochemicals.** They are used in products that our families use. Petrochemicals can be found in clothing, housing, food production and storage, transportation, and recreation.

Many of our clothes are made from petrochemicals. Fabrics like nylon and vinyl may look like cotton or leather, but they are made from oil products. The detergents we use to clean our clothes are produced from petrochemicals.

Many materials in our houses are made from petrochemicals. Paints, plastic pipes and carpets contain chemicals made from oil.

The most important use of petroleum products in the home you do not see directly. Oil is a major fuel source in the United States. Petroleum fuels include heating oil, kerosene, and natural gas. Electricity is produced by plants powered by fuel oil.

Our food is fertilized, protected, and stored in plastic produced from petrochemicals. Petrochemicals are used to kill pests and weeds and to make fertilizer. Plastic is used to wrap food.

We use petroleum fuels for transportation. From the neighborhood gasoline station to jet fuels for airliners, vehicles run on petroleum. The cost of petroleum affects the price of almost anything we buy, since it takes fuel to carry goods to local stores.

Petrochemical plastics are used in boats and luggage. Television sets, computers, and radios contain plastic parts.

There are many forms of petrochemicals. Because they are part of, or used to make other products, it is hard to estimate how much we use of them. We need to understand and manage this vital natural resource well.

PRODUCTS WE USE

DIRECTIONS: In each box write products we use for each kind of need.

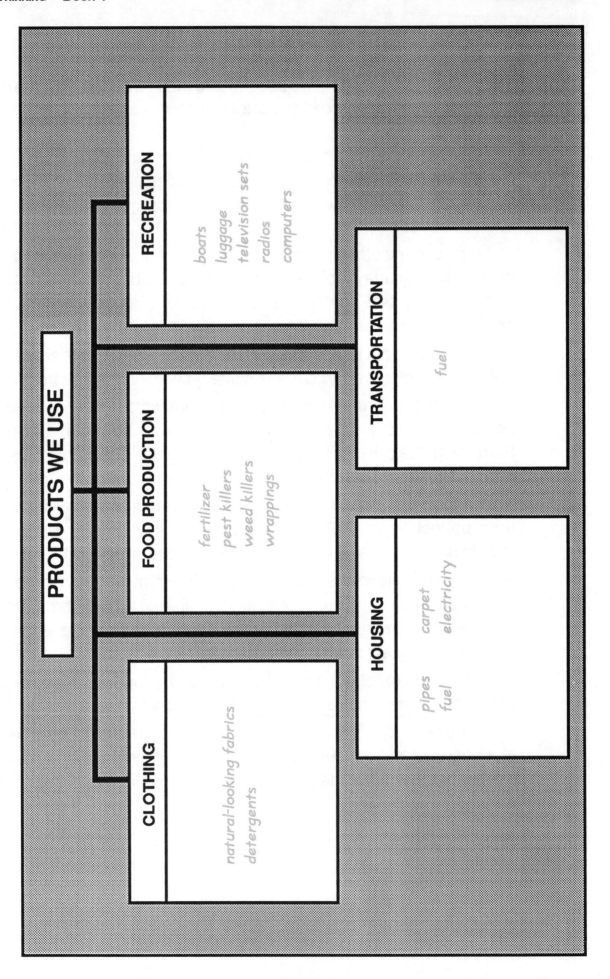

PRODUCTS WE USE

RECREATION
boats
luggage
television sets
radios
computers

FOOD PRODUCTION
fertilizer
pest killers
weed killers
wrappings

CLOTHING
natural-looking fabrics
detergents

TRANSPORTATION
fuel

HOUSING
pipes
fuel
carpet
electricity

NEEDS AND RESOURCES:
THE BUFFALO AS A SOURCE OF SUPPLY

NOTE: This lesson may be used as one in a series of lessons comparing the needs and sources of goods of today's families with the needs and sources of goods of Plains Indian families one hundred years ago.

THINKING SKILL: Verbal classifications

OBJECTIVE: Students will use a branching diagram to identify products which Plains Indians obtained from the buffalo.

DISCUSSION: TECHNIQUE—Use a transparency of the branching diagram to record responses as students read the passage and discuss products which Plains Indians obtained from the buffalo.

DIALOGUE—Examine the variety of products that Plains Indians made from the buffalo and the economy of using every part of the animal. As you discuss each item, ask the student who suggested the item to identify the key characteristic required for that product.

What characteristic does this buffalo product offer? (The buffalo material may be warm, tough, waterproof, sticky, or lightweight; separated into strings; carved or drilled; folded and easily transported; cooked or dried; burned or melted for tallow; softened for leather; or capable of producing a sound when vibrated.)

After the class has discussed the types of needs and products available from the buffalo, compare the information on the *branching diagram* with that from the Plains Indians *webbing diagram* in the last lesson.

To what extent were Plains Indians dependent on the buffalo for basic needs? (Identify the number and significance of products which Plains Indians needed for which the buffalo was the source of supply.) **What goods were not secured from the buffalo? What other sources of goods were available to them?** (Students will recognize that a culture which secures most of its needs from a single source becomes significantly dependent on that source.) **As natural and man-made conditions reduced or eliminated the number of buffalo, what effect did that have on the life-style and/or survival of the Plains Indians? What conditions reduced the buffalo herds of the nineteenth century?** (Students may discuss the exploitative hunting of the buffalo and the encroachment by American settlers on their grazing and migration lands.)

Students should recognize that any culture must strive to make efficient use of its available resources, whether those resources are petrochemicals in contemporary society or the buffalo one hundred years ago. This lesson demonstrates that the Plains Indians used all of the body materials of the buffalo for some needed product.

Why was it necessary to use all of the body materials of the buffalo for some needed product? How did the life-style of the Plains Indians limit the processing of most goods to the site of the slaughter of the animal? How might they have learned to use all of the materials so cleverly?

Discussion may extend to the efficient use of the entire whale in the nineteenth century or cows in modern stockyards. Although these comparisons are not quite so strong as the diversity and prevalence of today's petrochemical by-products, they emphasize the significance of animal products in the past and in present times.

Students should recognize that since many products made from the buffalo were necessary for the survival of Plains Indians people, the buffalo became significant in their religion, customs, and art.

Help students identify contemporary situations which cause families to travel in search of sources of economic support. The life-style of migrant families who follow the harvests is not unlike that of the Plains Indians families of a century ago. Each must be unusually knowledgeable about the source of their livelihood, whether vegetables or buffaloes. Each must travel to find available sources. Each is at the mercy of natural and man-made conditions which may affect the supply of their needed goods.

RESULT—A culture must make efficient use of the resources available to it. Plains Indians were resourceful in using all of the body materials of the buffalo for some needed product. Since products made from the buffalo were necessary for the survival of Plains Indians people, the buffalo became significant in their religion, their customs, and their art. If a culture is dependent on a source of supply, people become knowledgeable about the source, able to secure the goods, and, to some extent, dependent on natural and man-made conditions which may effect their supply.

WRITING EXTENSION
- Describe how Plains Indians used the buffalo to meet their survival needs.
- Discuss the significance of the efficient use of materials to produce needed goods.

THINKING ABOUT THINKING
- What does their efficient use of buffalo materials suggest about the values and ingenuity of Plains Indian people?
- What kinds of thinking do you expect they would value? Why?
- How does knowing about their creativity and economy change your understanding of their culture?
- How did using the diagram help you understand and remember the needs and sources of supply of Plains Indians?
- Suggest another lesson in which using this diagram would help you understand what you are learning.
- Design another diagram that would help you organize information to describe needs and sources of supply.

SIMILAR SOCIAL STUDIES LESSONS
- To depict branches or divisions of governments, institutions, or social science disciplines.
- To depict classes/subclasses of dwellings, weapons, household articles, or tools belonging to various eras or cultures.
- To depict part/whole relationships of dwellings, artifacts, costumes, communities, governments, and social systems.
- To describe the functions of architectural structures, governmental divisions, or community institutions.
- To describe people, events, artifacts, groups, or eras.

NEEDS AND RESOURCES:
THE BUFFALO AS A SOURCE OF SUPPLY

DIRECTIONS: **Read the passage carefully to determine how the Plains Indians used the buffalo. Use the branching diagram to record the uses of items which the Plains Indians made from the buffalo.**

Long ago the Plains Indians tribes followed herds of buffalo for food. The tribes used every bit of the buffalo's body to make products which they needed.

The buffalo's hide was a source of clothing material for Plains Indians people. The strong hide provided belts, clothes, shirts, and winter robes.

The Plains Indians used buffalo products to build shelters and to keep warm. The warm, strong, waterproof buffalo hides were used as tent covers to keep out the winter cold. Hides were used for bed covers and rugs.

The Plains Indians used buffalo products to defend themselves against attackers. The muscle tissue was used for bow strings. The strong hide was stretched across a frame to make a shield.

Buffalo hide was used for travel equipment. The hides were used as saddle blankets for the comfort and health of horses.

The Plains Indians used buffalo products as tools or utensils within the home. They made cups and spoons from horns. They created paint brushes by chewing a small bone until it was soft. Ropes for houses and animals, and tie-strings for the doors of tents, were all made from buffalo hide. Plains Indians made glue by boiling the buffalo hoofs.

Products Which Plains Indians Obtained from the Buffalo

DIRECTIONS: Read the passage carefully to determine how the Plains Indians used the buffalo. Write each item in the box which best describes its use.

bed covers, belts, bow strings, cups, glue, paint brushes, ropes, rugs, saddle blankets, shields, shirts, spoons, tent covers, tie strings, winter robes.

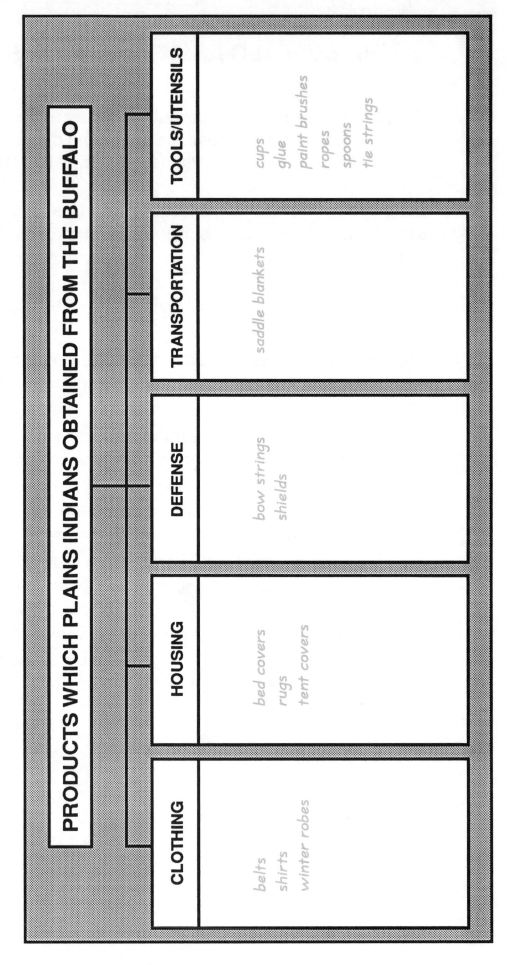

PRODUCTS WHICH PLAINS INDIANS OBTAINED FROM THE BUFFALO

CLOTHING
belts
shirts
winter robes

HOUSING
bed covers
rugs
tent covers

DEFENSE
bow strings
shields

TRANSPORTATION
saddle blankets

TOOLS/UTENSILS
cups
glue
paint brushes
ropes
spoons
tie strings

WHAT GOVERNMENT DOES

THINKING SKILL: Verbal classifications

OBJECTIVE: Students will use a branching diagram to list what government does.

DISCUSSION: TECHNIQUE—Use a transparency of the branching diagram to record responses as students read the passage and discuss what government does.

DIALOGUE—Before the students read the passage, list what they know about the functions of government. In this lesson no distinction is made between local or national government.

RESULT—The government makes rules, provides needed services, and judges how well the rules are followed.

WRITING EXTENSION
- **Of the services mentioned, which are provided by local government and which by the national government?**
- **Find out what kinds of laws are made by local government and by the national government.**

THINKING ABOUT THINKING
- **How did using the diagram help you understand and remember the functions of government?**
- **Suggest another lesson in which using this diagram would help you understand what you are learning.**
- **Design another diagram that would help you organize information to describe the functions of government.**

SIMILAR SOCIAL STUDIES LESSONS
- To depict branches or divisions of governments, institutions, or social science disciplines.
- To depict classes/subclasses of dwellings, weapons, household articles, or tools belonging to various eras or cultures.
- To depict part/whole relationships of dwellings, artifacts, costumes, communities, and social systems.
- To describe the functions of architectural structures or community institutions.
- To describe people, events, artifacts, groups, or eras.

WHAT GOVERNMENT DOES

DIRECTIONS: Read the passage carefully to find out what government does. Use the branching diagram to write in your answers.

Government is a group of people who are elected by the rest of the people to run things. There are three things that the government does: it makes rules, provides services, and judges how the rules are followed.

Rules that the government makes are called **laws**. Besides making laws concerning crimes, the government decides who should pay taxes. Taxes are needed to provide the services that the government provides.

The government builds roads, pays for schools, provides police and fire protection, and maintains the armed forces for national defense.

The judging branch of the government decides if the rules are fair and if crimes have been committed.

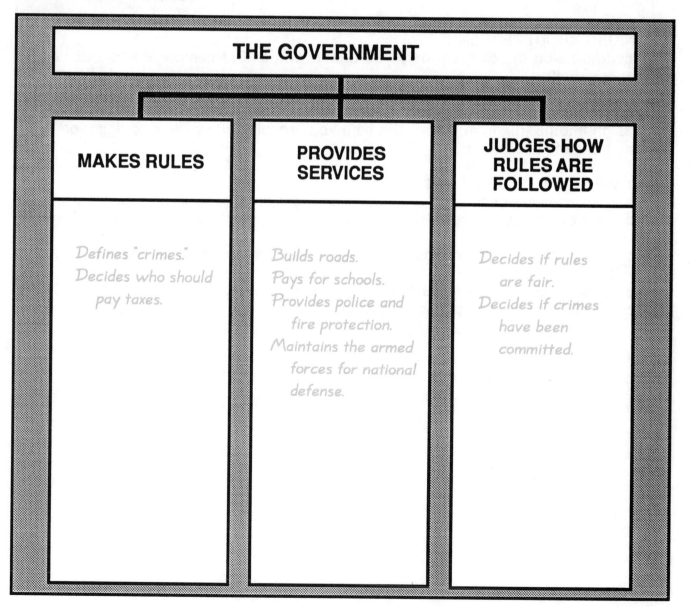

THE GOVERNMENT

MAKES RULES	PROVIDES SERVICES	JUDGES HOW RULES ARE FOLLOWED
Defines "crimes." Decides who should pay taxes.	Builds roads. Pays for schools. Provides police and fire protection. Maintains the armed forces for national defense.	Decides if rules are fair. Decides if crimes have been committed.

CITY, STATE, AND NATIONAL GOVERNMENTS

THINKING SKILL: Verbal classifications

CONTENT OBJECTIVE: Students will use a matrix to differentiate among city, state, and national governments.

DISCUSSION: TECHNIQUE—Use a transparency of the matrix diagram to record responses as students discuss the leaders, locations, and buildings of city, state, and federal governments. Few primary students know these terms and can distinguish among levels of government. Use this opportunity to list the names of local elected (city) officials and to discuss your community's terms and titles for agencies and officials.

DIALOGUE—Some elementary students do not realize that in the United States "federal" and "national" mean the same thing. Some students believe that "federal" refers to a branch of the government, another level of government, or relates only to Washington, D.C.

Help students understand the purposes of distinguishing among the elected officials, locations, and buildings of local, state, and federal agencies. Encourage students to identify the individuals who serve in local, state, and federal positions. Bulletin boards or picture displays of individuals, buildings, vehicles, or symbols may help students identify the various levels of government.

RESULT—To understand the effectiveness of public services and policies, one must know which type of government is providing it.

WRITING EXTENSION
• Select either city, state, or national government and describe the chief official, the location of that form of government, and the building in which the lawmakers meet.

THINKING ABOUT THINKING
• How did using the diagram help you understand significant differences between city, state, and federal governments?
• Suggest another lesson in which you think that recording information this way would help you understand what you are learning.
• Suggest another lesson in which you think that using this graph would help you understand what you are learning.

SIMILAR SOCIAL STUDIES LESSONS
• To describe primary grade information about cultures, governments, economic systems, historical trends, or characteristics of any two cultures, historical figures, discoveries or technological change, historical events, geographical features or natural resources.

CITY, STATE, AND NATIONAL GOVERNMENTS

DIRECTIONS: In the correct boxes in the chart, write the chief official, the city, and the building where lawmakers meet. Do this for city, state, and national governments.

There are three major levels of government in the United States. Each has a chief official, meets in a particular city, and has a special building.

The chief official of a city is called the **mayor.** Mayors are usually elected to that position, although in some cities the mayor may be appointed by the city council. The mayor and the city council make laws for the city at the **city hall.**

The **governor** is the chief official of a state. The governor sees that the laws made by the state legislature are carried out. The state government is located in the state capital. The state legislature meets in the **state capitol building.**

The chief official of the national government is the **President of the United States,** who carries out laws passed by the Congress. Congress meets in the **Capitol Building** in Washington, D.C.

	CITY	STATE	NATIONAL
CHIEF OFFICIAL	Mayor	Governor	President
CITY WHERE LAWMAKERS MEET	Same city you live in	State capital	Washington, D.C.
BUILDING WHERE LAWMAKERS MEET	City Hall	State Capitol building	United States Capitol building

CHAPTER 5—MATHEMATICS LESSONS

USING A NUMBER LINE TO "FEEL" ADDITION AND SUBTRACTION (interval graph)		CHECKING SUBTRACTION (flowchart)
	FINDING A MATHEMATICAL RULE (matrix)	
FACTOR TREE (branching diagram)		COMMON FACTORS (overlapping classes diagram)
	REVIEWING THE GCF and LCM (compare and contrast diagram)	
VALUE OF FRACTIONS (transitive order graph)		CLASSIFYING SHAPES (branching diagram)
	DESCRIBING QUADRILATERALS (matrix)	
CLASSIFYING SHAPES BY SIDES AND ANGLES (overlapping classes diagram)		COMPARING UNITS OF MEASURE (matrix)
	HEADS OR TAILS? (matrix)	
EFFECT OF INFLATION ON KID'S BUYING POWER (grid graph)		DO YOU HAVE THE RIGHT CHANGE? (branching & overlapping classes diagrams)
	WRITING A FLOWCHART FOR A WORD PROBLEM (flowchart)	

USING A NUMBER LINE TO "FEEL" ADDITION AND SUBTRACTION

THINKING SKILL: Number operations

CONTENT OBJECTIVE: Students will use the number line to add and subtract.

DISCUSSION: TECHNIQUE—Introduce the number line by drawing one on a chalkboard. Use a transparency of the number line to illustrate how to add and subtract.
    DIALOGUE—Emphasize that the number line begins with zero.

What direction must you move your pencil when drawing a number that is added to another number? (To the right.) **What direction must you move your pencil when drawing a number that is subtracted from another number?** (To the left. Prompt students to use the terms "add," "subtract," "sum," "total," and "difference." Encourage them to describe adding as moving to the right and subtracting as moving to the left.)

    If students are uncertain about adding and subtracting, encourage them to use the number line to check their homework.
    RESULT— Using a number line helps one "feel" how to add and subtract.

WRITING EXTENSION
• **Explain how a thermometer is like a number line.**

THINKING ABOUT THINKING
• **How would you represent 4 + 3 + 2 on a number line?**
• **How would you represent 9 – 4 – 3 on a number line?**
• **How does moving your pencil along the line "show" that you are adding or subtracting?**

SIMILAR MATHEMATICS LESSONS
• To depict transitive order in inequality statements or in the value of decimals.
• To depict order of occurrence in preparing flow charts of computer operations.
• To solve word problems involving transitive order.
• To describe geometric proportions in angle, length, area, or volume.

USING A NUMBER LINE TO "FEEL" ADDITION AND SUBTRACTION

DIRECTIONS: Read the examples below. To represent the first number in a problem, it is important to begin at zero.

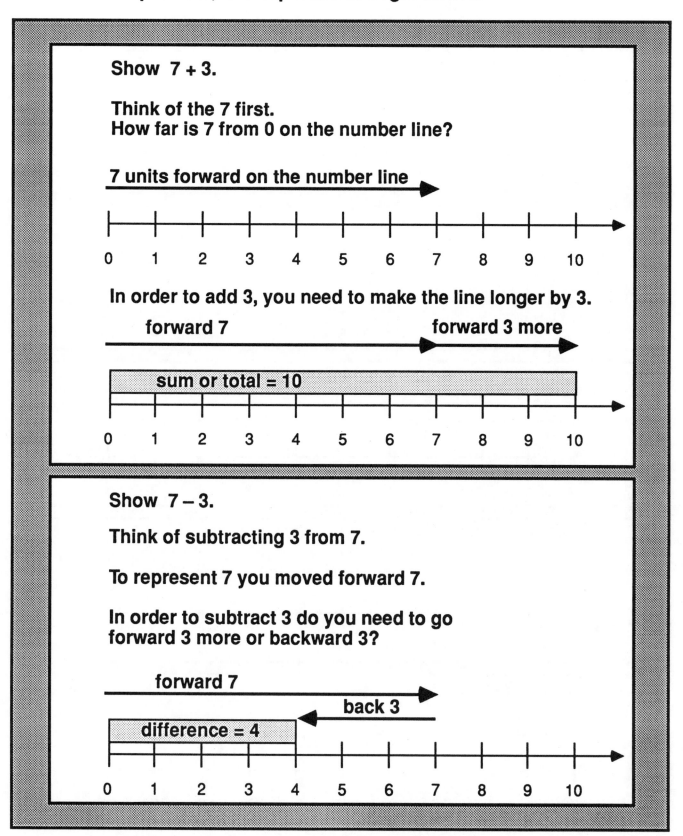

Show 7 + 3.

Think of the 7 first.
How far is 7 from 0 on the number line?

7 units forward on the number line

0   1   2   3   4   5   6   7   8   9   10

In order to add 3, you need to make the line longer by 3.

forward 7   **forward 3 more**

sum or total = 10

0   1   2   3   4   5   6   7   8   9   10

Show 7 – 3.

Think of subtracting 3 from 7.

To represent 7 you moved forward 7.

In order to subtract 3 do you need to go forward 3 more or backward 3?

forward 7

back 3

difference = 4

0   1   2   3   4   5   6   7   8   9   10

© 1992 CRITICAL THINKING PRESS & SOFTWARE • P.O. Box 448, Pacific Grove, CA 93950

USING A NUMBER LINE TO "FEEL"
ADDITION AND SUBTRACTION

DIRECTIONS: Draw arrows on the dotted lines below to show adding and subtracting. Use the examples on the page before to help you draw in your answers to each of the exercises.

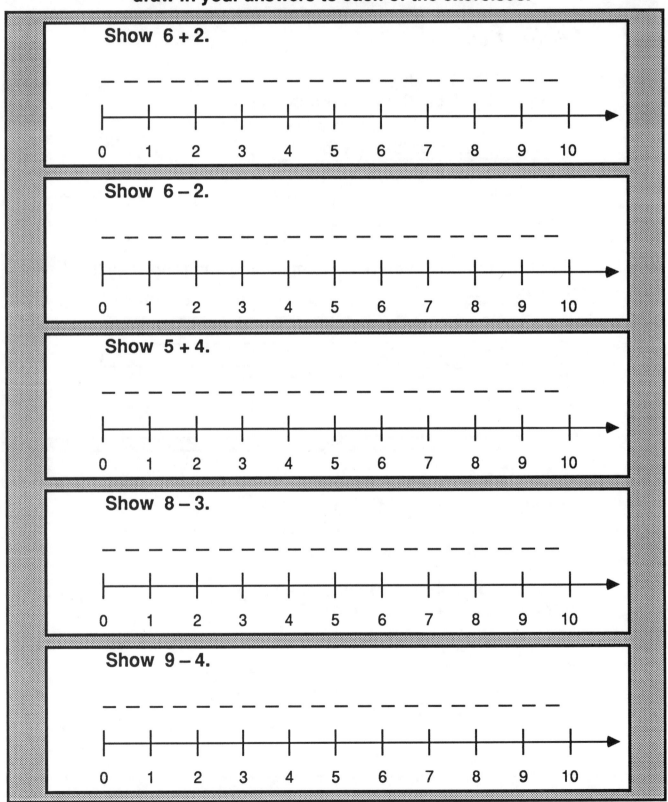

CHECKING SUBTRACTION

THINKING SKILL: Operation analysis

CONTENT OBJECTIVE: Students will use a step flowchart to show how to check subtraction.

DISCUSSION: TECHNIQUE—Reproduce the step flowchart. Have students cut apart the steps and glue them to the step flowchart. Identify other multistep mathematics operations which can be clarified by a flowchart.

DIALOGUE—Relate the symbols and sequential steps of this exercise to flowcharting activities in the computer literacy exercises in your mathematics texts. Review the flowchart symbols with your students. Remind students that subtraction is checked by adding. Example: 5 – 2 = 3. To see if 3 is the correct answer, ask "What do you add to 3 to get 5? or "To see if your answer is correct, add the smaller of the numbers in the problem to your answer. The sum of these should equal the largest number."

RESULT— Upon completion of the flowchart, students have a graphic reminder of the steps that must be followed when checking subtraction.

WRITING EXTENSION
- Identify the steps in checking subtraction.
- Tell what might happen if the sequence of steps in checking subtraction were not correctly followed.

THINKING ABOUT THINKING
- How did using the flowchart help you remember the steps in checking subtraction?
- What other mathematics operations can be pictured by using a flowchart?
- Suggest another lesson in which using a flowchart would help you understand what you are learning.

SIMILAR MATHEMATICS LESSONS
- To illustrate steps in solving multistep mathematics problems.
- To illustrate steps in classifying polyhedra or types of numbers.
- To illustrate using computer software.
- To check computations by determining whether correct procedures were followed.

CHECKING SUBTRACTION

DIRECTIONS: Study the number line below, then decide how to arrange the steps in checking a subtraction problem. Remember that you check subtraction by adding.

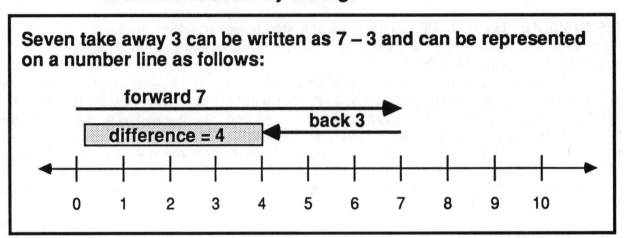

Seven take away 3 can be written as 7 – 3 and can be represented on a number line as follows:

forward 7

back 3

difference = 4

0   1   2   3   4   5   6   7   8   9   10

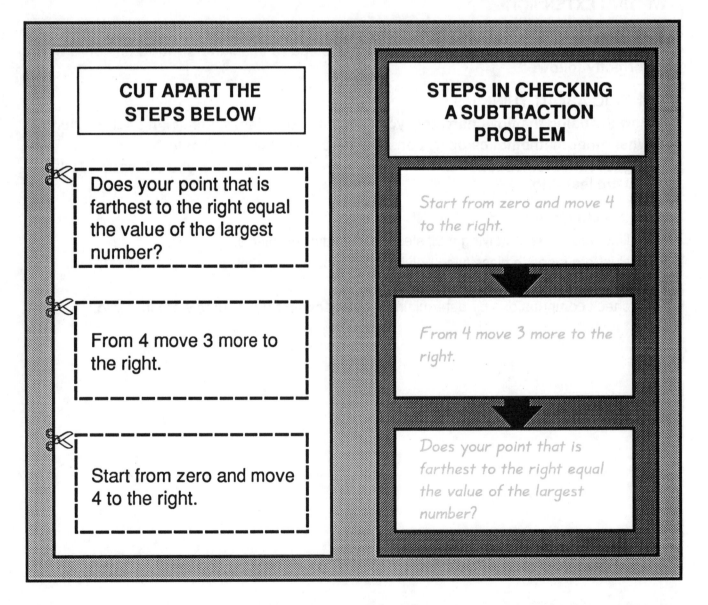

CUT APART THE STEPS BELOW

Does your point that is farthest to the right equal the value of the largest number?

From 4 move 3 more to the right.

Start from zero and move 4 to the right.

STEPS IN CHECKING A SUBTRACTION PROBLEM

Start from zero and move 4 to the right.

From 4 move 3 more to the right.

Does your point that is farthest to the right equal the value of the largest number?

FINDING A MATHEMATICAL RULE

THINKING SKILL: Symbol sequences, inferring rules or patterns

CONTENT OBJECTIVE: Students will use a matrix to discover a mathematical rule.

DISCUSSION: TECHNIQUE—Encourage students to identify the clues to find the rule and to prepare their own "rules" for other students. Use subtraction, division, or combinations of any two operations.

DIALOGUE—Encourage students to explain how they discovered the rule.

Look at the matrix. Along the top and along the left side you see the numbers 2, 3, 4, and 5. How are these numbers related to the four numbers shown in the small squares? For example, how are 2 and 2 related to 4? (2 + 2 = 4 or 2 x 2 = 4.) **How are 2 and 3 related to 6?** (2 x 3 = 6.) **Does this rule work for 3, 3, and 9?** (Yes, 3 x 3 = 9.)

RESULT—Students can discover number patterns and create mathematical puzzles to challenge their classmates' ability to find a rule.

WRITING EXTENSION
• Tell when might it be useful to recognize number rules or patterns?

THINKING ABOUT THINKING
• How did using the matrix help you figure out the rule?
• What was your first clue about the rule in each matrix?
• How did the difference between the numbers in the two matrices suggest that addition is the operation in the second matrix?
• In what way did making your own rule help you understand number patterns?
• Suggest another lesson in which using a matrix might help you understand what you are learning.

SIMILAR MATHEMATICS LESSONS
• To set up problems which allow students to discover a number rule.
• To classify numbers or polygons by more than one variable.
• To use or construct probability, statistical, or arithmetic charts.

FINDING A MATHEMATICAL RULE

DIRECTIONS: Four numbers are filled in on each matrix below. Determine how those numbers were obtained and fill in the rest of each matrix.

	2	3	4	5
2	4	6	8	10
3	6	9	12	15
4	8	12	16	20
5	10	15	20	25

	2	3	4	5
2	4	5	6	7
3	5	6	7	8
4	6	7	8	9
5	7	8	9	10

CREATE A RULE

DIRECTIONS: Use the top matrix to create your own number puzzle. In the bottom matrix write in just enough clues for another student to figure out your number rule. Leave as many boxes blank as possible. Ask another student to identify your number rule and fill in the rest of the matrix.

Your completed puzzle

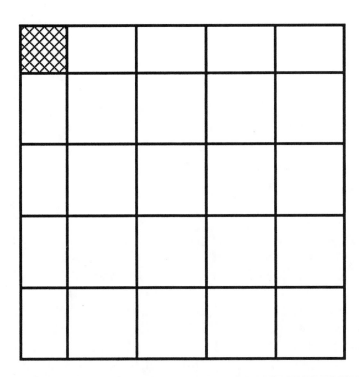

Your challenge puzzle

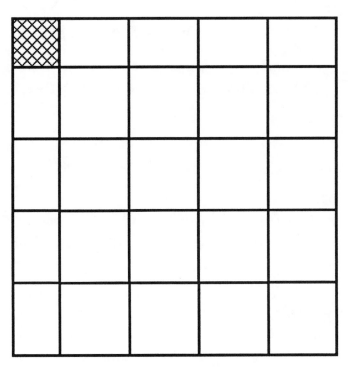

FACTOR TREE

NOTE: This is one of three lessons used as the operations occur in your mathematics text to discriminate between the greatest common factor (GCF) and the least common multiple (LCM). Use the third lesson (Reviewing GCF and LCM) after instruction on GCF and LCM.

THINKING SKILL: Attributes of numbers

CONTENT OBJECTIVE: Students will use a branching diagram to represent a number as a product. This lesson reviews factors and distinguishes between the greatest common factor and the least common multiple.

DISCUSSION: TECHNIQUE—Use a copy of the branching diagram to record answers as students identify factors of each complex number.

DIALOGUE—Encourage students to describe how using the diagram helps them "see" the factoring process. Use two branching diagrams side-by-side to factor the numbers in the denominators of two fractions and to compute the least common multiple.

Example: 1/6 + 3/8 =

```
        6               8
      __|__           __|__
     |     |         |     |
     2     3         2     4
```

Pretend that you want to drop only one of each factor "into a bowl." By multiplying all the factors "in the bowl" together, you find the lowest number that is a multiple of both 6 and 8. (2 x 3 x 4= 24) 24 is the smallest number that can be the new denominator for 1/6 and 3/8. 24 is the least common multiple of 6 and 8.

What do you have to do to 6 to make 24? (Multiply by 4.) **Now multiply the numerator by the same number. (1 x 4 = 4) The fraction 4/24 equals 1/6.**

What do you have to do to 8 to make 24? (Multiply by 3.) **Now multiply the numerator by the same number. (3 x 3 = 9) The fraction 9/24 equals 3/8.**

Therefore, 4/24 + 9/24 = 13/24.

Prompt students to link the appearance of the diagram to the steps in calculating the LCM. Students often confuse the LCM and the GCF. The next lesson in the series uses the overlapping class diagram to show the GCF. (See the "Common Factors" lesson.)

RESULT— The diagram shows what the LCM means and how to calculate it.

WRITING EXTENSION
- **What are factors? When is it helpful to be able to identify them?**
- **What is the least common multiple? Why is it helpful?**

THINKING ABOUT THINKING
- **How does the branching diagram help you "see" factors?**
- **What other mathematics operations could you see more easily if you drew them?**
- **Suggest another lesson in which using the branching diagram would help you understand what you are learning.**

SIMILAR MATHEMATICS LESSONS
- To classify polygons.
- To describe set/subset relationships, geometric and number properties.

FACTOR TREES

DIRECTIONS: Fill in the missing factors for the factor trees below. Do not use 1 as a factor.

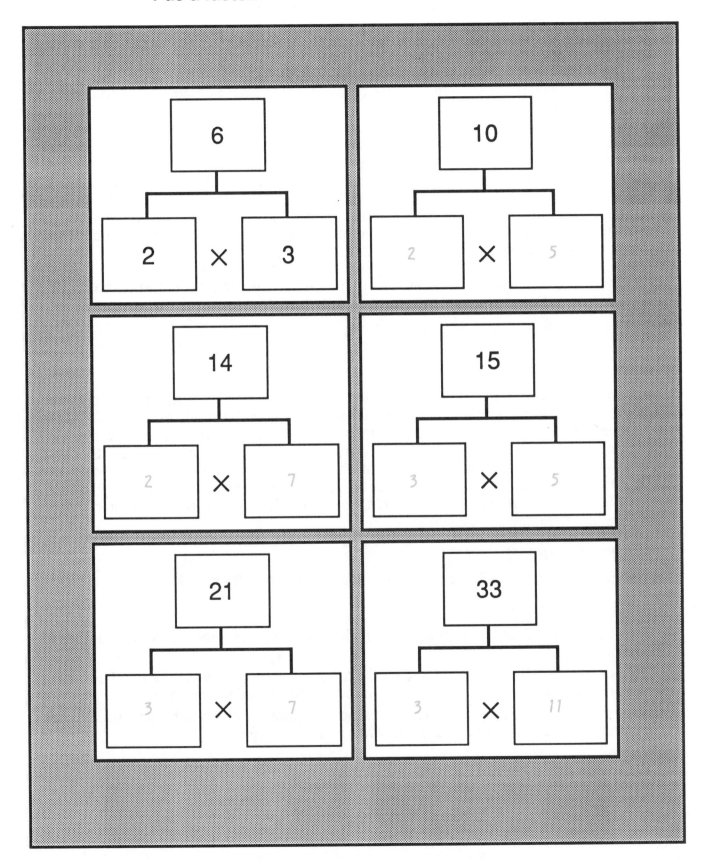

COMMON FACTORS

NOTE: This is one of three lessons used as the operations occur in your mathematics text to discriminate between the GCF and the LCM Use the third lesson (Reviewing GCF and LCM) after instruction on GCF and LCM.

THINKING SKILL: Symbol classification

CONTENT OBJECTIVE: Students will use an overlapping classes diagram to find common factors of two numbers.

DISCUSSION: TECHNIQUE—The diagram shows that two numbers may have several factors in common and leads students to identify the greatest common factor that two numbers share. Finding the greatest common factor is helpful in reducing fractions to the simplest form.

DIALOGUE—To explain the example, ask students to list all combinations of factors that will produce 6 and 8. The overlapping diagram has been produced by merging the factors of the two numbers together. The numbers in the intersection are common factors of both 6 and 8. Repeat this process to find the common factors of other numbers.

Reduce the fraction 6/8 to its simplest form. Since 2 is the greatest common factor of 6 and 8, divide both 6 and 8 by 2 to reduce it to its simplest form.

$$\frac{6}{8} \div \frac{2}{2} = \frac{6 \div 2}{8 \div 2} = \frac{3}{4}$$

The numbers shown in the intersection of the overlapping classes diagrams are common factors. If there are more than one common factors in the intersection, then the GCF is the product of those factors. Students often confuse the greatest common factor and the least common multiple. The overlapping classes diagram is one way of showing the GCF. Students may use the diagrams as visual reminders of what the two terms mean and how to calculate them. Prompt students to link the appearance of the diagram to the steps in calculating the GCF.

RESULT—The overlapping classes diagram helps identify the greatest common factor and reminds students how to calculate it.

WRITING EXTENSION
• **Tell how finding the GCF helps you reduce a fraction to its simplest form?**

THINKING ABOUT THINKING
• **How does using the overlapping classes diagram help you "see" common factors of two numbers?**
• **How does using the overlapping classes diagram help you "see" the least common factor? How can you use the least common factor in fraction problems?**
• **Suggest another lesson in which showing information on an overlapping classes diagram would help you understand what you are learning.**

SIMILAR MATHEMATICS LESSONS
• To illustrate or explain sets or set theory.
• To illustrate multiples or factors of numbers, geometry terms, or polygons.

COMMON FACTORS

DIRECTIONS: Fill in the factors of the following numbers. You may use the results of the "Factor Tree" lesson.

Number	Factor 1	Factor 2
6	2	3
10	2	5
15	3	5
21	3	7

DIRECTIONS: There is a number in a box in each circle. Each factor of this number is to be placed in one of the two parts of its circle. In the example below, 2 and 3 are in the 6 circle while 2 and 5 are in the 10 circle. Notice where the common factor, 2, is placed.

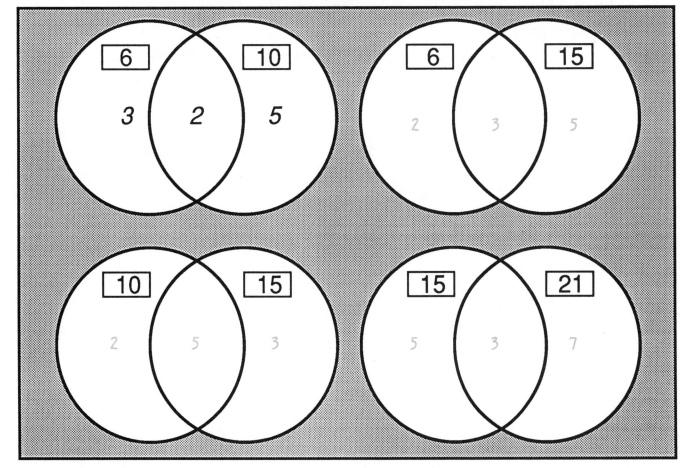

REVIEWING THE GREATEST COMMON FACTOR AND LEAST COMMON MULTIPLE

NOTE: This is the third lesson in a series of three. Use this review lesson only after the concepts of greatest common factor and least common multiple have been fully explained and students can accurately compute the GCF and LCM.

THINKING SKILL: Verbal similarities and differences

CONTENT OBJECTIVE: Students will use a compare and contrast diagram to see how the LCM and the GCF are alike and how they are different.

DISCUSSION: TECHNIQUE—As students discuss the lesson, record each idea on a transparency of the compare and contrast graph.

DIALOGUE—One purpose of the compare and contrast lesson is to clarify concepts or terms that are likely to be confused. By naming similarities, students are alerted to the source of possible confusion. By naming differences, the student confirms what the terms or concepts really mean and how to use them. This study skill helps students think about and manage their own learning.

RESULT—Reminding ourselves how the GCF and LCM are alike and how they are different helps us remember how to use them correctly.

WRITING EXTENSION
- **Tell how finding the GCF helps you reduce a fraction to its simplest form?**

THINKING ABOUT THINKING
- **How does using the compare and contrast diagram help you remember the difference between the GCF and LCM?**
- **How does using the overlapping classes diagram for the GCF and the factor tree for the LCM help you remember the difference?**
- **Suggest another lesson in which showing information on a compare and contrast diagram would help you understand what you are learning.**

SIMILAR MATHEMATICS LESSONS
- To compare operations, geometry terms, or polygons.

REVIEWING THE GCF AND THE LCM

DIRECTIONS: Read the passage and complete the compare and contrast diagram on the next page.

We have learned how to find the greatest common factor (GCF) and the least common multiple (LCM). Both the GCF and the LCM have factors, three initials to describe them, and have "common" as a middle name. Both are helpful in working fraction problems.

Knowing the factors of a number is helpful in working fraction problems. If you want to reduce a fraction like 6/15 to lowest terms, you need to divide both the 6 and the 15 by 3, which is the largest number that will divide evenly into both 6 and 15. The number "3" is called the greatest common factor (GCF). You can find the GCF by using an overlapping circles diagram. Notice that the GCF "3" is smaller than either the 6 or the 15.

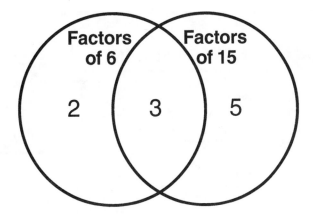

You also need to know about factors in order to add unlike fractions. If you want to add 1/6 and 1/8 it is necessary to convert both fractions to the same denominator. Use two factor trees to find the factors of 6 and 8.

The least common multiple (LCM) is found by using the factors in each number only once. Imagine you are dropping only one of each factor into a bowl. You would then have a "2," a "3," and a "4" in the bowl. By multiplying these factors (2 x 3 x 4), you get 24, which is the least common multiple of 6 and 8. Notice that the LCM "24" is larger than either the 6 or the 8.

REVIEWING THE GCF AND THE LCM

| GREATEST COMMON FACTOR | LEAST COMMON MULTIPLE |

HOW ALIKE?

Both involve factors.

Both have three initials with "common" in the middle.

Both are used in solving fraction problems.

HOW DIFFERENT?

WITH REGARD TO

Although GCF has "greater" in its name, it is smaller than either number being tested.	**SIZE**	Although LCM has "least" in its name, it is larger than either number being tested.
The GCF is used to reduce a fraction to lowest terms.	**APPLICATION**	The LCM is used to find a common denominator when adding fractions.
Use an overlapping classes diagram to find the GCF.	**HOW FOUND**	Use a factor tree branching diagram to find the LCM.

VALUE OF FRACTIONS

THINKING SKILL: Number sequences

CONTENT OBJECTIVE: Students will use the transitive order graph to arrange fractions in order from smallest to largest.

DISCUSSION: TECHNIQUE—Use a transparency of the transitive order graph to illustrate the relative value of fractions. The lesson is designed to clarify students' misconceptions about the relative value of common fractions. It demonstrates that, if the numerator remains the same, the value of the fraction gets smaller as the denominator gets larger.

DIALOGUE—Encourage students to use their own words to describe the pattern that emerges as the numerator of a fraction increases.

What relationship did you see between the value of the fraction and the value of the numerator? How did using a common denominator help you to check the relative value of the fractions?

If students are still uncertain about the relationship between the value of a fraction and the size of the denominator, encourage them to use the graph to confirm the relative value of other fractions.

RESULT—Picturing various fractions confirms the principle that, if the numerator stays the same, the larger the denominator, the smaller the value of the fraction.

WRITING EXTENSION
* **Explain why the value of a fraction gets smaller as the number in the denominator gets larger?**

THINKING ABOUT THINKING
* **What clues did you find to help you see the relationship between the value of the fraction and the size of the denominator?**
* **How did using the graph help you understand the relative value of fractions?**
* **Suggest another lesson in which using a transitive order graph would help you understand what you are learning.**
* **Why do people sometimes believe that 3/4 is smaller than 3/8? How does using the graph prevent that mistake?**

SIMILAR MATHEMATICS LESSONS
* To depict transitive order in inequality statements or in the value of decimals.
* To depict order of occurrence in preparing flow charts of computer operations.
* To solve word problems involving transitive order.
* To describe geometric proportions in angle, length, area, or volume.

VALUE OF FRACTIONS

DIRECTIONS: Cut the bars apart. Arrange the bars in order from smallest part shaded to largest part shaded.

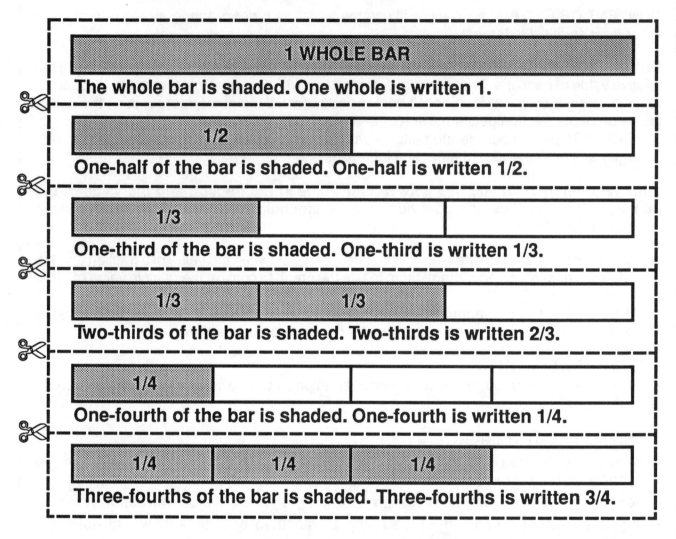

1 WHOLE BAR

The whole bar is shaded. One whole is written 1.

1/2

One-half of the bar is shaded. One-half is written 1/2.

1/3

One-third of the bar is shaded. One-third is written 1/3.

1/3   1/3

Two-thirds of the bar is shaded. Two-thirds is written 2/3.

1/4

One-fourth of the bar is shaded. One-fourth is written 1/4.

1/4   1/4   1/4

Three-fourths of the bar is shaded. Three-fourths is written 3/4.

DIRECTIONS: Use the transitive order graph below to record the following fractions in order of value from smallest to largest.

FRACTIONS: 1/2, 1/3, 1/4, 2/3, 3/4

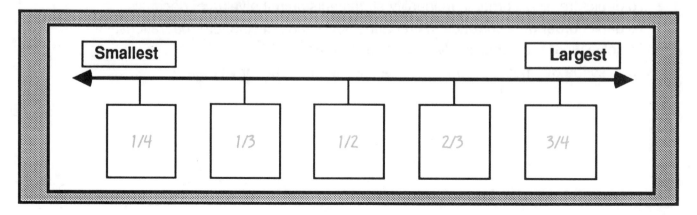

Smallest   Largest

| 1/4 | 1/3 | 1/2 | 2/3 | 3/4 |

CLASSIFYING SHAPES

THINKING SKILL: Figural and verbal classification

CONTENT OBJECTIVE: Students will use a branching diagram to sort triangles, quadrilaterals, and pentagons. *NOTE: Students may need colored pens or crayons for this exercise.*

DISCUSSION: TECHNIQUE—The goal of this lesson is to define polygons by the correct number of sides and to categorize shapes appropriately. Students tend to identify any shape by its general appearance (peaks, slanted sides, regularity). In this lesson students must count the number of sides in each polygon, cut it out, and paste it in the appropriate category of the branching diagram. To make the figures more visible, students may use felt-tip pens or crayons to color the class and the shapes in that class the same color. This diagram is a visually attractive design for bulletin boards. Ask the students to add additional polygons. Add magazine pictures of objects in which the various polygons have been identified and outlined.

DIALOGUE—After students have drawn each shape in the appropriate category, ask them to label each shape with the given number. Class discussion of each category should include identifying and defining each type of polygon. Students should state why the term applies to a given shape.

Not all primary mathematics textbooks use the term "polygon." Young children can understand and use what adults perceive as technical language easily and accurately if such terms are clearly explained. If you choose to use "polygon" rather than "shape," define "polygons" appropriately.

The shapes in this lesson are all polygons. A polygon is a closed shape which has straight sides. Polygons can have different numbers of sides. (Distinguish polygons from other shapes by examining some examples of common polygons and non-polygons [lightning designs, open curves, spirals, arches, or polygons which are missing a side].)

Each time a student identifies a polygon as a triangle, a quadrilateral, or a pentagon, confirm the term by prompting the student to apply the definition to the characteristics of the given figure. For example, to describe the first shape in the exercise, ask:

Is this figure a quadrilateral? (Yes.) **What makes you think so?** (A quadrilateral has four sides. This figure has four sides.)

RESULT—Shapes can be classified by counting the number of sides.

WRITING EXTENSION
• **Explain why it is helpful to call shapes by their correct names.**

THINKING ABOUT THINKING
• **Suggest another lesson in which using a branching diagram would help you understand what you are learning? How did drawing the shapes help you remember their names?**

SIMILAR MATHEMATICS LESSONS
• To compare units of weight or measure.

CLASSIFYING SHAPES

DIRECTIONS: We describe a shape by the number of its sides. Triangles have three sides. Quadrilaterals have four sides. Shapes with five sides are called pentagons. For each shape, count the number of sides. Decide whether it is a triangle, quadrilateral, or a pentagon. Cut out the boxes containing the shapes and paste each on the branching diagram on the next page.

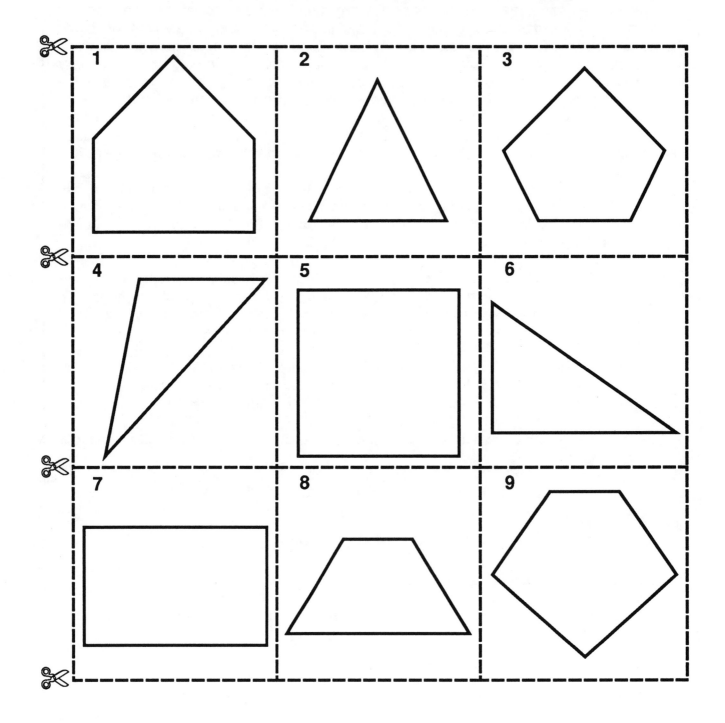

CLASSIFYING SHAPES

DIRECTIONS: Use the branching diagram below to classify the shapes you cut out from the previous page.

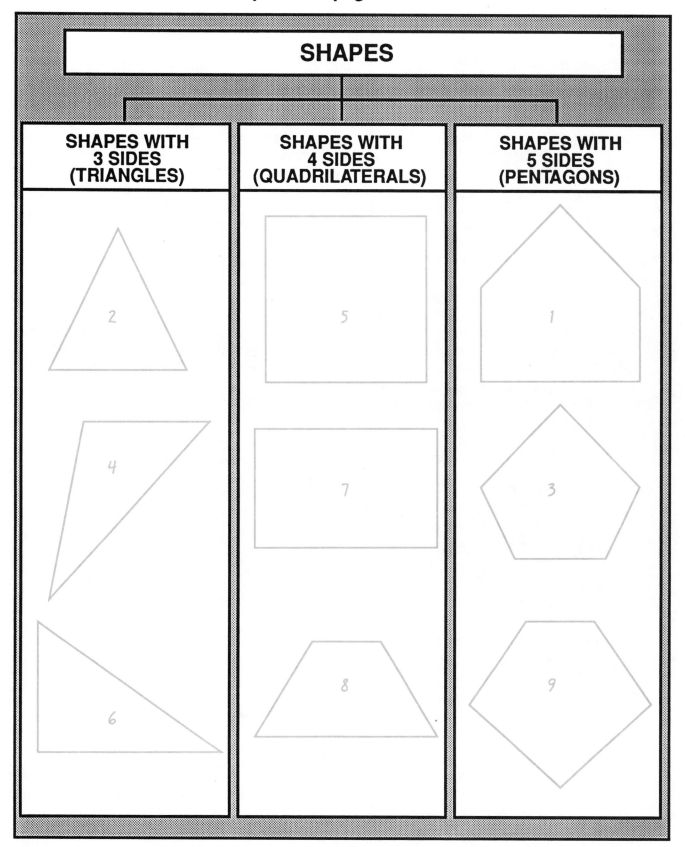

DESCRIBING QUADRILATERALS

THINKING SKILL: Figural and verbal classification

CONTENT OBJECTIVE: Students use a matrix diagram to define and categorize four-sided figures.

DISCUSSION: TECHNIQUE—The goal of this lesson is to define terms that accurately describe quadrilaterals and to recognize that many quadrilaterals can be described by more than one term. Not realizing that several of these terms apply to broader categories, students tend to associate a term with one particular polygon. For example, students attach the term "parallelogram" to quadrilaterals with slanted sides. They sometimes do not recognize that rectangles and squares are also parallelograms and are also quadrilaterals, or that squares are also rectangles.

DIALOGUE—Check the matrix through class discussion of each shape. Ask students to define the term each time and to state why each term does or does not apply to the given shape. Discussion of the first shape might proceed in this manner.

Is this shape a parallelogram? (No.) **How do you know?** (A parallelogram has two sets of parallel sides. This shape has only one.) **Is this figure a quadrilateral?** (Yes.) **Why do you think so?** (A quadrilateral is a polygon that has four sides. This shape has four sides.) **Is this shape a rectangle?** (No.) **How do you know?** (A rectangle has two sets of parallel sides and four right angles. This shape has one set of parallel sides and no right angles.) **Is this shape a square?** (No.) **How do you know?** (A square has two sets of parallel, equal sides and four right angles. This shape has one set of parallel sides, two equal sides and no right angle.) **Is this shape a trapezoid?** (Yes.) **Why do you think so?** (A trapezoid has only one set of parallel sides. This shape has one set of parallel sides. This shape also has two equal sides, but not all trapezoids need to have two equal sides.)

RESULT—More than one term can be used to describe quadrilaterals.

WRITING EXTENSION
- Explain why more than one geometric term can describe a rectangle.

THINKING ABOUT THINKING
- How did using the diagram help you understand that more than one term can describe a square?
- How did using the diagram help you understand and remember the difference in the names of the shapes?
- Suggest another lesson in which a matrix diagram would help you understand what you are learning.

SIMILAR MATHEMATICS LESSONS
- To compare addition, multiplication, subtraction, and division.
- To compare geometric terms.
- To compare English measure with metric measure.

DESCRIBING QUADRILATERALS

DIRECTIONS: Put a check mark in the box of each geometry term which applies
to each quadrilateral (four-sided shape).

DEFINITIONS

Parallelogram: a quadrilateral with two sets of parallel sides.
Quadrilateral: any closed, four-sided shape.
Rectangle: a parallelogram with four right angles.
Square: a rectangle with four equal sides.
Trapezoid: a quadrilateral with only one pair of parallel sides.

	PARALLELOGRAM	QUADRILATERAL	RECTANGLE	SQUARE	TRAPEZOID
(trapezoid)		✓			✓
(rectangle)	✓	✓	✓		
(square)	✓	✓	✓	✓	
(parallelogram)	✓	✓			

CLASSIFYING SHAPES BY SIDES AND ANGLES

THINKING SKILL: Figural and verbal classification

CONTENT OBJECTIVE: Students will use an overlapping classes diagram to classify shapes according to number of sides and equality of angles.

DISCUSSION: TECHNIQUE—Reproduce the lesson in classroom quantity so that each student may cut out the boxes containing the shapes and move them to the correct region of the diagram. When students have finished, have a student review the lesson using a transparency which can be cut apart.
     DIALOGUE—Inform students that all of the shapes may not belong inside the diagram. Cut out the parallelogram with the slanted sides.

How many sides does this shape have? (four) **Is this a triangle, a quadrilateral, or a pentagon?** (quadrilateral) **Does this quadrilateral have a special name?** (parallelogram) **Does this parallelogram have four equal angles?** (No. It has two pairs of equal angles, but not four equal angles.) **Where on the diagram should the parallelogram be placed?** (Inside the "SHAPES WITH FOUR SIDES" circle but outside the "SHAPES WITH ALL EQUAL ANGLES" circle.)

Repeat this line of questioning during the review lesson.
     RESULT—The square has four sides and four equal angles and belongs in the overlapping part of the diagram. The pentagon does not have four sides or all equal angles and belongs outside the overlapping circles diagram.

WRITING EXTENSION
• **Describe the important characteristics of shapes.**

THINKING ABOUT THINKING
• **How does using the overlapping classes diagram help you "see" the common properties of two shapes?**
• **Suggest another lesson in which you think that using the overlapping classes diagram would help you understand what you are learning.**

SIMILAR MATHEMATICS LESSONS
• To illustrate or explain sets or set theory.
• To illustrate multiples or factors of numbers.
• To illustrate geometry terms which define types of polygons or polyhedra.

CLASSIFYING SHAPES BY SIDES AND ANGLES

DIRECTIONS: Cut apart the boxes containing the shapes. Paste the boxes in the region of the overlapping circles diagram that best describes the shape.

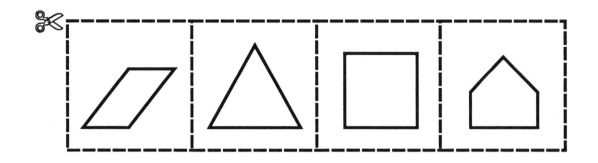

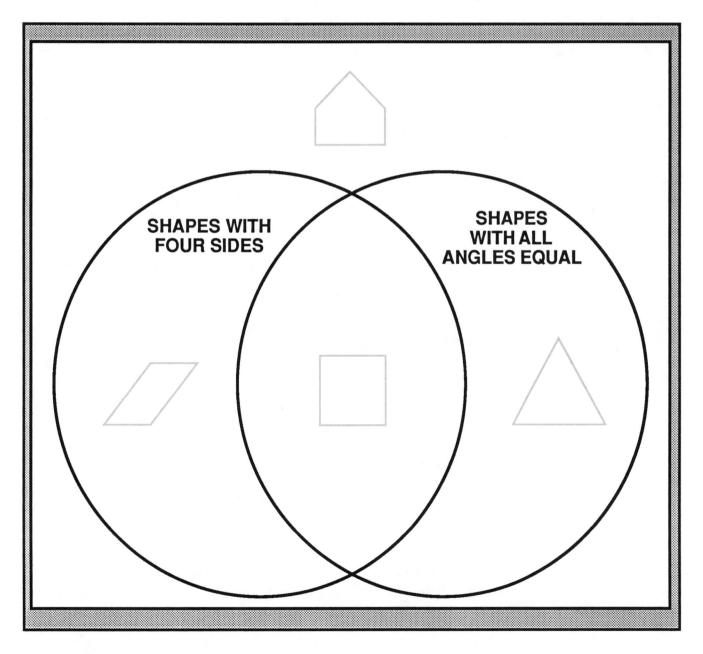

COMPARING UNITS OF MEASURE

THINKING SKILL: Cross-classification

CONTENT OBJECTIVE: Using the matrix, students will describe time, distance, or weight in terms of small, average, and large.

DISCUSSION: TECHNIQUE—Use a transparency of the matrix to record student responses as the class reviews accurate definitions. Ask each student reporting an answer to use the word in a sentence.

DIALOGUE—Ask students to identify what type of object should go in each cell of the matrix. Use that criterion to search the choice list for appropriate examples. Define unit of measure. A **unit of measure** is a standard of measure that is the same all over the world and represents an amount that everyone understands. Standard units of measure insure that things built in one part of the world will fit with things built in other locations. There are many units of measure designed to fit the object being measured. Small amounts of material are measured with small units, whereas large amounts are measured with large units.

What kind of word should we list in the first box? (Smallest or shortest time.) **Which definitions did you use?** (If there are 24 hours in a day, then a day is longer and the hour is shorter.) **How can you use another definition to check your answer?** (If there are 365 days in a year, then the year is longer than a day. So the time units from shortest to longest are hour, day, year.)

This process encourages students to look systematically for relationships rather than guessing or randomly writing words in the cells.

Identify students' working vocabulary of size connotations in common words. Encourage students to add additional terms in each category to describe small, average, and large units of time, distance, or weight. Ask students to identify other objects identified with these units. Use a transitive order graphic to show additional units if needed.

Size may be a significant characteristic in conveying meaning. Not understanding size may result in humorous or misleading explanations.

Why is it important that we know the size of something to picture it in our minds and describe it to other people accurately? Give an example of a funny or unfortunate mistake that might occur if you used the wrong size term. (Example: suppose a grocery shopper claimed he had a list "a mile long." Is he using the measuring unit to be funny or for emphasis?)

The second exercise is an optional one to depict the relative size of terms which students use or have recently learned.

For additional examples of comparing terms by degree of meaning, see the *Building Thinking Skills*® series.

RESULT—In order to recognize units of measure, it is necessary to understand its size compared to similar things.

WRITING EXTENSION

• **Write a short story that contains a long time, a long distance, or a large weight.**

• **Rewrite the story using a short time, a short distance, or a small weight. How does your story seem different when you change the size?**

THINKING ABOUT THINKING

- **How did using the diagram help you understand the correct units of measure for different things being measured?**
- **Suggest another lesson in which using a diagram like this would help you understand what you are learning.**
- **Design another diagram that would help you picture the relative size of objects.** (Suggestion: Students may find that the transitive order diagram illustrates degree in objects, actions, or characteristics.)

SIMILAR MATHEMATICS LESSONS

- To set up problems which allow students to discover a number rule.
- To classify numbers, or polygons, by more than one variable.

ALTERNATE LESSONS

- Use the second blank graphic following this lesson to list various units of measure. For example (This will require that students look up the metric/English conversions. For your convenience the approximate conversions are listed):

Distance: centimeter, foot, inch, kilometer, meter, millimeter, one mile, ten miles, yard

ANSWERS: ten miles, one mile, kilometer, meter, yard, foot, inch, centimeter, millimeter

approximate conversions: 1 mile = 1.61 kilometers, 1 kilometer = .62 miles, 1 kilometer = 1000 meters, 1 meter = 3.28 feet, 1 yard = 3 feet, 1 foot = 12 inches, 1 inch = 2.54 centimeters, 1 centimeter = 0.4 inches, 1 centimeter = 1/100 meter, 1 millimeter = 1/1000 meter.

Time: century, day, decade, hour, minute, month, second, week, year

ANSWERS: century, decade, year, month, week, day, hour, minute, second

conversions: one century = 100 years, one year = 12 months, one month = 4.33 weeks, one week = 7 days, one day = 24 hours, one hour = 60 minutes, one minute = sixty seconds.

Weight: gram, milligram, one kilogram, one ounce, one ton, pound, ten kilograms, ten ounces, ten tons

ANSWERS: ten tons, one ton, ten kilograms, one kilogram, pound, ten ounces, one ounce, gram, milligram

approximate conversions: 1 ton = 2000 pounds, 1 kilogram = 2.2 pounds, one pound = 16 ounces, 1 ounce = 28.3 grams, 1 gram = 0.035 ounces, one gram = 1000 milligrams, 1 milligram = 1/1000 gram.

NOTE: The blank graphic has nine blanks. In order to have nine entries in each category, multiples of various units have been used such as ten miles and one mile, etc.

COMPARING SIZE

DIRECTIONS: Use the definitions in the Choice Box to fill in the matrix below.

There are 12 inches in a foot and 5280 feet in a mile. There are 24 hours in a day and 365 days in a year. There are 16 ounces in a pound and 2000 pounds in a ton.

CHOICE BOX

day, foot, hour, inch, mile, ounce, pound, ton, year

	TIME	DISTANCE	WEIGHT
SMALLEST	hour	inch	ounce
LARGER	day	foot	pound
LARGEST	year	mile	ton

© 1992 CRITICAL THINKING PRESS & SOFTWARE • P.O. Box 448, Pacific Grove, CA 93950

COMPARING UNITS OF MEASURE

DIRECTIONS: Use this transitive order diagram to compare other units of measure.

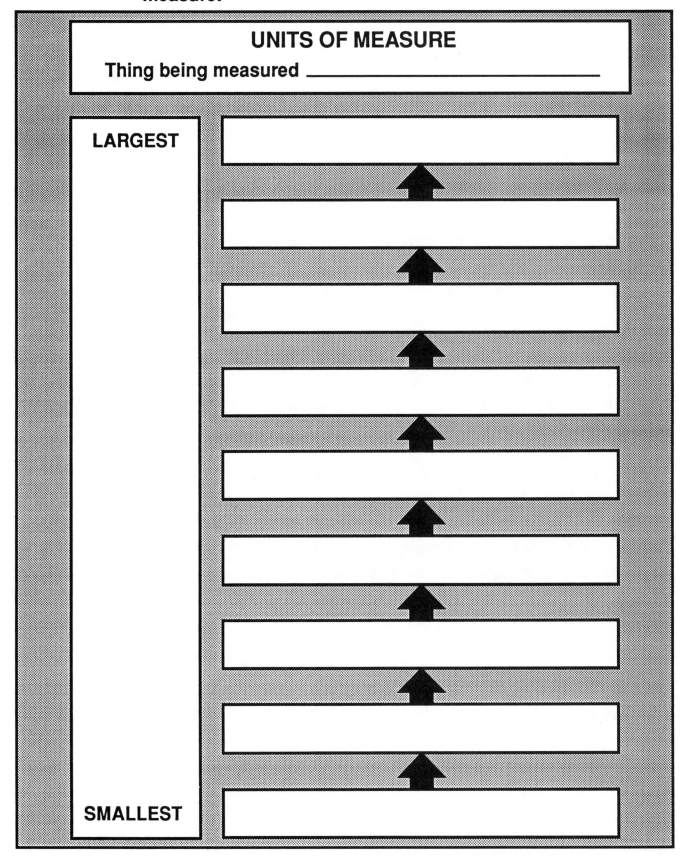

EFFECT OF INFLATION ON KIDS' BUYING POWER

THINKING SKILL: Depicting number values

CONTENT OBJECTIVE: Students will recognize the effect of inflation on their purchases by using an interval graph to compare the prices of items they commonly buy.

DISCUSSION: TECHNIQUE—Use a transparency of the blank graph to assist students in planning their graphs. Use three different colored markers to represent costs in 1980, 1985, and 1990. Model the procedure by graphing the cost of ten items in 1980.

DIALOGUE—When students have completed their graphs, encourage them to draw inferences from the graph.

What trend in inflation is suggested by your graph? (Prices keep going up.)

Discuss the effect of increasing prices on our purchasing things we want and need. List options students exercise in coping with increasing prices. These options may include: deciding not to buy the item, borrowing or using other available items, finding a lower cost substitute, comparison shopping to find another less expensive source, deciding not to buy other things in order to pay the higher price, saving for purchases, finding additional income by chores, recycling, etc.

RESULT—Bar graphs are excellent tools for making comparisons.

WRITING EXTENSION

- **Explain the effect of increased prices on your buying power as the result of inflation? Tell what you do to reduce the effect of inflation in purchasing these items.**

THINKING ABOUT THINKING

- **Suggest another lesson in which using a grid graph would help you understand what you are learning.**
- **How does using the graph help you "see" the price comparisons?**

SIMILAR MATHEMATICS LESSONS

- To depict economic, demographic, geographic, political, social, or meteorological statistics.

EFFECT OF INFLATION ON KIDS' BUYING POWER

DIRECTIONS: To see what inflation (rising prices) is doing to your buying power, examine this list of things that students often buy. Record the total purchases for each year on the graph. Use a different color for each year and record the color for each year on the key.

ITEM	1980	1985	1990
Fast-food lunch (hamburger, small fries, small soft drink)	$1.39	$1.97	$2.56
Gum (5 sticks)	.25	.35	.50
Soft drink (vending machine)	.40	.50	.75
Chocolate bar	.25	.40	.50
Milk (at school)	.10	.25	.35
Postage stamp	.15	.22	.25
Crayons (8 pack)	.45	.79	.89
Glue (1.25 ounce)	.50	.69	.75
Comic Book	.50	.75	1.25
Movie ticket (child's price)	2.00	2.50	3.00
TOTALS	$5.99	$8.42	$10.80

COMPARING THE TOTAL COST OF TEN ITEMS
IN 1980, 1985, AND 1990

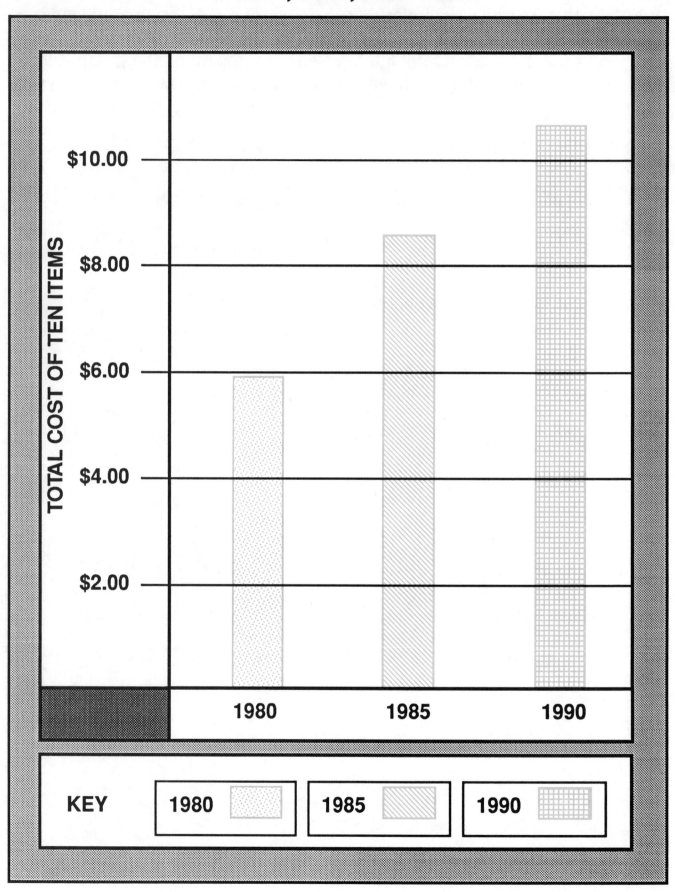

   © 1992 CRITICAL THINKING PRESS & SOFTWARE • P.O. Box 448, Pacific Grove, CA 93950

HEADS OR TAILS?

THINKING SKILL: Figural similarities and differences, probability

CONTENT OBJECTIVE: Students will use a matrix chart to record the number of heads or tails that occur when a coin is flipped a number of times.

DISCUSSION: TECHNIQUE—As a class activity, use a transparency of the matrix chart to record the results of flipping a coin until either six heads or six tails come up. As an individual or paired activity, have each student or pair of students toss a coin enough times to fill in the matrix chart.

DIALOGUE—Class activity: After the results have been obtained, find the fraction of times that heads or tails came up. For example: if 6 heads and 4 tails come up, then the coin has been tossed 6 + 4 or 10 times. The fraction of times that it came up heads is 6 of 10 or 6/10. The fraction of times that tails came up is 4 of the 10 times or 4/10. The fraction of heads (6/10) is the probability of tossing a head. The fraction of tails (4/10) is the probability of tossing a tail. (Note that the probability of tossing a head [6/10] plus the probability of tossing a tail [4/10] = 10/10 or 1 or 100%.)

Weather reporters state probabilities as percentages. If there is a 30 percent chance of rain, then the probability of rain is 30/100 or 3/10. If there is a 30 percent chance of rain, then there is a 70 percent (100% – 30% = 70%) of it not raining.

If an event is impossible—such as Christmas occurring in July—then there is no chance that it can happen and the probability of that event happening is zero. If an event is a "sure thing"—such as New Year's Day coming on January 1—then the probability of that event happening is 1 or 100%.

Individual activity: Make a chart of the totals for the entire class. If you have 15 pairs of students, then the total number of trials will be about 150 and about 75 of the 150 trials will come up heads and about 75 of the 150 will come up tails.

RESULT—If this exercise is repeated many times so that the total number of coin tosses is 100 or larger, then the fraction for the time that heads comes up gets close to 1/2. For example: if heads comes up 49 times out of 100 trials, then the probability of tossing a head is the fraction 49/100 which is close to 50/100 which equals 1/2.

WRITING EXTENSION
- **Explain how to find the chances of flipping a head.** (The chances of flipping a head, or the probability of getting a head, equals the number of times heads came up divided by the total number of times the coin was flipped.)

THINKING ABOUT THINKING
- **How did you determine the number of times the coin was flipped?**
- **How did using the chart help you keep track of your results?**

SIMILAR MATHEMATICS LESSONS
- To compare fractions.

HEADS OR TAILS?

DIRECTIONS: **Flip a penny. Each time you flip it, write either "H" for heads or "T" for tails in one of the circles. Mark H's on the left side of the chart and T's on the right.**

HEADS – (H)			TAILS – (T)		
◯	◯	◯	◯	◯	◯
◯	◯	◯	◯	◯	◯

TOTAL NUMBER OF HEADS = _____   TOTAL NUMBER OF TAILS = _____

Number of times heads came up = _____

Number of times tails came up = _____

TOTAL NUMBER OF FLIPS = _____

MAKE A FRACTION OUT OF:

Number of heads and total number of flips   _____

MAKE A FRACTION OUT OF:

Number of tails and total number of flips   _____

Are the two denominators the same?   _____

ADD THE TWO FRACTIONS. $+$ $=$ _____

DO YOU HAVE THE RIGHT CHANGE?

THINKING SKILL: Number value

CONTENT OBJECTIVE: Students will determine the value of different coin combinations.

DISCUSSION: TECHNIQUE—Use play money coins or have students make play coins to see and feel the various combinations. Use a transparency of the combinations table to record student answers.

DIALOGUE—Encourage students to produce each combination by moving coins.

Why is it helpful to combine coins differently? (To check that you have the right change for something you want to buy.) **Pennies and nickels don't seem very valuable. Predict how purchasing things would be different if our government eliminated nickels or pennies.**

RESULT—There are many ways to combine two pennies and two nickels to produce different values.

WRITING EXTENSION
• **Explain how the number of combinations changes if more coins are used?**

THINKING ABOUT THINKING
• **Suggest another lesson in which you think that using a table would help you understand what you are learning.**

SIMILAR MATHEMATICS LESSONS
• To record numerical data.
• To schedule time.

DO YOU HAVE THE RIGHT CHANGE?

DIRECTIONS: You have four coins—two pennies and two nickels. What are the prices of different things you could buy using either two coins or three coins?

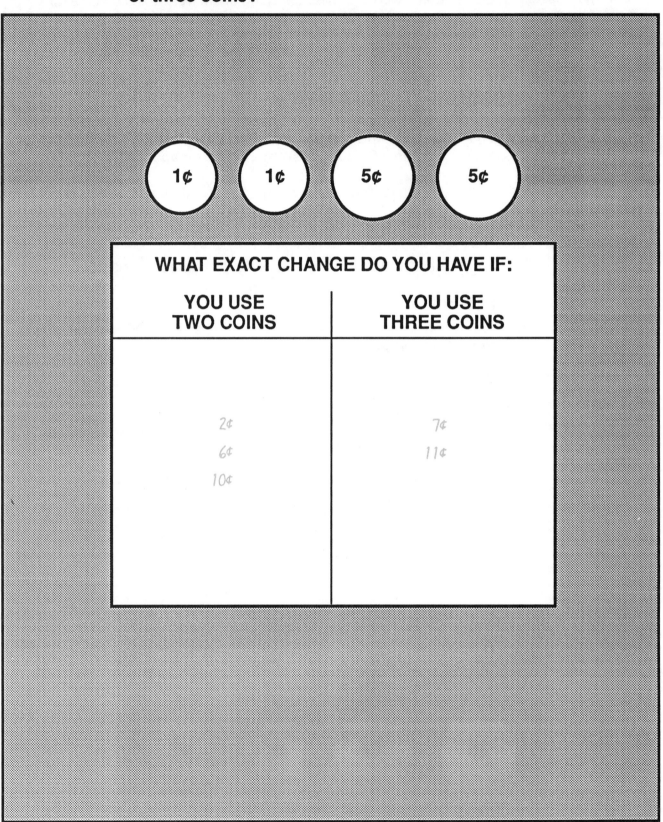

WHAT EXACT CHANGE DO YOU HAVE IF:	
YOU USE TWO COINS	YOU USE THREE COINS
2¢	7¢
6¢	11¢
10¢	

DO YOU HAVE THE RIGHT CHANGE?

DIRECTIONS: You have six coins—two pennies, two nickels, and two dimes. What are the prices of different things you could buy using either two coins or three coins?

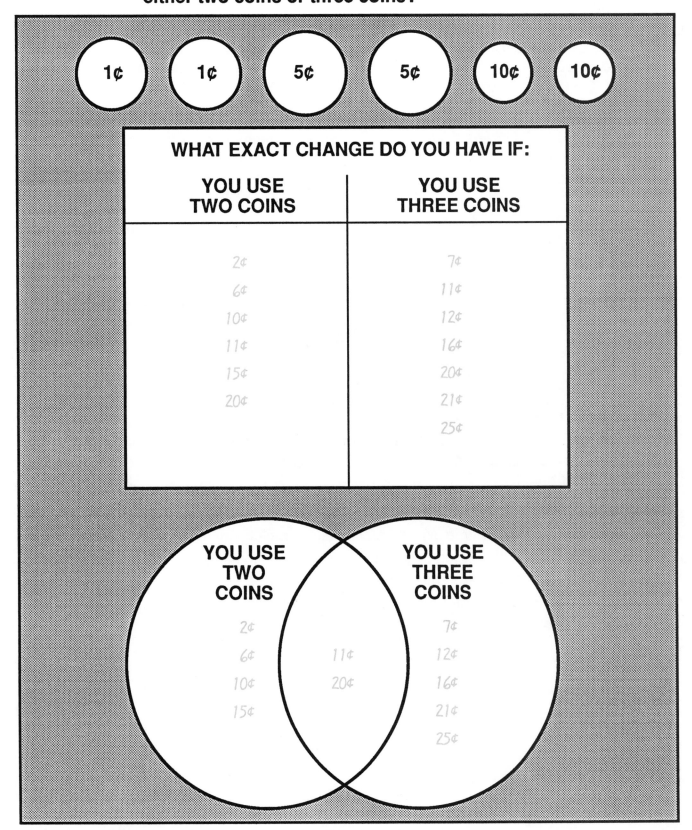

1¢   1¢   5¢   5¢   10¢   10¢

WHAT EXACT CHANGE DO YOU HAVE IF:

YOU USE TWO COINS	YOU USE THREE COINS
2¢	7¢
6¢	11¢
10¢	12¢
11¢	16¢
15¢	20¢
20¢	21¢
	25¢

YOU USE TWO COINS

YOU USE THREE COINS

2¢
6¢   11¢
10¢   20¢
15¢

7¢
12¢
16¢
21¢
25¢

WRITING A FLOWCHART FOR A WORD PROBLEM

THINKING SKILL: Operation analysis

CONTENT OBJECTIVE: Students will use a step flowchart to show the steps in thinking through a word problem.

DISCUSSION: TECHNIQUE—Explain the symbols used in making a flowchart. For more details on creating flowcharts, see Chapter 1, page 24, *Using Flowchart Diagrams.* Use a transparency of the first flowchart to talk through the steps in adding a duration of time measured in minutes to a duration of time measured in hours and minutes. Use a transparency of the second flowchart to talk through the steps in adding a length measured in inches to a length measured in feet and inches. Identify other multistep mathematics operations which can be clarified by a flowchart.

DIALOGUE—Relate the symbols and sequential steps of this exercise to flowcharting activities in the computer literacy exercises in your mathematics texts. Review the flowchart symbols with your students.

RESULT—Upon completion of the flowchart, students have a graphic reminder of the steps that must be followed when thinking through a word problem.

WRITING EXTENSION
- Identify the steps in adding lengths measured in different units of measure.
- Tell what might happen if the units of measure were not the same in all parts of a problem.

THINKING ABOUT THINKING
- How did using the flowchart help you remember the steps in adding lengths measured in different units of measure?
- What other mathematics operations can be pictured by using a flowchart?
- Suggest another lesson in which using a flowchart would help you understand what you are learning.

SIMILAR MATHEMATICS LESSONS
- To illustrate steps in solving multistep mathematics problems.
- To illustrate steps in classifying polyhedra or types of numbers.
- To illustrate steps in troubleshooting computer operations.
- To illustrate operational steps in programming a computer.
- To check computations by determining whether correct procedures were followed.

SYMBOLS USED FOR FLOWCHARTS

DIRECTIONS: Study the symbols below that are used in producing flowcharts.

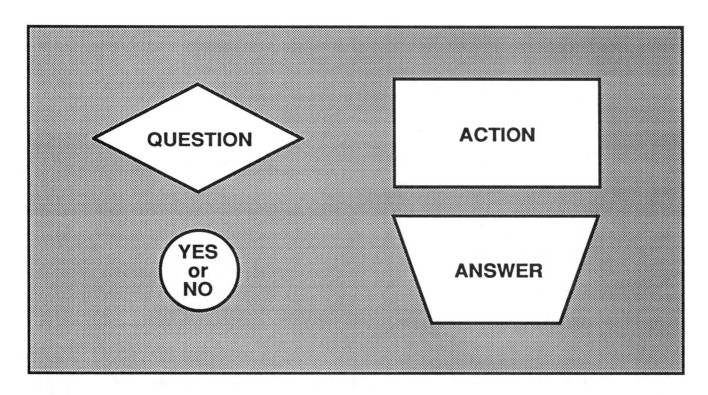

DIRECTIONS: Fill in the flowchart symbols below to represent the following situation: The teacher asks, "Do you need help? If you do, raise your hand."

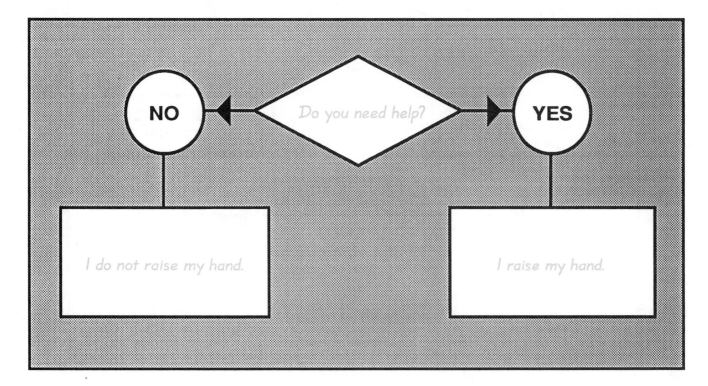

221

WRITING A FLOWCHART FOR A WORD PROBLEM

DIRECTIONS: Follow the flowchart for adding a length of time measured in minutes to a length of time measured in hours and minutes.

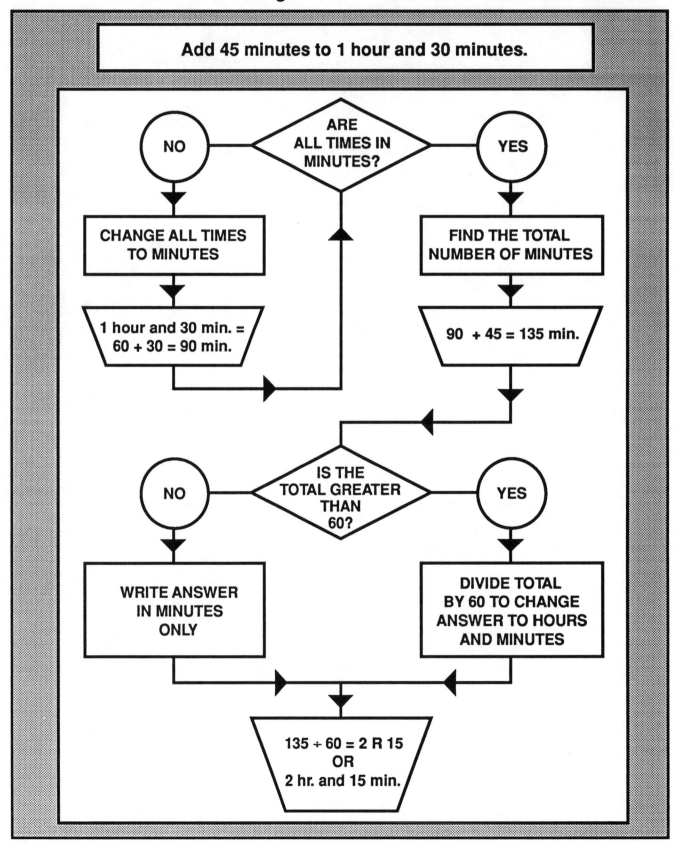

Add 45 minutes to 1 hour and 30 minutes.

ARE ALL TIMES IN MINUTES?

NO

YES

CHANGE ALL TIMES TO MINUTES

FIND THE TOTAL NUMBER OF MINUTES

1 hour and 30 min. = 60 + 30 = 90 min.

90 + 45 = 135 min.

IS THE TOTAL GREATER THAN 60?

NO

YES

WRITE ANSWER IN MINUTES ONLY

DIVIDE TOTAL BY 60 TO CHANGE ANSWER TO HOURS AND MINUTES

135 ÷ 60 = 2 R 15
OR
2 hr. and 15 min.

WRITING A FLOWCHART FOR A WORD PROBLEM

DIRECTIONS: Complete the flow chart for adding a length measured in inches to a length measured in feet and inches.

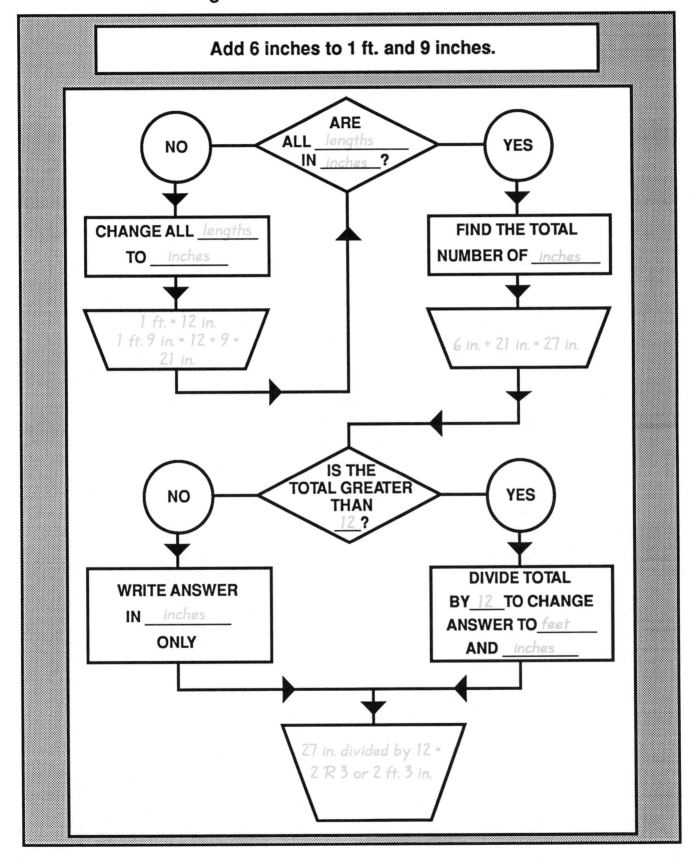

Add 6 inches to 1 ft. and 9 inches.

ARE ALL _lengths_ IN _inches_ ?

NO   YES

CHANGE ALL _lengths_ TO _inches_

FIND THE TOTAL NUMBER OF _inches_

1 ft. = 12 in.
1 ft. 9 in. = 12 + 9 = 21 in.

6 in. + 21 in. = 27 in.

IS THE TOTAL GREATER THAN _12_ ?

NO   YES

WRITE ANSWER IN _inches_ ONLY

DIVIDE TOTAL BY _12_ TO CHANGE ANSWER TO _feet_ AND _inches_

27 in. divided by 12 = 2 R 3 or 2 ft. 3 in.

CHAPTER 6—SCIENCE LESSONS

	CLASSIFYING THINGS (matrix)	
COMPARING LIVING AND NON-LIVING THINGS (compare and contrast)		CONTRASTING PLANTS AND ANIMALS (contrast graph)
	HOW ANIMALS MOVE (branching diagram)	
LIFE CYCLE OF A PLANT (cycle graph)		HOW SEEDS TRAVEL (branching diagram)
	WHAT PART OF A PLANT DO WE EAT? (branching diagram)	
FRUIT OR VEGETABLE? (overlapping classes diagram)		THE FOUR FOOD GROUPS (matrix)
	FOOD CHAIN (cycle diagram)	
MEAT-EATING AND PLANT-EATING DINOSAURS (contrast graph)		SOLIDS, LIQUIDS, AND GASES (matrix)
	HEATING AND COOLING WATER (cycle graph)	
WATER CYCLE (cycle graph)		ENERGY CHANGES (flowchart)
	SIMPLE MACHINES (central idea graph)	
WHICH SOUND IS LOUDER? (transitive order graph)		WEATHER OBSERVATIONS (matrix)
	STARS AND PLANETS (compare and contrast)	

CLASSIFYING THINGS

THINKING SKILL: Verbal classification

CONTENT OBJECTIVE: Students will use a matrix chart to classify animals by habitat.

DISCUSSION: TECHNIQUE—Use a transparency of the matrix chart to classify things in nature according to two variables. Fill in the chart as the students discuss each object.

DIALOGUE—Bring in items to be classified, see how many of them fit on one of the two matrix charts.

Discuss how and why organisms and materials in science are described by more than one variable. Have students bring in pictures to make a bulletin board display illustrating classification, such as:

	ANIMALS THAT LIVE IN THE SEA	ANIMALS THAT LIVE IN THE FOREST	ANIMALS THAT LIVE IN THE DESERT
BIRDS			
MAMMALS			
REPTILES			

Why is it important to accurately describe the things we study in science? (Our descriptions confirm important characteristics and convey understanding to others accurately.)

RESULT—A matrix chart is useful to classify things in nature.

WRITING EXTENSION

• **In this lesson, things were classified by pairs of characteristics (roughness and hardness or weight and size). Explain what other pairs of characteristics can be used to classify things in nature.**

THINKING ABOUT THINKING

• **How did using the diagram help you understand classification?**
• **Suggest another lesson in which depicting information on a matrix chart would help you understand what you are learning.**
• **Design another graph that would help you classify.**

SIMILAR SCIENCE LESSONS

• To record, summarize, and evaluate experimental or observational results or statistical data.
• To describe plants, animals, minerals, chemical elements, or physical phenomena by two characteristics.

CLASSIFYING THINGS

DIRECTIONS: Classify the following things using the chart below. Glass is both hard and smooth. Look where it is on the chart.

ice cube, jagged rock, river rock, sand, still water, wet sponge

	Smooth	**Rough**
Hard	*glass* *ice cube* *river rock*	*jagged rock*
Soft	*still water*	*sand* *wet sponge*

- -

DIRECTIONS: Classify the following things using the chart below.

cloud, fishing float, iceberg, lead sinker, submarine

	Heavy	**Light**
Large	*iceberg* *submarine*	*cloud*
Small	*lead sinker*	*fishing float*

COMPARING LIVING AND NON-LIVING THINGS

THINKING SKILL: Verbal similarities and differences

CONTENT OBJECTIVE: Students will use the compare and contrast graph to differentiate between living and non-living things.

DISCUSSION: TECHNIQUE—Use a transparency of the compare and contrast graph to record responses as students discuss the similarities and differences between living and non-living things. Encourage them to identify additional similarities or differences between living and non-living things.

DIALOGUE—Discuss the differences between living and non-living things by naming the quality that is different. Establish this pattern: **"With regard to** (quality), (item one and its distinction), **but** (item two and its distinction)."** For example, **"With regard to nutrition, living things need nourishment but non-living things do not."**

Encourage students to identify things which might appear to be living but aren't, like rolling rocks or windblown objects. Identify living things that seem non-living but are alive, like coral. Clarify the difference between the self-propelled motion of animals as compared to motion caused by outside forces.

RESULT—Understanding the similarities and differences between living and non-living things helps one identify which things are living.

WRITING EXTENSION
- **Describe how living and non-living things are alike and how they are different.**

THINKING ABOUT THINKING
- **How does identifying characteristics help you understand significant differences between living and non-living things?**
- **How did using the diagram help you understand and remember the characteristics of the living things?**
- **Suggest another lesson in which using this diagram would help you understand what you are learning.**

SIMILAR SCIENCE LESSONS
- To compare phyla of plants, animals, and microorganisms.
- To compare systems within the human body with those in less complex life forms.
- To distinguish between plants and animals; comparing predators and prey.
- To compare land formations or types of rocks.
- To compare weather phenomena.
- To compare physical science phenomena: types of energy, types of machines, types of instruments; comparing energy, work, and power; comparing electrical measuring units.
- To compare relative distances of planets from the sun.
- To compare scientific procedures or experiments.

COMPARING LIVING AND NON-LIVING THINGS

DIRECTIONS: Read the passage carefully, then use the diagram on the next page to record how living and non-living things are alike and how they are different.

All things have weight and take up space. Both living and non-living things come in many sizes and shapes. There are tiny plants, tiny animals, and tiny grains of sand. There are large plants, large animals, and large lakes and mountains.

Most animals can move themselves from place to place. Plants must be moved from place to place by wind, by water, or by animals. No non-living thing can move itself from place to place. Like plants, non-living things must also be moved by other forces.

All living things breathe, but plants breath differently from animals. Non-living things do not breathe. Breathing is called respiration.

Non-living things do not eat and do not give birth. Giving birth is known as reproduction. All plants and animals reproduce themselves. Plants and animals need nourishment but get their food in different ways.

COMPARING LIVING AND NON-LIVING THINGS

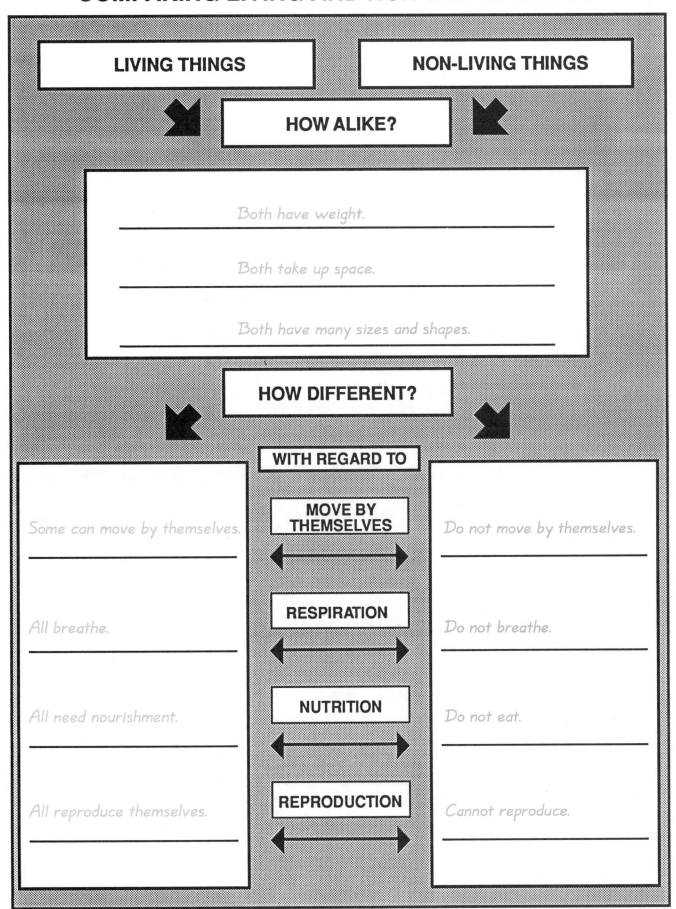

| LIVING THINGS | NON-LIVING THINGS |

HOW ALIKE?

Both have weight.

Both take up space.

Both have many sizes and shapes.

HOW DIFFERENT?

WITH REGARD TO

Some can move by themselves.	**MOVE BY THEMSELVES**	Do not move by themselves.
All breathe.	**RESPIRATION**	Do not breathe.
All need nourishment.	**NUTRITION**	Do not eat.
All reproduce themselves.	**REPRODUCTION**	Cannot reproduce.

CONTRASTING PLANTS AND ANIMALS

THINKING SKILL: Verbal similarities and differences

CONTENT OBJECTIVE: Students will use the contrast graph to differentiate between plants and animals.

DISCUSSION: TECHNIQUE—Use a transparency of the contrast graph to record responses as students discuss the similarities and differences between plants and animals. Encourage them to identify additional similarities or differences between plants and animals.

DIALOGUE—Discuss the differences between living and non-living things by naming the quality that is different. Establish this pattern: **"With regard to** (quality), (item one and its distinction), **but** (item two and its distinction)**."** For example, **"With regard to motion, plants cannot move themselves from place to place but animals usually can."**

Discuss why it is important to distinguish plants from animals, such as understanding whether the organism makes food or must obtain food.
Identify some animals that look like plants, such as sea anemones.

RESULT—It is important to understand the differences between plants and animals.

WRITING EXTENSION
• Describe how plants and animals are alike and how they are different.

THINKING ABOUT THINKING
• How does identifying characteristics help you understand significant differences between plants and animals?
• How did using the diagram help you understand and remember the characteristics of the plants and animals?
• Suggest another lesson in which using this diagram would help you understand what you are learning.

SIMILAR SCIENCE LESSONS
• To compare phyla of plants, animals, and microorganisms.
• To compare systems within the human body with those in less complex life forms.
• To distinguish between plants and animals; comparing predators and prey.
• To compare land formations or types of rocks.
• To compare weather phenomena.
• To compare physical science phenomena: types of energy, types of machines, types of instruments; comparing energy, work, and power; comparing electrical measuring units.
• To compare relative distances of planets from the sun.
• To compare scientific procedures or experiments.

CONTRASTING PLANTS AND ANIMALS

DIRECTIONS: Read the following passage carefully and use the information to complete the contrast diagram below.

Animals can usually move around, but plants stay in one place. Both plants and animals breathe. Breathing is called respiration. Plants take in carbon dioxide and give off oxygen. Animals take in oxygen and give off carbon dioxide.

Plants make their own food from sunlight, water, and minerals from the ground. Animals eat plants or other animals. Both plants and animals reproduce (give birth to similar kinds). Plants produce seeds which grow into new plants. Animals lay eggs, which hatch later, or give birth to live young.

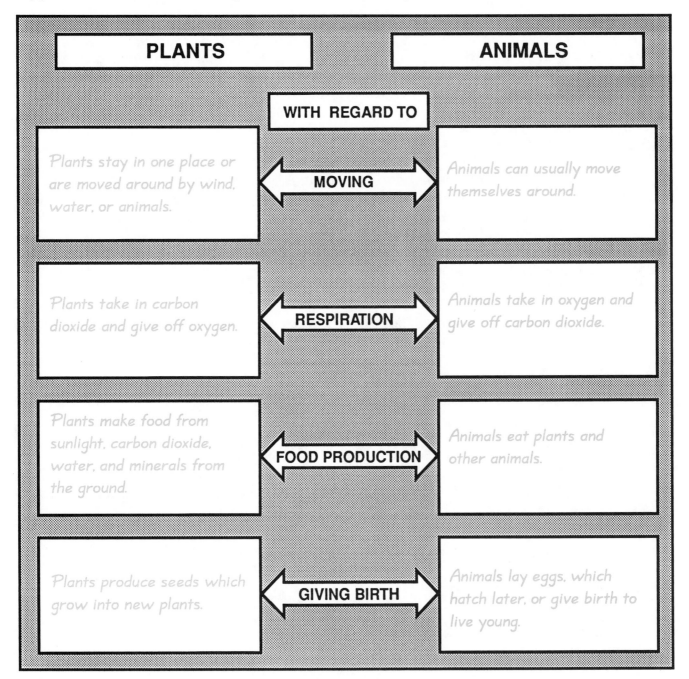

PLANTS	WITH REGARD TO	ANIMALS
Plants stay in one place or are moved around by wind, water, or animals.	MOVING	Animals can usually move themselves around.
Plants take in carbon dioxide and give off oxygen.	RESPIRATION	Animals take in oxygen and give off carbon dioxide.
Plants make food from sunlight, carbon dioxide, water, and minerals from the ground.	FOOD PRODUCTION	Animals eat plants and other animals.
Plants produce seeds which grow into new plants.	GIVING BIRTH	Animals lay eggs, which hatch later, or give birth to live young.

HOW ANIMALS MOVE

THINKING SKILL: Verbal classification

CONTENT OBJECTIVE: Students will use the branching diagram to classify animals by the way they move.

DISCUSSION: TECHNIQUE—Use a transparency of the branching diagram to record responses as students discuss how land and water animals move.

    DIALOGUE—Discuss the type of animal, the habitat in which it lives, and its means of locomotion. Clarify locomotion as an animal's ability to move itself. A key distinction in this lesson involves subtle differences between types of movement. Clarify with students the differences in the following terms:

What is the difference between walking and crawling? (Walking means to move by steps with the body above the ground; crawling means to move slowly by dragging the body along the ground.) **What is the difference between running and scampering?** (Running means to move on foot at a pace faster than walking; scampering means to run quickly for a short distance with frequent changes in direction.) **What is the difference between floating and swimming?** (Floating is to drift or rest on or near the surface of the water. Floating suggests little activity or control of speed or direction. Swimming means to propel oneself through the water; it suggests voluntary speed and direction.)

    Make similar distinctions between swimming and diving, running and leaping, swinging and climbing. Emphasize the advantages and limitations of each form of movement and the body structures and animal characteristics required for each. Identify examples of animals' use of more than one kind of locomotion.

    Encourage students to list as many additional animals as they can identify on the diagram. Use student-colored pictures (enlarged pictures from the exercises or original drawings) or magazine pictures of animals moving to create a bulletin board display using the diagram in the lesson.

    RESULT—The movement of animals differs by type and by habitat. Each kind of movement has advantages and disadvantages for the survival of the animal.

WRITING EXTENSION
- **Identify the characteristics used to describe how animals move.**

THINKING ABOUT THINKING
- **Why is knowing the type of animal and where it lives important in understanding its means of moving?**
- **How did using the diagram help you understand and remember how animals move?**
- **Suggest another lesson in which using this graph would help you understand what you are learning.**
- **Design another diagram to help you describe how animals move.**

SIMILAR SCIENCE LESSONS
- To illustrate types of characteristics among organisms in the plant or animal kingdoms.
- To illustrate types of characteristics among chemical elements.
- To illustrate various branches of science.

HOW ANIMALS MOVE

DIRECTIONS: Use the pictures below to help you fill in the branching diagram to classify these animals by how they move.

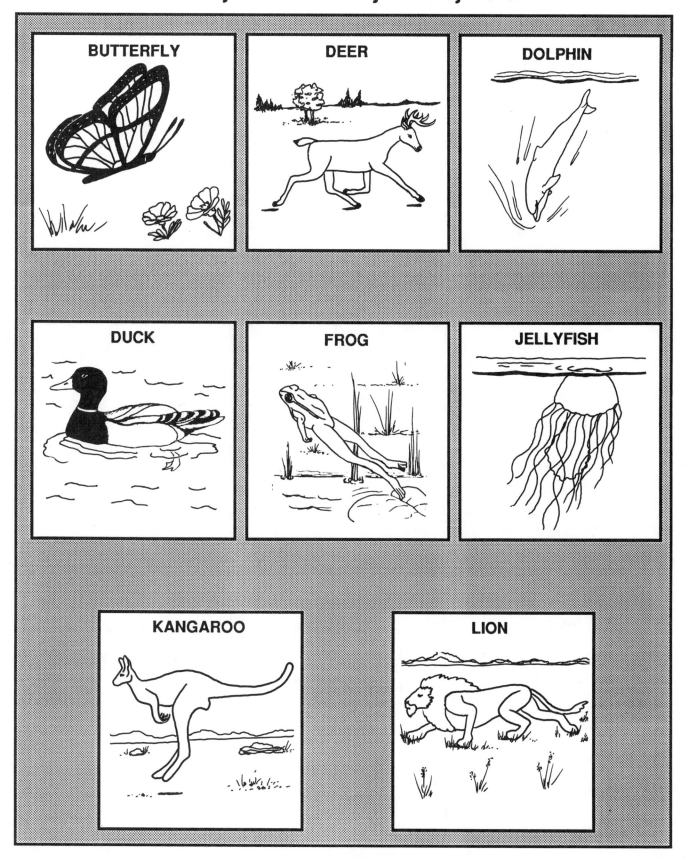

HOW ANIMALS MOVE

DIRECTIONS: Use the pictures below to help you fill in the branching diagram to classify these animals by how they move.

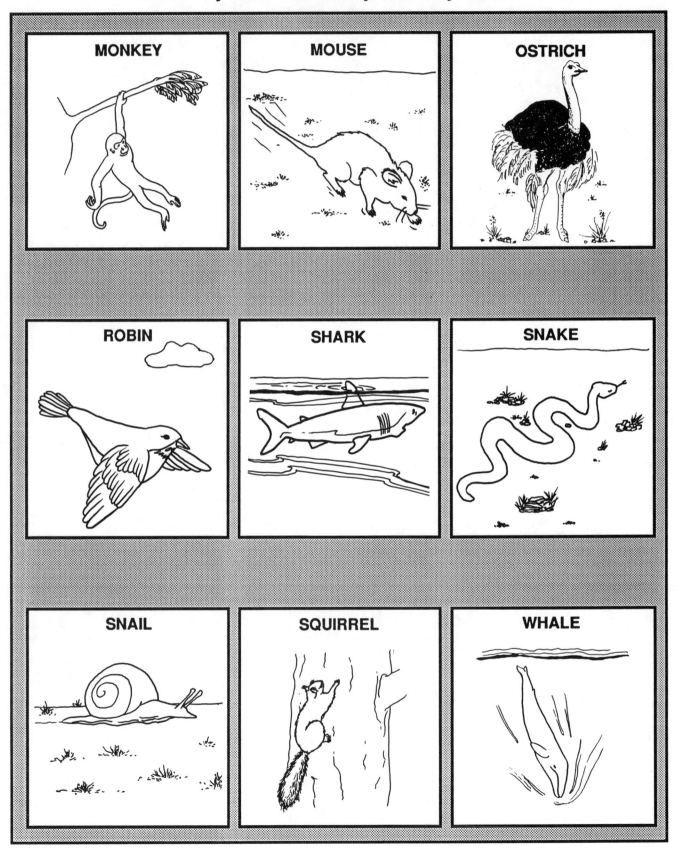

HOW ANIMALS MOVE

DIRECTIONS: Use the pictures from the picture dictionary to fill in the branching diagram to classify animals by how they move.

```
HOW ANIMALS MOVE
│
├── IN THE WATER
│     ├── DIVE
│     │     └── Whale
│     ├── SWIM
│     │     ├── Dolphin
│     │     └── UNDER
│     │           └── Shark
│     └── FLOAT
│           ├── Jellyfish
│           └── ON TOP
│                 └── Duck
│
├── ON THE GROUND
│     │
│     ├── WALK
│     │     ├── ON 4 LEGS
│     │     │     ├── HOP
│     │     │     │     ├── Kangaroo
│     │     │     │     └── Frog
│     │     │     └── RUN
│     │     │           ├── Lion
│     │     │           └── Deer
│     │     ├── SCAMPER
│     │     │     └── Mouse
│     │     └── ON 2 LEGS
│     │           └── Ostrich
│     └── CRAWL
│           ├── Snail
│           └── Snake
│
└── ABOVE THE GROUND
      ├── CLIMB
      │     └── Squirrel
      ├── FLY
      │     ├── Butterfly
      │     └── Robin
      └── SWING
            └── Monkey
```

LIFE CYCLE OF A PLANT

THINKING SKILL: Verbal classification

CONTENT OBJECTIVE: Students will use the cycle diagram to follow the life cycle of a plant.

DISCUSSION: TECHNIQUE—Use a transparency of the cycle diagram to record responses as students discuss the stages in the life of a plant. Select seeds and plants with which students are familiar and describe their appearance at various stages in the cycle. Fruits, vegetables, and cone-bearing plants can illustrate the cycle.

Discuss the effect of breaking the cycle at any point. Identify natural and man-made conditions which might interrupt the cycle.

DIALOGUE—Have students collect many different kinds of seeds. Discuss the stages in the life of a plant. Growing seeds is a useful parallel activity. If seeds are not grown, ask for student observations of the changes in plants that they are growing.

RESULT—Plants pass through stages necessary for the continued survival of the plant.

WRITING EXTENSION
• **Identify the stages in the life of a plant. Give examples of each part of the cycle.**

THINKING ABOUT THINKING
• **How did using the diagram help you understand and remember the life stages of a plant?**
• **Suggest another lesson in which using a cycle diagram would help you understand what you are learning.**

SIMILAR SCIENCE LESSONS
• To depict natural cycles (e.g., water cycle, seasonal cycle)

LIFE CYCLE OF A PLANT

DIRECTIONS: Read the following passage, then fill in the cycle diagram.

Many plants produce seeds. If a seed falls on the ground and has enough water, light, and space it can grow into a seedling.

The seedling grows and becomes an adult plant. This stage may take one growing season or many years.

When the plant has become an adult, it can produce seeds which make new plants.

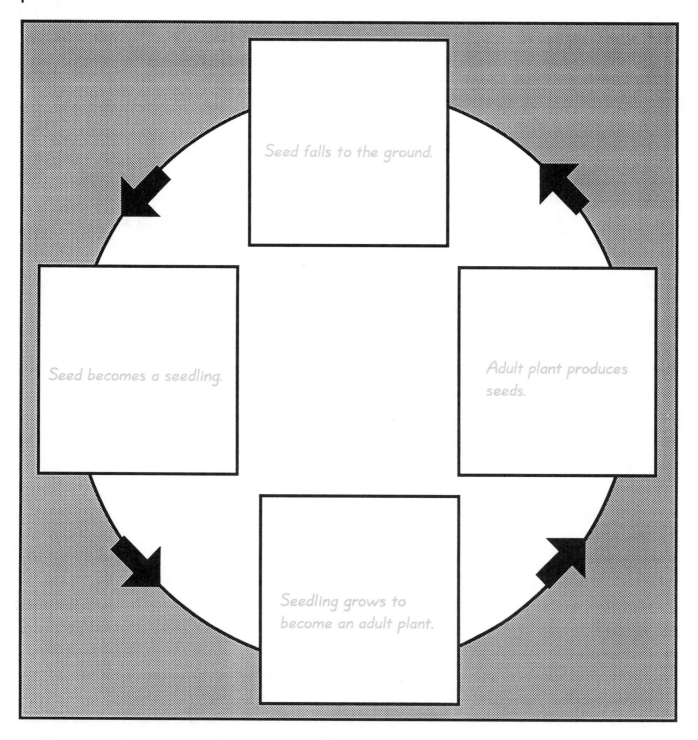

Seed falls to the ground.

Seed becomes a seedling.

Adult plant produces seeds.

Seedling grows to become an adult plant.

HOW SEEDS TRAVEL

THINKING SKILL: Verbal classification

CONTENT OBJECTIVE: Students will use the branching diagram to classify plants by the way their seeds travel.

DISCUSSION: TECHNIQUE—Use a transparency of the branching diagram to record responses as students discuss how seeds travel. Students may write in their answers or paste pictures in the correct categories.

DIALOGUE—Discuss the ways seeds travel. You may need to bring in a coconut in order to demonstrate that coconuts float. Identify the parts of a plant that assist its dispersal.

Encourage students to list on the diagram as many additional plants as they can identify in each category.

RESULT—Plants cannot move by themselves, but have a number of ways of distributing their seeds. Each way of moving seeds has advantages and disadvantages for the survival of the plant.

WRITING EXTENSION
• How do a seed's characteristics affect how it travels.

THINKING ABOUT THINKING
• Why is knowing where plants grow important in understanding how their seeds travel?
• How did using the diagram help you understand and remember how seeds travel?
• Suggest another lesson in which using this graph would help you understand what you are learning.
• Design another diagram to help you describe how seeds travel.

SIMILAR SCIENCE LESSONS
• To illustrate types of characteristics among organisms in the plant or animal kingdoms.
• To illustrate types of characteristics among chemical elements.
• To illustrate various branches of science.

HOW SEEDS TRAVEL

DIRECTIONS: **Read the following passage and use the pictures on the next page to help you fill in the branching diagram to classify seeds by how they travel.**

In order to grow into a new plant, a seed must have a good place to grow. Some seeds fall close to the parent plant. There may not be enough space, light, or water under the parent plant for all the seeds to grow into plants. Most plants produce many seeds but only a few of these seeds come to rest in a place where a new plant can grow.

Since seeds can't move by themselves, they must be carried to their new growing place. Seeds travel by water, animals, wind, or by the plant itself.

Some seeds are light and can float on water. Water-carried seeds can be small like milkweed seeds or big like coconuts. They can float long distances.

Other seeds, such as burrs, have stickers that can hook onto animal's fur or people's clothes. These seeds are called "hitchhikers." Some seeds stick in the mud and are picked up by the feet of wading birds.

When animals carry off fruit to eat, the part that is not eaten, or is eaten but not digested, may contain seeds. These seeds can fall to the ground a great distance from the parent plant.

Some seeds are carried easily by the wind. These light seeds may have special shapes like wings or parachutes to help them float in the wind.

Other seeds are shot out from the plant when the fruit pod dries and bursts. These seeds pop out far enough from the parent plant to get the space, light, and water they need.

HOW SEEDS TRAVEL

DIRECTIONS: Cut out the pictures below and use them to help you fill in the branching diagram to classify seeds by how they travel.

HOW SEEDS TRAVEL

DIRECTIONS: Use the pictures from the picture dictionary to complete this branching diagram.

HOW SEEDS TRAVEL

SHOT OUT BY OR FALL FROM THE PLANT

CARRIED BY WIND

CARRIED BY ANIMALS

FLOAT ON WATER

WHAT PART OF A PLANT DO WE EAT?

THINKING SKILL: Verbal classification

CONTENT OBJECTIVE: Students will use the branching diagram to classify plants according to the part that we eat.

DISCUSSION: TECHNIQUE—Use a transparency of the branching diagram to record responses as students discuss the part of the plant that we eat. For language-limited students, use an enlarged and hand-colored copy of the picture dictionary to create a bulletin board display of the completed matrix.

DIALOGUE—According to a commonly used second grade science textbook:

Many children have misconceptions about plant roots, stems, and leaves. For example, they may believe that any underground part of a plant is a root and only leafy parts are leaves. Thus, if they eat a plant part that grows underground, they might assume it must be a root. If the vegetable is stiff and straight, they might assume it must be part of a stem.

Help students understand that plants and plant parts do not always fit into tidy categories. Point out that onions are actually underground leaves. Roots can be found growing at the base of the onion. A potato is a specialized, food-storing underground stem called a tuber. A celery stalk is another example of a long leaf base, not a stem.*

Have students name other plants and the parts of that plant that are eaten. Confirm that some seeds are edible while others are not. Take this opportunity to introduce fruits and vegetables not commonly eaten by your students. Differentiate among the seeds (beans, grains, nuts). Dried beans are hard and must be soaked before they are cooked or else cooked a long time. Grains are hard and must be cracked or ground before they can be used to make bread. Nuts can be eaten raw, roasted, or boiled. Nuts vary in size. Grains are usually small while beans are intermediate in size.

How does knowing what part of the plant we're eating affect our understanding of the nutritional value of foods? (Knowing which part we eat helps us understand whether or how it should be cooked or prepared.) **How does knowing what part of the plant we're eating affect our understanding of how to cook the food?** (Roots are hard and will need to be cooked longer than other parts of the plant.)

Identify uncommon foods from plants and the cultures that include them in their diet. Discuss which plants we eat more than one part of, such as turnips.

RESULT—In each edible plant one or more parts is preferred to be eaten.

WRITING EXTENSION
• Identify the various parts of a plant that are eaten.

THINKING ABOUT THINKING
• How did using the diagram help you understand and remember parts of a plant?
• Suggest another lesson in which using a branching diagram would help you understand what you are learning.

SIMILAR SCIENCE LESSONS
• To classify plants or animals according to selected characteristics.
• To depict a balanced diet.

*Addison Wesley Science, Teachers Edition 2. Menlo Park, CA, 1989. p. 54B

WHAT PART OF A PLANT DO WE EAT?

DIRECTIONS: Use the pictures on this and the next page to help you fill in the branching diagram for sorting plants according to part of the plant that we eat.

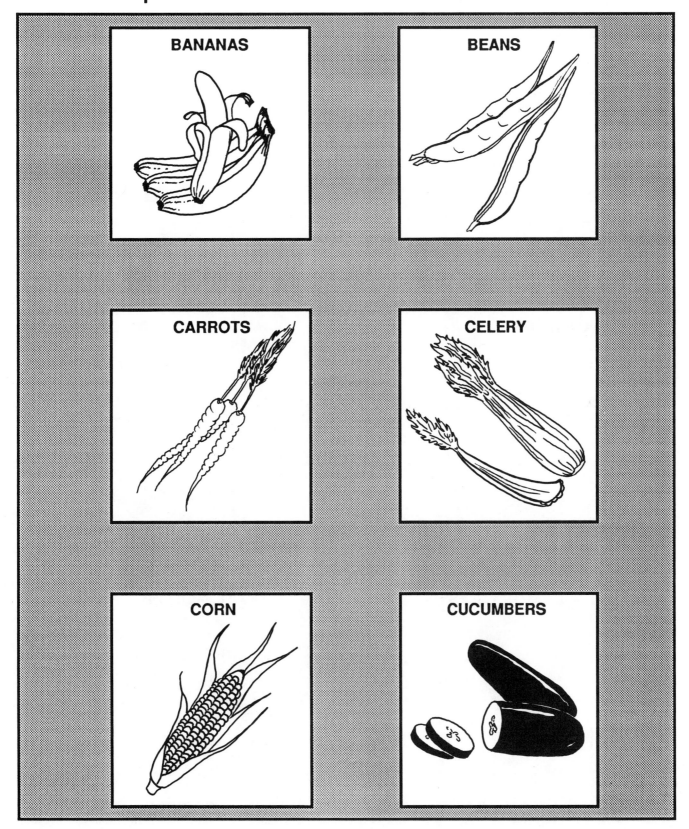

WHAT PART OF A PLANT DO WE EAT?

DIRECTIONS: Use the pictures on this and the previous page to help you fill in the branching diagram for sorting plants according to the part of the plant that we eat.

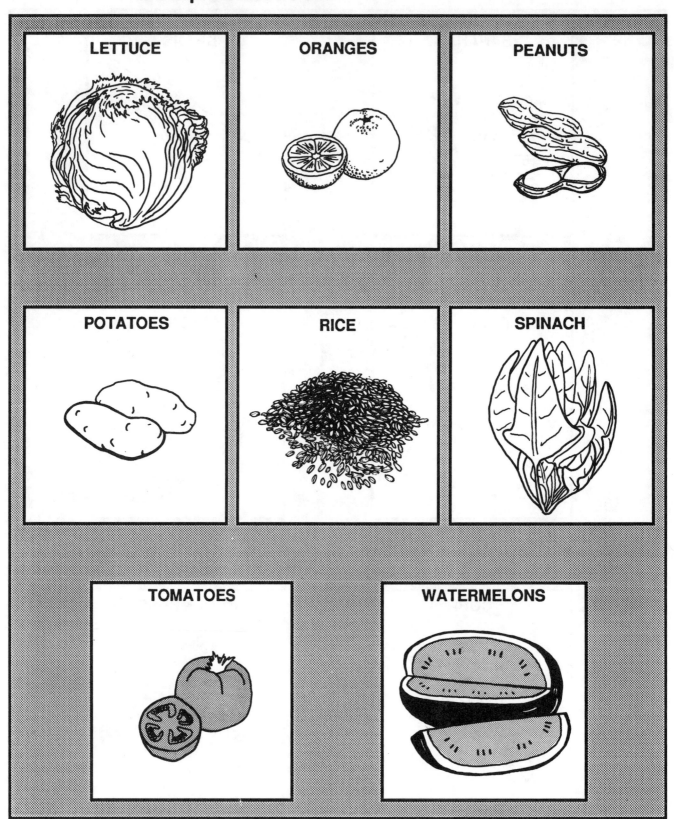

LETTUCE

ORANGES

PEANUTS

POTATOES

RICE

SPINACH

TOMATOES

WATERMELONS

WHAT PART OF A PLANT DO WE EAT?

DIRECTIONS: Sort the following plants according to the part that is eaten.

banana, beans, carrots, celery, corn, cucumbers, lettuce, orange, peanuts, potatoes, rice, spinach, tomato, watermelon

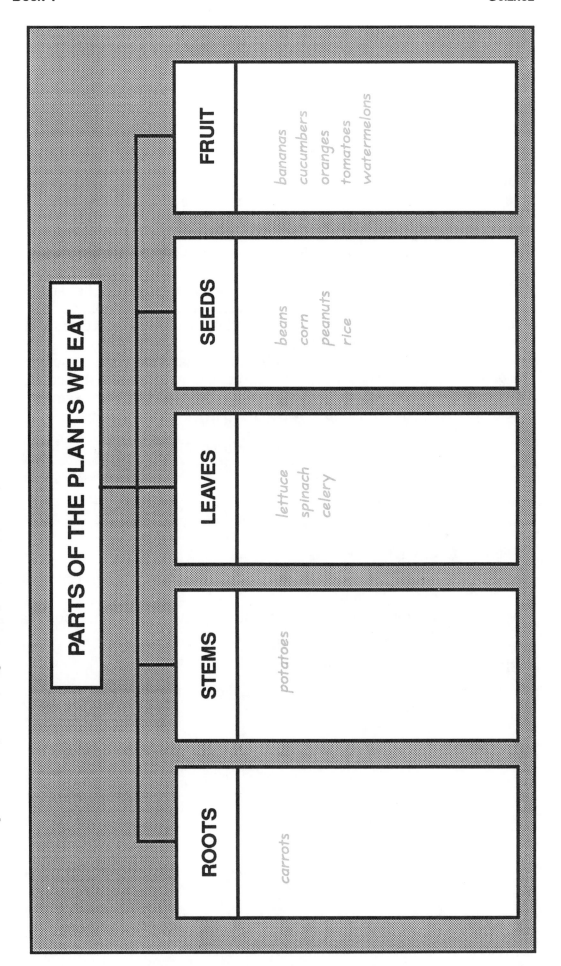

PARTS OF THE PLANTS WE EAT

FRUIT
bananas
cucumbers
oranges
tomatoes
watermelons

SEEDS
beans
corn
peanuts
rice

LEAVES
lettuce
spinach
celery

STEMS
potatoes

ROOTS
carrots

FRUIT OR VEGETABLE?

THINKING SKILL: Verbal classification

CONTENT OBJECTIVE: Students will use an overlapping classes diagram to classify fruits and vegetables.

DISCUSSION: TECHNIQUE—Use a transparency of the overlapping classes diagram to record responses as students discuss the differences between fruits and vegetables. It is helpful to bring in examples of fruit so that students can see the skin, pulp, and seeds.

DIALOGUE—Discuss the differences between fruits and vegetables. Use this opportunity to introduce fruits and vegetables not commonly eaten by your students.

Various ethnic groups use fruit and vegetables differently. For example, plantains (a starchy, less sweet member of the banana family) are fried in batter and eaten as a vegetable in Cuban dishes. Southerners sometimes substitute sweet potatoes for pumpkin in pies or turnovers. Tomatoes, which are actually a fruit, are used by most cultures as a salad vegetable and cooked as a sauce vegetable.

RESULT—A fruit is the part of a plant that contains the seeds. Whether a fruit is considered a fruit or a vegetable depends on the part of the meal in which it is consumed and results in the use of the popular term rather than the scientific one. For example, a tomato is by the scientific definition a "fruit," but by popular use it is called a "vegetable."

Which plants do we eat more than one part of? (Example: turnips—both the roots and the leaves [turnip greens] are eaten by some people.)

WRITING EXTENSION

- Discuss the differences between fruits and vegetables.

THINKING ABOUT THINKING

- How did using the diagram help you understand the difference between fruits and vegetables?
- Suggest another lesson in which using an overlapping classes diagram would help you understand what you are learning.

SIMILAR SCIENCE LESSONS

- To illustrate relationships within the plant or animal kingdoms.

FRUIT OR VEGETABLE?

DIRECTIONS: Read the following description of fruits and vegetables. Then fill in the diagram by writing the names of foods from the choice box below that are considered only vegetables on the left. Foods that are only fruits should be listed on the right. Foods that are both fruits and vegetables should be listed in the overlapping part of the diagram.

Vegetables are plants whose different parts can be eaten. We may eat one or two parts of the whole plant. We may prefer to eat the leaves, stem, roots, fruit, or seeds.

Fruits are the part of the plant that contains the seeds of the plant. The seeds are usually surrounded by a fleshy pulp which is often sweet. The pulp is covered on the outside by the tougher skin or rind. We usually eat the pulp of a fruit in salads, desserts, or as a snack.

> apples, bananas, beets, broccoli, cabbage, carrots, celery, cucumbers, lettuce, oranges, potatoes, squash, tomatoes, watermelons

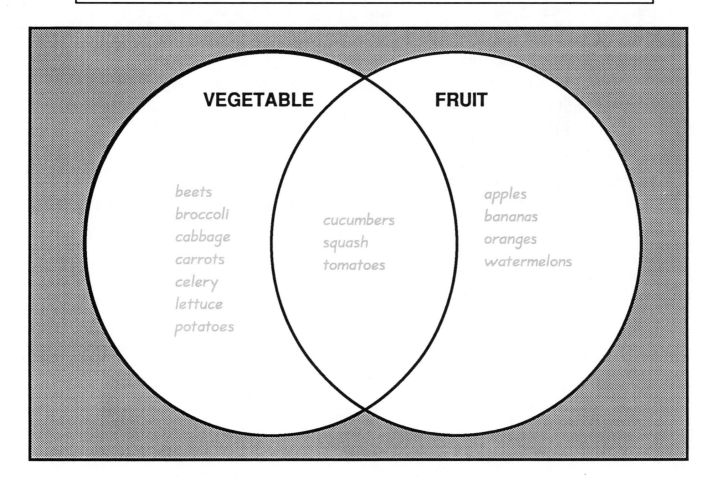

VEGETABLE   **FRUIT**

beets
broccoli
cabbage
carrots
celery
lettuce
potatoes

cucumbers
squash
tomatoes

apples
bananas
oranges
watermelons

THE FOUR FOOD GROUPS

THINKING SKILL: Verbal classification

CONTENT OBJECTIVE: Students will use the matrix chart to match foods with their groups and the function of each group.

DISCUSSION: TECHNIQUE—Use a transparency of the matrix to record responses as students discuss food groups and the function of foods.

DIALOGUE—Encourage students to name a variety of foods and classify them by food groups. This lesson offers an opportunity for students from a variety of ethnic backgrounds to describe foods that are not commonly known to the whole class or featured in textbooks or offered in fast-food restaurants.

The key concept of this lesson is the relationship between the food group and a balanced meal. Students should understand that we select foods from each group because different foods provide different nutrients for different purposes to promote good health. Students tend to memorize foods by group with little understanding that it is a variety of nutrients that is needed, not an arbitrary selection of foods from different groups. Distinguish food groups by discussing the nutrients that are common to that group.

Science texts and students from families with vegetarian preferences may identify nuts and beans as meat because they contain some of the proteins usually found in meat. Nutritionally the meat group includes nuts and beans, as well as animal products.

RESULT—Foods from all groups are necessary to provide the nutrients for good health.

WRITING EXTENSION

- **Describe a balanced lunch that contains your favorite foods from each food group. Explain why the lunch is balanced.**

THINKING ABOUT THINKING

- **How did using the diagram help you understand and remember the four food groups?**
- **Suggest another lesson in which using a matrix chart would help you understand what you are learning.**

SIMILAR SCIENCE LESSONS

- To record, summarize, and evaluate measurements or observations.
- To describe plants, animals, minerals, chemical elements, or physical phenomena by two characteristics.

THE FOUR FOOD GROUPS

DIRECTIONS: Read the following passage and fill in the matrix chart below.

There are four basic food groups. It is important to eat foods from each of the four groups in order to stay healthy.

The fruit and vegetable group is necessary to have healthy eyes, skin, teeth and gums.

The meat group is necessary for building and maintaining your muscles. The meat group includes beef, pork, fish, chicken, and turkey.

The milk group is important for the health of your teeth and bones. Milk, cheese, ice cream, and yogurt are members of the milk group.

The bread and cereal group gives you energy. Cereals such as wheat, rice, and oats are good breakfast foods to give you energy for school.

FOOD GROUP	COMMON FOODS	HELPS TO BUILD OR PROVIDE
FRUIT AND VEGETABLE GROUP	*See the two previous lessons.*	*Eyes, skin, teeth, and gums*
MEAT GROUP	*Beef, pork, fish, chicken and turkey*	*Building and maintaining muscles*
MILK GROUP	*Milk, cheese, ice cream, and yogurt*	*Teeth and bones*
BREAD AND CEREAL GROUP	*Wheat, rice, and oats*	*Energy*

FOOD CHAIN

THINKING SKILL: Transitive order

CONTENT OBJECTIVE: Students will use a cycle diagram to depict the steps in the food chain.

DISCUSSION: TECHNIQUE—Use a transparency of the Cycle Graph to record responses as students discuss the steps in the food chain.
　　DIALOGUE—Ask students to trace the steps in the food chain cycle and explain why each step is necessary. Identify what each organism contributes. Discuss the nature of cycles.

What makes a cycle different from other patterns? (A cycle is a repeating process that flows in one direction and requires each step to maintain its action. Cycles can remain constant, slow down or stop, or expand.) **What makes a cycle work? What would happen if there were a break in the cycle? Is there a point in the cycle in which a break might be more likely to occur? Why do you think so? What other examples of cycles can you think of?** (water cycle, photosynthesis/respiration cycle, seasonal cycle.)

　　RESULT—Each living thing provides food for another in an efficient cycle that supports life and decomposes waste.

WRITING EXTENSION
• Describe the food chain cycle. Give examples of each part of the cycle.

THINKING ABOUT THINKING
• How does a cycle show how living things depend on each other for food?
• Suggest another lesson in which using this graph would help you understand what you are learning.

SIMILAR SCIENCE LESSONS
• To depict natural cycles (e.g., water cycle, photosynthesis/respiration cycle, seasonal cycle, raw material trade, electrical current cycle, gasoline engine cycle).

FOOD CHAIN

DIRECTIONS: Read the passage carefully, then use the information to complete the food chain cycle diagram. List the sequence of events in order on the lines below.

In the food chain, plants produce food for animals who eat plants (herbivores). A corn plant uses sunlight and fertilizer to make food. Corn is a food source for many plant-eaters, including worms.

Meat-eating animals (carnivores) feed on plant-eating animals or other meat-eaters. Worms are eaten by sparrows which are eaten by hawks.

When a hawk or another member of a food chain dies, they become food for decomposers (fungi or bacteria). These decomposers break down dead organisms and animals. The decomposed materials go back into the soil or water and provide fertilizer for the corn. The corn grows and the food chain cycle repeats.

LIST THE EVENTS IN ORDER

1. Corn is eaten by worms. _____

2. _____

3. _____

4. _____

5. _____

6. _____

FOOD CHAIN

DIRECTIONS: Complete the food chain cycle diagram using the information from the page before this one.

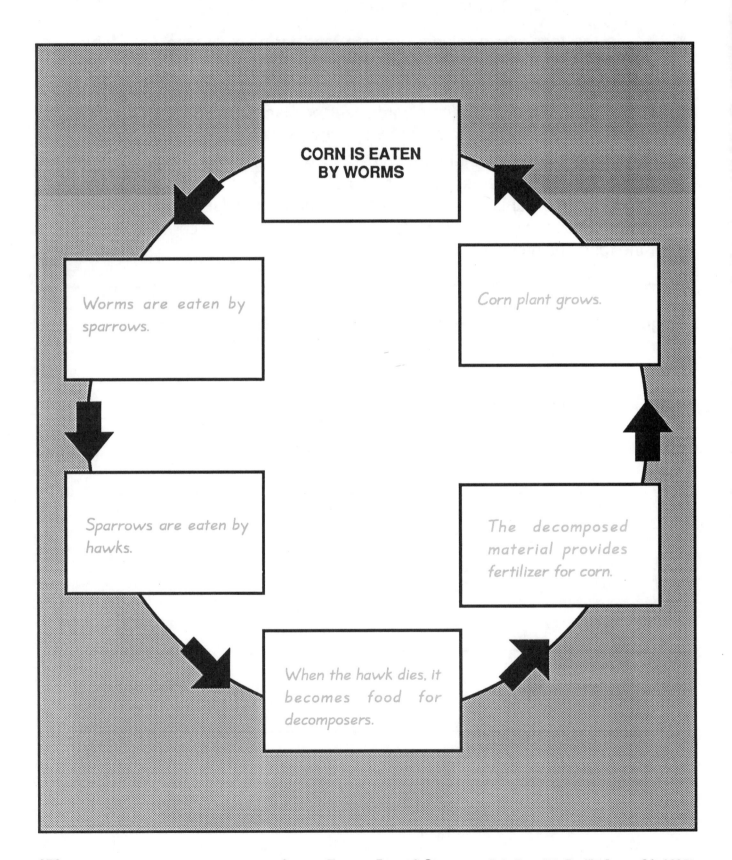

MEAT-EATING AND PLANT-EATING DINOSAURS

THINKING SKILL: Verbal similarities and differences

CONTENT OBJECTIVE: Students will use the contrast graph to differentiate between amphibians and reptiles.

DISCUSSION: TECHNIQUE— Use a transparency of the contrast graph to record responses as students discuss the similarities and differences between meat-eating and plant-eating dinosaurs.

DIALOGUE—Discuss the differences between meat-eating and plant-eating dinosaurs by naming the quality that is different. Establish this pattern: **"With regard to** (quality), (item one and its distinction), **but** (item two and its distinction)." For example, **"With regard to teeth, meat eating dinosaurs have sharp teeth, but plant eating dinosaurs have flat teeth."**

RESULT—Identifying the differences between meat-eating and plant-eating dinosaurs promotes the clearer understanding of the feeding habits of these two kinds of dinosaurs.

WRITING EXTENSION

• Describe how meat-eating and plant-eating dinosaurs are alike and how they are different.

THINKING ABOUT THINKING

• How does identifying characteristics help you understand significant differences between meat-eating and plant-eating dinosaurs?

• If you saw a picture of a dinosaur how could you tell if it was a meat-eating or a plant-eating dinosaur?

• How did using the diagram help you understand and remember the characteristics of the dinosaurs?

• Suggest another lesson in which using this diagram would help you understand what you are learning.

• Design another diagram that would help you describe animals.

SIMILAR SCIENCE LESSONS

• To compare phyla of plants or animals.

• To compare systems within the human body with those in less complex life-forms comparing bone formation or location.

• To compare living and nonliving things; distinguishing between plants and animals; comparing predators and prey.

• To compare land formations or types of rocks.

• To compare weather phenomena.

• To compare physical science phenomena: types of energy, types of machines, types of instruments; comparing energy, work, and power; comparing electrical measuring units.

• To compare relative distances of planets from the sun.

• To compare scientific procedures or experiments.

MEAT-EATING AND PLANT-EATING DINOSAURS

DIRECTIONS: Read the following passage to learn how meat-eating and plant-eating dinosaurs are alike and how they are different. Fill in the compare and contrast diagram on the next page.

Many dinosaurs lived at different times long ago. Some of the dinosaurs ate the meat of other animals while other dinosaurs were plant eaters.

Meat eaters like Tyrannosaurus ran long distances on two strong legs to catch its prey. It used two short legs to hold its kill. It used its sharp teeth to eat its catch. Tyrannosaurus was a large animal standing taller than a two-story house.

Plant eaters like Brontosaurus walked slowly on four short legs. Brontosaurus was longer than three school busses and stayed in or near the water. When it was in the water it could move more easily. It ate plants which grew in or near the water and ate them with its flat teeth.

BRONTOSAURUS　　　　　　　　　　TYRANNOSAURUS

　　　© 1992 CRITICAL THINKING PRESS & SOFTWARE • P.O. Box 448, Pacific Grove, CA 93950

MEAT-EATING AND PLANT-EATING DINOSAURS

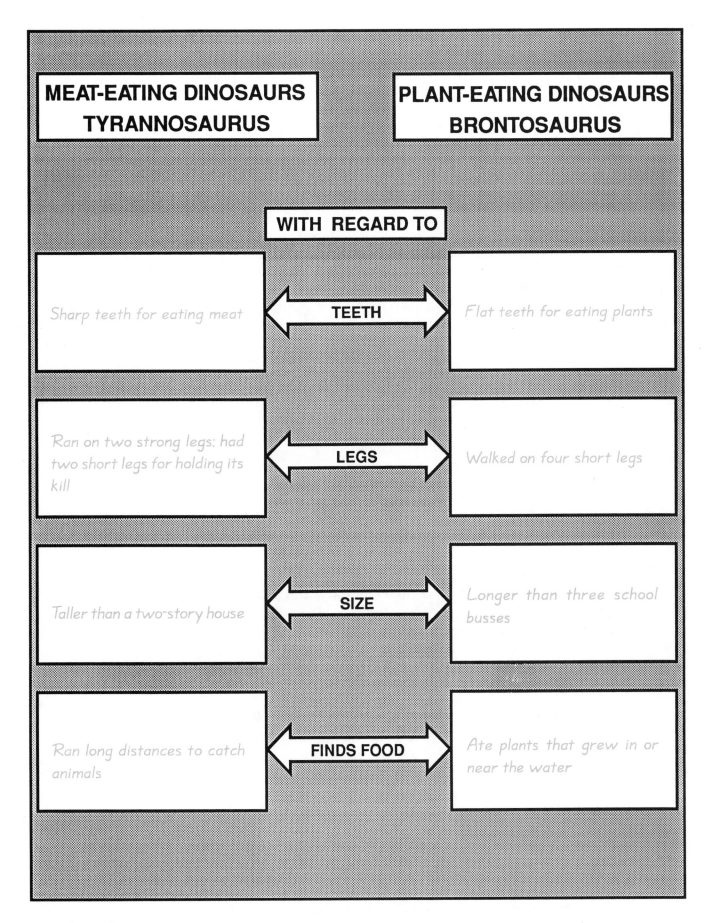

MEAT-EATING DINOSAURS TYRANNOSAURUS

PLANT-EATING DINOSAURS BRONTOSAURUS

WITH REGARD TO

Sharp teeth for eating meat	**TEETH**	Flat teeth for eating plants
Ran on two strong legs; had two short legs for holding its kill	**LEGS**	Walked on four short legs
Taller than a two-story house	**SIZE**	Longer than three school busses
Ran long distances to catch animals	**FINDS FOOD**	Ate plants that grew in or near the water

SOLIDS, LIQUIDS, AND GASES

THINKING SKILL: Verbal classification

CONTENT OBJECTIVE: Students will read a passage about the properties of matter and record what they have learned on a matrix graph.

DISCUSSION: TECHNIQUE—Use a transparency of the matrix graph to record student responses as you discuss the lesson.

DIALOGUE—The key concept in this lesson is clarification of the characteristics of each state of matter and then distinguishing among them. Using water and other common substances which children recognize in different states helps young children understand this principle.

The most frequent misconception that young children hold is their inability to recognize that gases take up space and have weight. Our usual procedures for weighing don't commonly include weighing a gas in some container. Children are accustomed to food or material being weighed; weighing a gas is an abstract and uncommon experience for an elementary child. Students may recognize that a flat, deflated basketball weighs less than a fully inflated one. This is difficult to demonstrate because it requires a very sensitive scale. There are science films which demonstrate the weighing of air.

Each example in the student passage should be demonstrated if that perception is beyond the common experience of your students. Demonstrate that gases take up space by inverting a glass full of air in an aquarium. When the glass is turned upright under the water, the air escapes, as seen by bubbles in the water.

Why do lead weights sink? (Because lead is much heavier than water.)
Why do the bubbles rise in water? (Because air is much lighter than water.)

RESULT—All forms of matter have weight and take up space.

WRITING EXTENSION
- **Select a common substance and describe it as a solid, a liquid, and a gas.**

THINKING ABOUT THINKING
- **How did using the diagram help you remember the properties of matter?**
- **Suggest another lesson in which depicting information on a matrix graph would help you understand what you are learning.**
- **Design another graph that would help you describe the states of matter.**

SIMILAR SCIENCE LESSONS:
- To record, summarize, and evaluate measurements and observations.
- To describe plants, animals, minerals, chemical elements, or physical phenomena by two characteristics.

SOLIDS, LIQUIDS, AND GASES

DIRECTIONS: Read the following passage then check the correct boxes in the matrix.

Water can be a solid, a liquid, or a gas. When water is frozen into hard ice, it is a solid. Solid ice has a definite shape. You can take it out of its container and pick it up. It will keep its shape as long as it is kept very cold. You know it has weight because you can feel it press on your hand.

When water is a liquid, it takes the shape of the container it is in. If you try to take it out of the container, it flows all over. You cannot pick it up with your hand. You can pour liquid water from one container to another. You can feel its weight when you pick up a container of water.

When water is boiled, you can see it turn first into hot steam and then disappear into the air as a gas When the water gas rises up into the atmosphere and becomes cooler, the tiny particles of water start gathering close together and we can see them in the sky as clouds. Sometimes a cloud forms on the ground. We call it fog. You cannot pick up this cloud in your hand but you can see the water droplets in the air around you as you walk through the thick fog. You know it has weight because it stays on the ground under plain air.

	SOLID	LIQUID	GAS
HAS WEIGHT	✓	✓	✓
TAKES UP SPACE	✓	✓	✓
CAN BE POURED		✓	
HAS A DEFINITE SHAPE	✓		
MANY ARE INVISIBLE			✓

HEATING AND COOLING WATER

THINKING SKILL: Verbal classification

CONTENT OBJECTIVE: Students will read a passage and fill in a cycle diagram.

DISCUSSION: TECHNIQUE—Use a transparency of the cycle diagram to record student responses as you discuss the heating and cooling of water.

     DIALOGUE—See the preceding lesson to review the three states of matter—solid, liquid and gas.

Name the process of water changing to steam. (boiling) **Name the process of steam changing to water.** (condensing) **Name the process of water changing to ice.** (freezing) **Name the process of ice changing to water.** (melting)

     RESULT—When water is heated to a high temperature, it boils. When water is cooled to a low temperature, it freezes.

WRITING EXTENSION

• **Select a material and describe the change from solid to liquid.**

THINKING ABOUT THINKING

• **How did using the diagram help you remember the terms used to describe the changes in the states of water?**
• **Suggest another lesson in which depicting information on a cycle diagram would help you understand what you are learning.**

SIMILAR SCIENCE LESSONS

• To depict natural cycles (e.g., water cycle, seasonal cycle).

HEATING AND COOLING WATER

DIRECTIONS: Read the following passage and fill in the cycle diagram below.

If water is heated long enough it boils away. The water has changed to steam. When steam hits a cool surface, it forms small drops of water. When the steam loses heat, we say it **condenses** to form water again. If you place water in a tray and put it in the freezer, the water will lose its heat and change to ice. When you use the ice cubes to cool a drink, the ice gains heat and changes back to water.

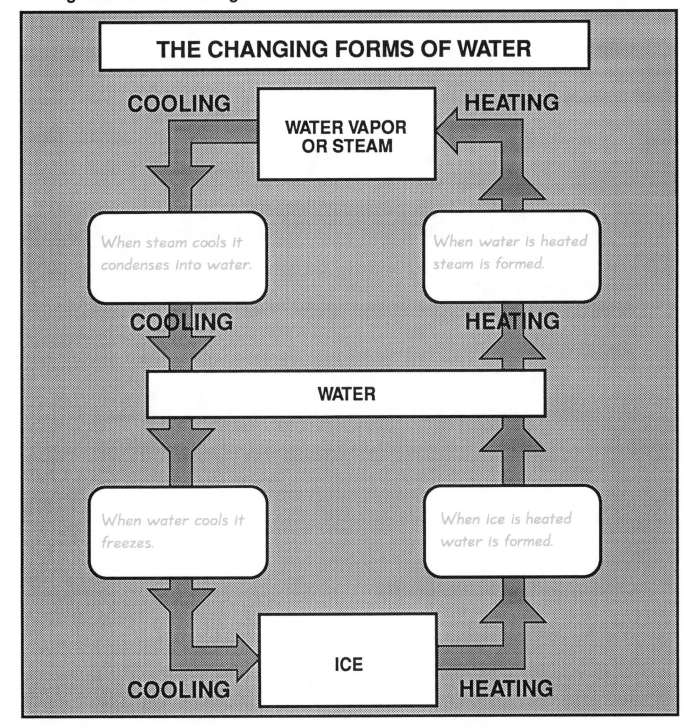

WATER CYCLE

THINKING SKILL: Verbal classification

CONTENT OBJECTIVE: Students will read a passage and fill in a cycle diagram.

DISCUSSION: TECHNIQUE—Use a transparency of the cycle diagram to record student responses as you discuss the water cycle.

DIALOGUE—**What causes the water in the lakes and oceans to warm up?** (The energy from the sun is taken up by the water). **What happens when water is heated?** (It rises up and becomes part of the air.) **What happens when warm moist air is cooled.** (The moisture condenses into tiny drops of water forming a cloud.) **Why are clouds important?** (Clouds are the source of rain.)

RESULT—Water is continually being evaporated from bodies of water and falling from the sky as rain.

WRITING EXTENSION
• **Describe how clouds are formed.**

THINKING ABOUT THINKING
• **How did using the diagram help you remember the water cycle?**
• **Suggest another lesson in which depicting information on a cycle diagram would help you understand what you are learning.**

SIMILAR SCIENCE LESSONS
• To depict natural cycles (e.g., growth cycles, seasonal cycle).

WATER CYCLE

DIRECTIONS: Read the passage and fill in the cycle diagram.

The sun causes water to evaporate from the lakes and oceans of the world. The warm, moist air from the lakes and oceans rises higher and higher. As it rises it cools. When moist air is cooled, clouds are formed and water droplets form within the clouds. When the water droplets grow large enough, they fall from the clouds as rain.

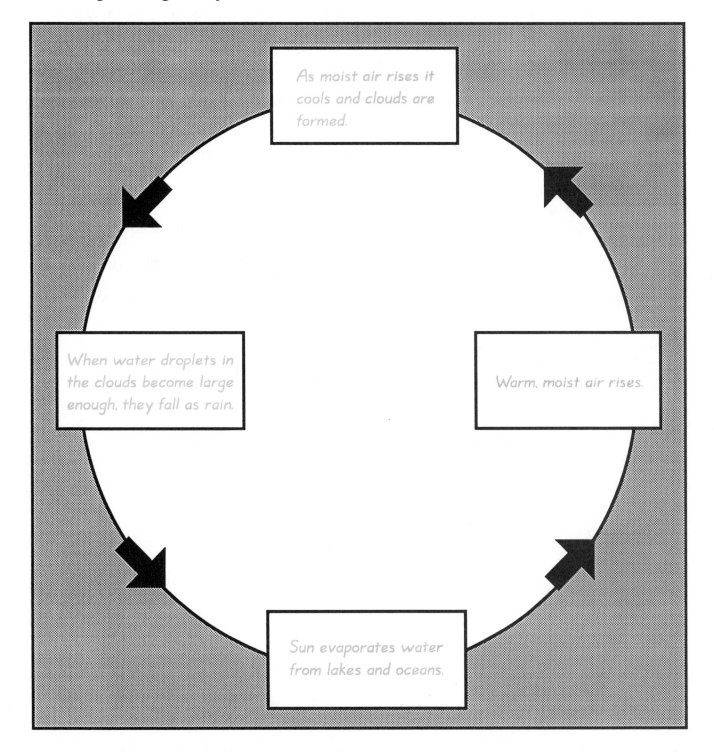

As moist air rises it cools and clouds are formed.

When water droplets in the clouds become large enough, they fall as rain.

Warm, moist air rises.

Sun evaporates water from lakes and oceans.

ENERGY CHANGES

THINKING SKILL: Verbal sequences

CONTENT OBJECTIVE: Students will determine the order in which energy transformations occur and list them on a flowchart.

DISCUSSION: TECHNIQUE—Have the students cut apart the matrix of energy transformations and arrange the list in order of occurrence on the flowchart. Make a transparency of the flowchart and the energy transformations. Cut apart the energy transformations and, during the discussion, use these pieces to overlay the flowchart transparency. Students may paste or write the sentences in the correct order.

   DIALOGUE—Help students identify the clues that suggest order. They may recognize that the last word or phrase of an earlier step becomes the first word or phrase of the next step.

   RESULT—There are many energy changes needed to lift a weight.

WRITING EXTENSION
• Identify the sequence of energy changes needed to lift a weight.

THINKING ABOUT THINKING
• Why is knowing about energy transformations important?
• How did using the diagram help you understand and remember the steps in lifting a weight?
• Suggest another lesson in which using a flowchart would help you understand what you are learning.
• Design another diagram that would help you describe energy transformations.

SIMILAR SCIENCE LESSONS
• To illustrate changes within the plant or animal kingdoms.
• To illustrate changes between elements in a compound or mixture.
• To illustrate similar changes in various branches of science.

ENERGY CHANGES

DIRECTIONS: Read the following passage then look at the six energy changes listed below. Cut them apart and arrange them in order of occurrence on the flowchart on the next page.

In a science class, the teacher demonstrates energy changes by burning a candle to produce heat. The heat from the candle is used to boil a bottle of water. The boiling water changes to steam. The steam from the bottle is carried by a hose to a small steam engine. The steam engine begins to turn. The turning engine is used to lift a weight.

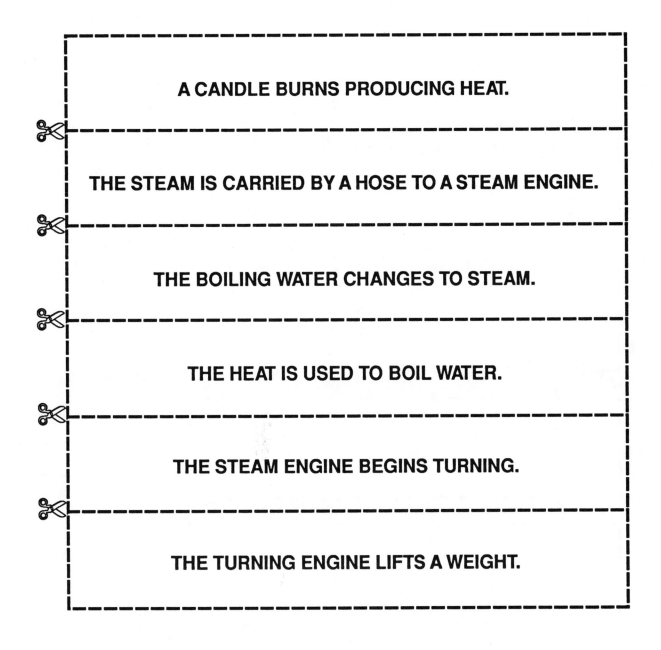

A CANDLE BURNS PRODUCING HEAT.

THE STEAM IS CARRIED BY A HOSE TO A STEAM ENGINE.

THE BOILING WATER CHANGES TO STEAM.

THE HEAT IS USED TO BOIL WATER.

THE STEAM ENGINE BEGINS TURNING.

THE TURNING ENGINE LIFTS A WEIGHT.

ENERGY CHANGES

DIRECTIONS: Use the sentences that you cut apart and arrange them in order of occurrence on the flowchart. Use the clues in the written passage.

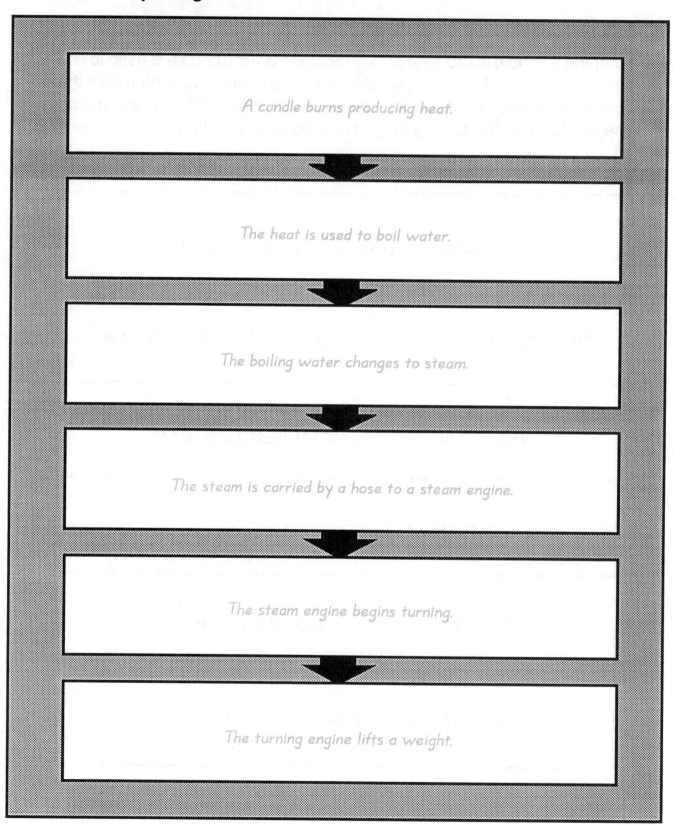

A candle burns producing heat.

The heat is used to boil water.

The boiling water changes to steam.

The steam is carried by a hose to a steam engine.

The steam engine begins turning.

The turning engine lifts a weight.

SIMPLE MACHINES

THINKING SKILL: Verbal classification

CONTENT OBJECTIVE: Students will use the central idea graph to identify different types of simple machines.

DISCUSSION: TECHNIQUE—Use a transparency of the central idea graph to record classes and examples of simple machines. Create a bulletin board display of simple machines using pictures of objects mentioned in the lesson and other common examples.

DIALOGUE—Encourage students to identify how force changes with the use of each type of simple machine. Identify other examples of each type.

Can you think of some objects or machinery which are made of more than one simple machine? (In less industrialized times, most complex machines were combinations of simple machines.) **Can you identify some objects which use electronic, not simple, machines?** (Compare a manual adding machine with a calculator, or compare a wound watch with an electronic one.)

RESULT—Knowing how simple machines put forces to work helps us do certain tasks more quickly and easily.

WRITING EXTENSION
- **Describe how simple machines use force efficiently to help us do tasks more easily and quickly.**
- **Describe and give examples of each type of simple machine.**

THINKING ABOUT THINKING
- **How did using the diagram help you understand and remember types of simple machines and examples?**
- **Suggest another lesson in which using this graph would help you understand what you are learning.**
- **Design another diagram that would help you describe simple machines.**

SIMILAR SCIENCE LESSONS
- To recognize main ideas and supporting details in critical reading activities from science texts.
- To illustrate classes and subclasses of organisms, minerals, weather phenomena, or chemical terms (elements, mixtures, or compounds).
- To illustrate part/whole relationships: parts of a microscope or other scientific equipment, parts of body systems, tissues, cells, organisms, atomic structure, structure of the earth, or the solar system.

SIMPLE MACHINES

DIRECTIONS: Read the passage below then fill in the central idea diagram on the next page.

Machines put forces to work which help us do things more easily. Simple machines are not driven by motors. They take advantage of simple forces to make work easier. Simple machines magnify a person's ability to move an object.

A **lever** is a bar used to pry up objects, like the claw of a hammer, pliers, or bottle openers.

A **wheel and axle**, like the pedals and chain of a bicycle, allows the small motion of the pedals to be changed into the larger motion of the bike wheel over the ground. A pencil sharpener is another example of a wheel and axle. It changes the small force on the handle into the larger force on the blades which sharpen the pencil.

A **pulley** is a set of wheels with a rope running over them. With a pulley, a person uses a small force through a long distance to lift a heavy load a short distance. The cords on Venetian blinds are wrapped around pulley wheels.

An **inclined plane** is a ramp that allows a person to slide an object that is too heavy to lift. The heavy object slides a long distance along the ramp and rises a short distance.

A **screw** is a coiled inclined plane that allows a small force on the big head to produce a large force on the small tip. For example, a hardware screw applies a great force to dig into wood.

A **wedge** is a narrow triangular blade used to split or cut wood or metal. Its shape allows a small force applied to the broad end to produce a large force at the blade end. Knives, scissors, and door stops are all wedges.

SIMPLE MACHINES

DIRECTIONS: Write one type of simple machine in each box on the diagram.
Add an example of each simple machine in parentheses.

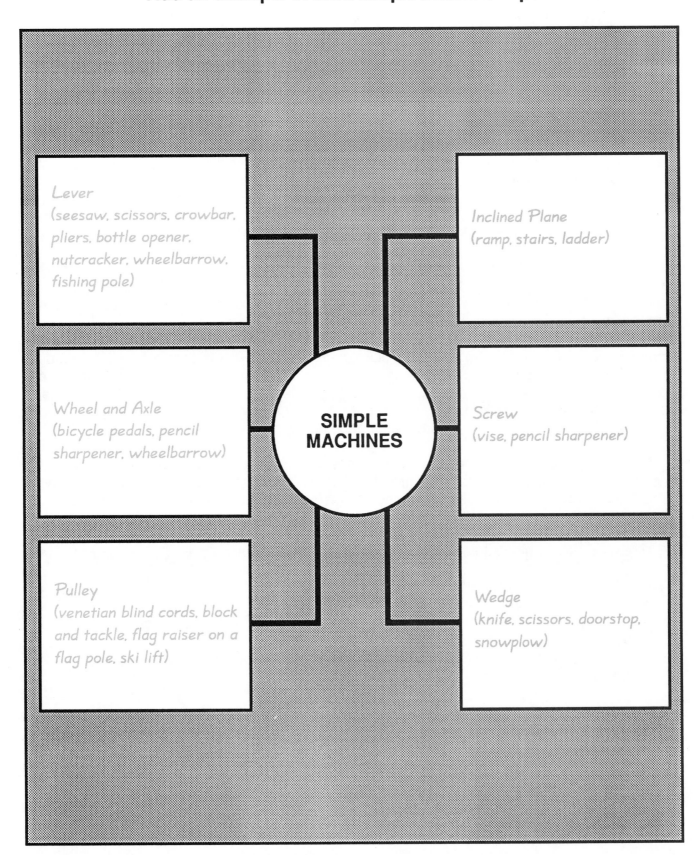

Lever
(seesaw, scissors, crowbar,
pliers, bottle opener,
nutcracker, wheelbarrow,
fishing pole)

Inclined Plane
(ramp, stairs, ladder)

Wheel and Axle
(bicycle pedals, pencil
sharpener, wheelbarrow)

SIMPLE
MACHINES

Screw
(vise, pencil sharpener)

Pulley
(venetian blind cords, block
and tackle, flag raiser on a
flag pole, ski lift)

Wedge
(knife, scissors, doorstop,
snowplow)

WHICH SOUND IS LOUDER?

THINKING SKILL: Verbal similarities and differences

CONTENT OBJECTIVE: Students will use the transitive order diagram to arrange sounds in order of increasing loudness.

DISCUSSION: TECHNIQUE—Use a transparency of the transitive order diagram to record responses as students discuss the relative loudness of sounds. Encourage students to identify additional examples of loud or soft sounds.

DIALOGUE—The transitive order diagram is useful in comparing anything that increases or decreases in size, weight, height, volume, or intensity. Small differences in the loudness of sounds is difficult to judge. Fourth grade science textbooks sometimes explain the use of decibels as a unit of volume.

In this lesson, sounds that differ greatly in loudness are used for comparison purposes. Sounds are compared as if heard from the same short distance. Encourage students to clarify the usefulness of understanding the relative loudness of sounds.

In what situations is it useful to understand the loudness of sounds? (To judge relative distance. For example, if we understand that the sound of an airplane engine is much louder than conversation between two people, then we know that an airplane engine that is hard to hear is a long distance away.)
What is the connection between the loudness of sounds and hearing safety? (To protect our ears against damage from long-term, high-intensity sounds, it is important to relate sounds we understand with a level of volume that can injure the ear. While a loud sound may be uncomfortable, the accumulated damage from prolonged exposure may result in a gradual hearing loss. Any sound as loud or uncomfortable as a nearby jet engine is damaging. Loud music in a small space may do more damage to hearing than students realize.)

RESULT—Small differences in the loudness of sounds are difficult to compare without special equipment. Sounds that differ greatly in loudness are compared more easily. Knowing relative loudness of sounds helps us judge distance and protect our hearing from damage.

WRITING EXTENSION
• Discuss the dangers of listening to very loud sounds for long periods of time.

THINKING ABOUT THINKING
• How did using the diagram help you compare sounds.
• Suggest another lesson in which you think that using this graph would help you understand what you are learning.
• Design another diagram that would help you compare other features of sound such as pitch or quality.

SIMILAR SCIENCE LESSONS
• To compare the relative distances to the planets.
• To compare the relative weights of materials.
• To compare the relative heights of clouds.
• To compare the relative sizes of plants.

WHICH SOUND IS LOUDER?

DIRECTIONS: Some sounds are louder than others. Which is louder, a whisper or conversation (talking)? Compare the following sounds. Arrange them from softest to loudest on the chart.

conversation, heavy traffic, jet airplane, thunder, whisper

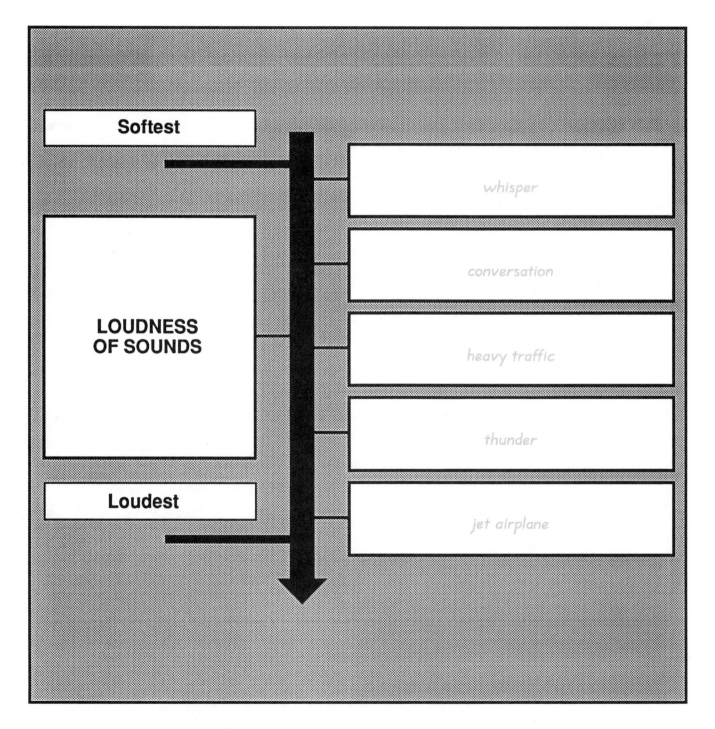

WEATHER OBSERVATIONS

THINKING SKILL: Verbal classification

CONTENT OBJECTIVE: Students will observe weather conditions and record their observations on a matrix graph.

DISCUSSION: TECHNIQUE—Use a transparency of the matrix graph to summarize weather observations for a two-week period. Encourage your students to draw inferences suggested by the information on the graph.
    DIALOGUE—Examine each variable and describe its effect in producing weather conditions for your locale. Encourage students to identify control factors and variables in a science demonstration.

Why was it important to record the weather at the same time each day? What factors changed during the two-week period? How did weather conditions reflect that change? If those conditions are present again, are we likely to have similar weather?

    RESULT—It is necessary to identify what remains constant and what changes in order to suggest a trend or principle in observing natural occurrences.

WRITING EXTENSION
- **Describe how one records and interprets weather information.**

THINKING ABOUT THINKING
- **How did using the diagram help you understand and suggest trends or principles about weather conditions?**
- **Suggest another lesson in which depicting information on a matrix graph would help you understand what you are learning.**
- **Design another graph that would help you describe weather conditions.**

SIMILAR SCIENCE LESSONS
- To record, summarize, and evaluate measurements and observations.
- To describe plants, animals, minerals, chemical elements, or physical phenomena by two characteristics.

WEATHER OBSERVATIONS

DIRECTIONS: A good scientist learns to make careful observations and to keep records. Use the matrix graph below to record weather conditions each day for a two-week period. Make sure all observations are made at the same time of day.

WEATHER RECORD FOR THE WEEK FROM _____ TO _____

DAY	SUNNY	RAINY	SNOWING	WINDY	WARM	CHILLY	FREEZING	CLOUDY	FOGGY
MON.									
TUE.									
WED.									
THU.									
FRI.									
SAT									
SUN.									

STARS AND PLANETS

THINKING SKILL: Verbal similarities and differences

CONTENT OBJECTIVE: Students will use the compare and contrast diagram to show similarities and differences between the stars and planets.

DISCUSSION: TECHNIQUE—Use a transparency of the compare and contrast diagram to record responses as students discuss the similarities of and differences between stars and planets.

DIALOGUE—Help the students use the passage to identify significant characteristics when describing a planet.

What characteristics might one discuss when describing a planet? (size, weight, distance from the sun, temperature, presence of satellites, geographical features, chemical composition.) **Why is it important to know the conditions on other planets?**

Encourage students to realize that our Sun is a star.

RESULT—Although the stars and planets look similar in the sky, planets revolve around stars like our Sun.

WRITING EXTENSION
• **Identify the characteristics that one uses to describe planets.**

THINKING ABOUT THINKING
• **How does using the diagram help you understand and remember the similarities and differences between stars and planets?**
• **Suggest another lesson in which using this graph would help you understand what you are learning.**
• **Design another graph that would help you describe planets.**

SIMILAR SCIENCE LESSONS
• To make comparisons within the plant or animal kingdoms.
• To make comparisons between chemical elements or compounds.

STARS AND PLANETS

DIRECTIONS: Use the compare and contrast diagram to illustrate the similarities and differences between the stars and planets.

When you look at the night sky, you see many tiny lights. If you watched night after night you would see that most of these tiny lights, that we call stars, always make the same shapes in the sky, like the Big Dipper. There are a few shiny objects that seem to move among the stars. These wandering objects are planets.

Both planets and stars are very far away from us, but the planets in our solar system are much closer to us than all of the stars, except for the star which we call the Sun.

Planets are smaller than stars and circle around the Sun. That's why the planets seem to move among the stars. Astronomers believe that many stars have planets circling around them just as the Sun does.

The Sun is an average-sized star. This means that some stars are larger than the Sun, some are smaller, and many are the same size.

STARS AND PLANETS

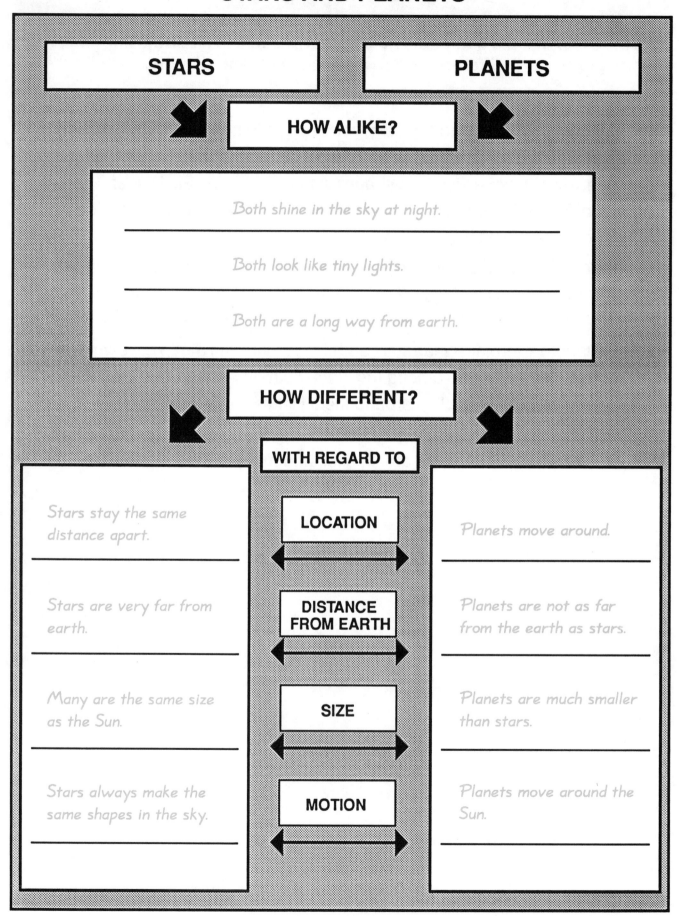

STARS	PLANETS

HOW ALIKE?

Both shine in the sky at night.

Both look like tiny lights.

Both are a long way from earth.

HOW DIFFERENT?

WITH REGARD TO

STARS		PLANETS
Stars stay the same distance apart.	**LOCATION**	Planets move around.
Stars are very far from earth.	**DISTANCE FROM EARTH**	Planets are not as far from the earth as stars.
Many are the same size as the Sun.	**SIZE**	Planets are much smaller than stars.
Stars always make the same shapes in the sky.	**MOTION**	Planets move around the Sun.

CHAPTER 7— ENRICHMENT LESSONS

THE TRUMPET AND
THE TUBA

(compare and contrast)

COMPARING NUMBER
AND MUSIC PATTERNS

(compare graph)

RECOGNIZING THE BEAT

(matrix)

DESCRIBING A
MUSICAL WORK

(central idea graph)

ELEMENTS OF
DESIGN

(branching diagram)

DESCRIBING A
PICTURE

(central idea graph)

THE TRUMPET AND THE TUBA

Note: The lessons in the Enrichment chapter require no specialized knowledge of music or art. They may also be used as critical reading lessons and for writing-across-the-curriculum activities.

THINKING SKILL: Verbal similarities and differences

OBJECTIVE: Students will use a compare and contrast graph to differentiate between the trumpet and the tuba.

DISCUSSION: TECHNIQUE—As students discuss the lesson, record each idea on a transparency of the compare and contrast graph. Listen to recordings or use films which feature the two instruments so that students can see and hear the difference.

　　DIALOGUE—Encourage students to identify additional similarities or differences. After students have reported differences between the trumpet and the tuba, discuss those differences by naming the quality that is different. Establish this pattern: "**With regard to** (quality), (item one and its distinction), **but** (item two and its distinction)." For example:

"**With regard to the pitch of the sounds produced, a trumpet produces high-pitched sounds, but a tuba produces low-pitched sounds.**"

　　RESULT—If one is clear about the differences between the structure and method of playing the trumpet and the tuba, one will not get these brass instruments confused.

WRITING EXTENSION
• **Describe how trumpets and tubas are alike and how they are different.**

THINKING ABOUT THINKING
• **How did using the diagram help you understand brass instruments?**
• **Suggest another lesson in which depicting information on this graph would help you understand what you are learning.**
• **Design another diagram that would help you describe brass instruments.**

SIMILAR ENRICHMENT LESSONS
• To compare two art media, works of art, design principles, styles of art, or artists' biographies.
• To compare architectural terms and styles.
• To compare elements of musical composition, forms of music, types of music, the development of musical styles, composers' or performers' biographies, or dance styles.

THE TRUMPET AND THE TUBA

DIRECTIONS: Read the passage carefully to determine how the trumpet and the tuba are alike and how they are different. Use the graph to record their similarities and differences.

The sound of a musical instrument is produced by vibrations. In brass instruments, these vibrations are made by blowing into the mouthpiece of the instrument.

The trumpet is one of the smaller brass instruments—light enough to be held easily with one hand. It is held straight out from the player's mouth. Trumpet players change the pitch by using their fingers to open and close three valves. The trumpet often carries the melody in a band and usually plays the higher-pitched tones.

The tuba is the largest brass band instrument. It is very heavy and often it is supported by a chair or a stand. Unlike the trumpet, the tuba is held with both hands and nearly straight up and down in front of the player. The sound comes out the top of the instrument. Tuba players also change the pitch by using their fingers to open and close three valves. The tuba seldom plays the melody and sometimes provides an "um pah pah" rhythm. The tuba usually plays the lower-pitched notes.

THE TRUMPET AND THE TUBA

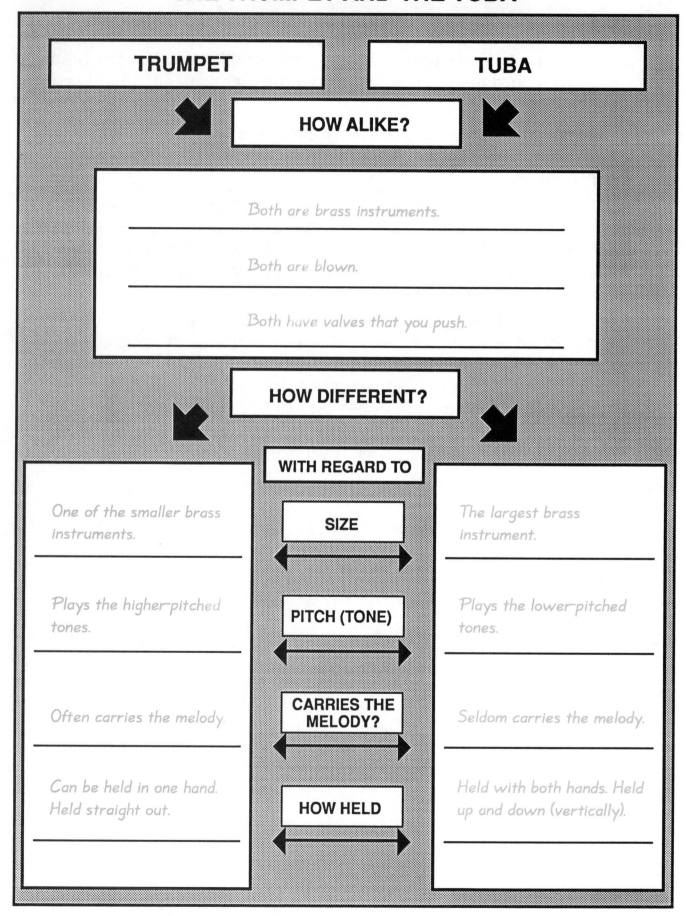

TRUMPET	TUBA

HOW ALIKE?

Both are brass instruments.

Both are blown.

Both have valves that you push.

HOW DIFFERENT?

WITH REGARD TO

TRUMPET		TUBA
One of the smaller brass instruments.	**SIZE**	The largest brass instrument.
Plays the higher-pitched tones.	**PITCH (TONE)**	Plays the lower-pitched tones.
Often carries the melody	**CARRIES THE MELODY?**	Seldom carries the melody.
Can be held in one hand. Held straight out.	**HOW HELD**	Held with both hands. Held up and down (vertically).

COMPARING NUMBER AND MUSIC PATTERNS

THINKING SKILL: Comparing symbol patterns

CONTENT OBJECTIVE: Students will use a comparison diagram to compare sequences of numbers with sequences of music notes.

DISCUSSION: TECHNIQUE—Use a transparency of the comparison diagram. Cut apart the transparency of the four groups of notes and the four number sequences. Illustrate the lesson by moving the transparency pieces for falling patterns of numbers and falling patterns of music notes onto the transparency of the comparison diagram.

Students will cut apart the pattern boxes and paste the appropriate patterns on the comparison diagram on page 281.

DIALOGUE—Encourage students to identify similar sequences as they listen to music.

How does the information on the diagram help you describe a melody?

Identify songs in which the melody line is similar to the patterns on the comparison diagram. Examples include, but are not limited to:
- falling melodies – the chorus of "Good Night Irene" and "Ceilito Lindo"
- repeating melodies – "Jingle Bells" and rap music
- rising melodies – "You Are My Sunshine" and "This Land is Your Land"
- rising, then falling, melodies – "Row, Row, Row Your Boat," "Frère Jacques," and "Twinkle, Twinkle Little Star"

Students may prefer to describe contemporary music. For additional discussion information, consult the music section of your school library, the district instructional materials center, or the following resource books:

Invitation to Music, Elie Siegmeister (Irvington-on-Hudson, N.Y.: Harvey House, 1961).
The Voice of Music, Robina Wilson (Atheneum, N.Y.: Margaret K. McElderry, 1977).
What To Listen For in Music, Aaron Copeland (New York: McGraw-Hill, 1957).

The patterns of numbers parallel patterns of music notes. In learning to read music, students will use letters, rather than numbers, to describe music notes. Using numbers or letters to describe music notes is helpful as students learning fingering on recorders and keyboards.

RESULT—Listening for patterns of notes helps one appreciate and understand a melody differently.

WRITING EXTENSION
- Select a song and describe the pattern of the melody.
- Describe how the pattern of the melody makes you feel.

THINKING ABOUT THINKING
- Suggest another lesson in which comparing things on a comparison diagram would help you understand what you are learning.
- Create a diagram to show the melody of a song.

SIMILAR ENRICHMENT LESSONS
- To classify music, art, architecture, or dance according to culture.
- To classify tools according to purpose, type, or function.
- To select music, art, flowers, decorations, or fashions appropriate to an occasion.
- To describe patterns in clothing design or clothing from different historical periods.

NUMBER AND MUSIC PATTERNS

DIRECTIONS: Cut out the four groups of numbers and the four groups of music notes below.

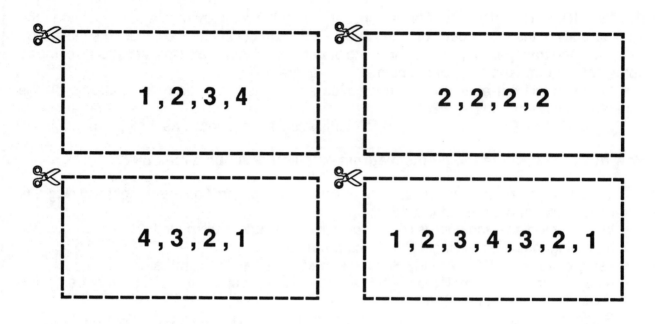

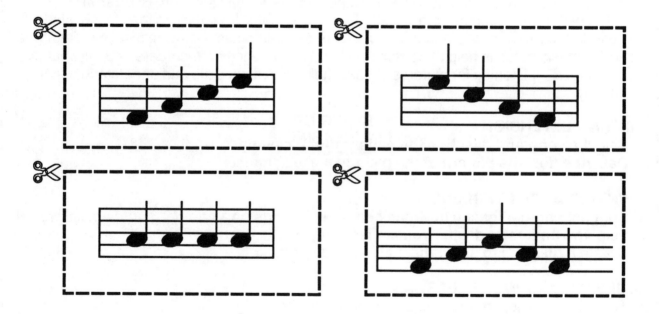

COMPARING NUMBER AND MUSIC PATTERNS

DIRECTIONS: Paste the four groups of numbers and the four groups of music notes in the box that best describes the pattern.

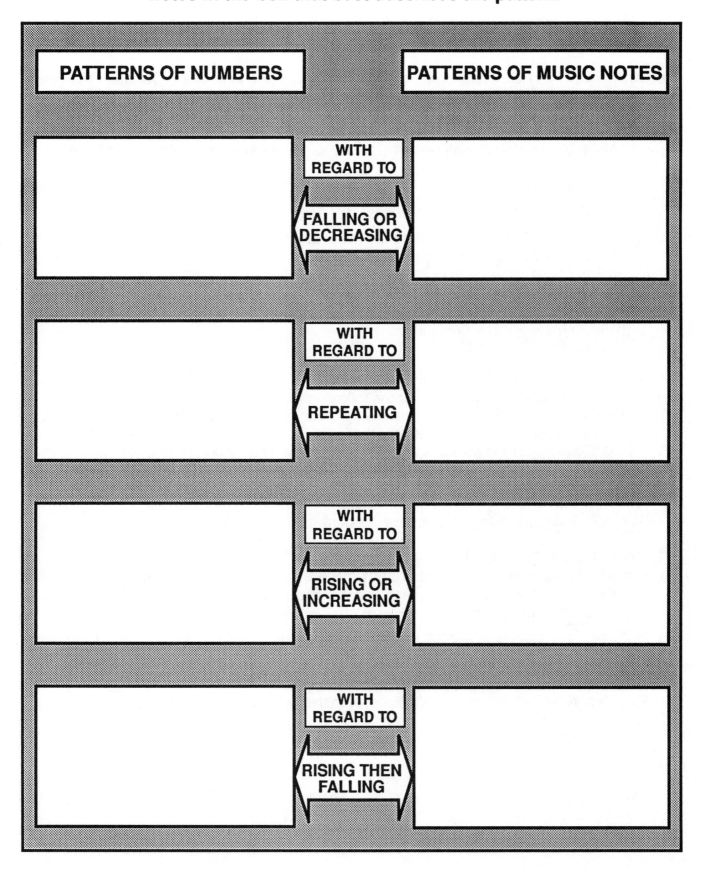

RECOGNIZING THE BEAT

THINKING SKILL: Figural sequences

CONTENT OBJECTIVE: Students will use a matrix chart to identify the beat as represented by dashes or by musical notes.

DISCUSSION: TECHNIQUE—Use a transparency of the matrix chart. Cut apart the nine possible answers. Have the students move them to the correct position on the matrix chart. There are seven blanks and nine possible answers. Encourage students to identify similar patterns in poems.
    DIALOGUE—Encourage students to identify similar sequences as they listen to music.

How did connecting the words, the beat, and the music notes help you describe the rhythm of a piece of music?

Use the same graphic organizer to describe the beat in common songs such as:
- "Row, Row, Row Your Boat" (3 long, steady beats)
- "On Top of Old Smoky" (long–short–short)
- "The Itsy-Bitsy Spider" (short–long–short)
- "Jingle Bells" (short–short–long)
- "This Old Man" (long–short–long)
- "Twinkle, Twinkle Little Star" (short–short)

For additional discussion information, consult the music section of your school library, the district instructional materials center, or the following resource books:
    Invitation to Music, Elie Siegmeister (Irvington-on-Hudson, N.Y.: Harvey House, 1961).
    The Voice of Music, Robina Wilson (Atheneum, N.Y.: Margaret K. McElderry, 1977).
    What To Listen For in Music, Aaron Copeland (New York: McGraw-Hill, 1957).
    RESULT—Listening for the beat in a song helps one understand and sing it better.

WRITING EXTENSION
- Select a piece of music and describe its beat.

THINKING ABOUT THINKING
- Suggest another lesson in which showing the beat on a diagram would help you understand it. (Apply to poems, other pieces of music, or recitation like the times table.)
- Draw the beat another way.

SIMILAR ENRICHMENT LESSONS
- To classify music, art, architecture, or dance according to culture.
- To classify tools according to purpose, type, or function.
- To select music, art, flowers, decorations, or fashions appropriate to an occasion.

RECOGNIZING THE BEAT

DIRECTIONS: Look at the top line in the matrix chart. The beat described as Short-Short-Long can be represented as two short lines and a long line or by musical notes. Cut apart the nine possible answers and use seven of them to complete the matrix chart.

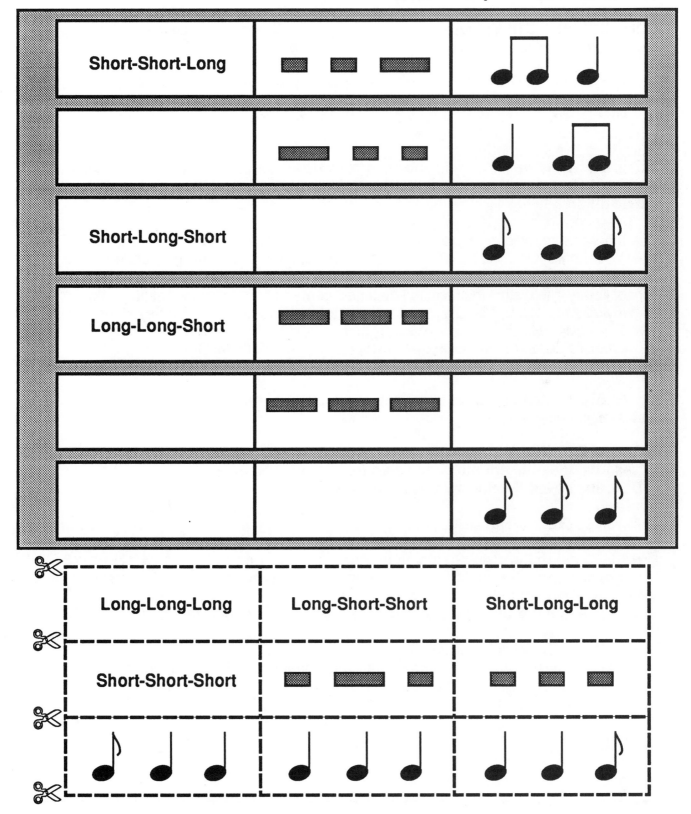

DESCRIBING A MUSICAL WORK

Note: This lesson requires no specialized knowledge of music. It may be used as a supplement to music instruction or as a critical reading or writing-across-the-curriculum lesson.

THINKING SKILL: Verbal classification

CONTENT OBJECTIVE: Students will use the central idea graph to describe elements of a musical work: melody, rhythm, harmony, tone color, form, and style.

DISCUSSION: TECHNIQUE—Use a transparency of the central idea graph to record responses as students discuss the elements of a musical work.
    DIALOGUE—Encourage students to apply these concepts as they listen to music.

How does the information on the diagram help you understand what to listen for in a musical work? How does it help you understand the differences between different works of music? How does knowing what to listen for in music help you enjoy and understand music differently?

Use the same graphic organizer to describe a simple piece of music, such as "Row, Row, Row Your Boat," "On Top of Old Smoky," or "Frère Jacques." Students may prefer to describe contemporary music. For additional discussion information, consult the music section of your school library, the district instructional materials center, or the following resource books:
    Invitation to Music, Elie Siegmeister (Irvington-on-Hudson, N.Y.: Harvey House, 1961).
    The Voice of Music, Robina Wilson (Atheneum, N.Y.: Margaret K. McElderry, 1977).
    What To Listen For in Music, Aaron Copeland (New York: McGraw-Hill, 1957).
Relate principles of describing music to describing poetry.

    RESULT—Knowing what to listen for in a piece of music helps one appreciate and understand it differently.

WRITING EXTENSION
• **Describe the different things to listen for in a piece of music.**
• **Describe how different rhythms make you feel.**

THINKING ABOUT THINKING
• **What other items could you organize quickly with a central idea graph?**
• **How did using the graph help you understand the elements of a musical work?**
• **Suggest another lesson in which depicting information on a central idea graph would help you understand what you are learning.**
• **Design another graph that would help you describe or analyze a musical work.**

SIMILAR ENRICHMENT LESSONS
• To classify music, art, architecture, or dance according to era, culture, or type.
• To classify tools according to purpose, type, function, or storage needs.
• To select music, art, flowers, decorations, or fashions appropriate to an occasion.

DESCRIBING A MUSICAL WORK

DIRECTIONS: Carefully read the passage below about the elements of a musical work: melody, rhythm, harmony, tone color, form, and style. In each box on the next page write words from the passage which describe each element.

Many elements make a musical piece special or different from others. These are **melody, rhythm, harmony, tone color, form, and style.**

Melody is the series of notes and rhythms arranged into the pattern that you recognize and remember as a particular song. A melody usually follows the familiar *do-re-mi-fa-sol-la-ti-do* **scale**.

Accent and **tempo** create **rhythm**, the steady beat that carries the music along. The strongest beat is called the accent. Where the accent falls changes the rhythm of the music. The accent in "On Top of Old Smoky" gives it a flowing sound; the regular accent in "Old Folks at Home" ("Way down upon the Swanee River") gives it a swinging sound. Tempo refers to the rate of speed at which music is played: a fast tempo, a slow tempo, or a changing tempo.

Harmony is the blending of tones, called **chords**, which are sounded at the same time. Gospel music and African music are familiar examples.

Tone color is the effect the composer achieves by choosing the **volume**, **pitch**, or combination of instruments to produce a mood or feeling. Volume refers to how loudly a piece is played. "The Star Spangled Banner" played softly and delicately would sound sad instead of rousing. Pitch refers to whether a melody uses high notes for light, cheerful sounds or low notes for serious sounds. In *Peter and the Wolf* the high notes of the flute suggest the bird, and the low notes of the bassoon sounds like the grumbling old grandfather.

Form refers to the length of the piece or the combination of instruments or voices required. **Symphonies** are the longest musical forms. They require many instruments and contain many melodies. Singing music forms may be a short **song** or a long musical story called an **opera.**

Style refers to types of music: the time in which it was composed, the purpose, and the intended audience. **Popular** music includes rock and roll, jazz, blues, and country and western. **Folk** music is traditional music, such as "On Top of Old Smoky." **Religious** music includes hymns or gospel songs.

DESCRIBING A MUSICAL WORK

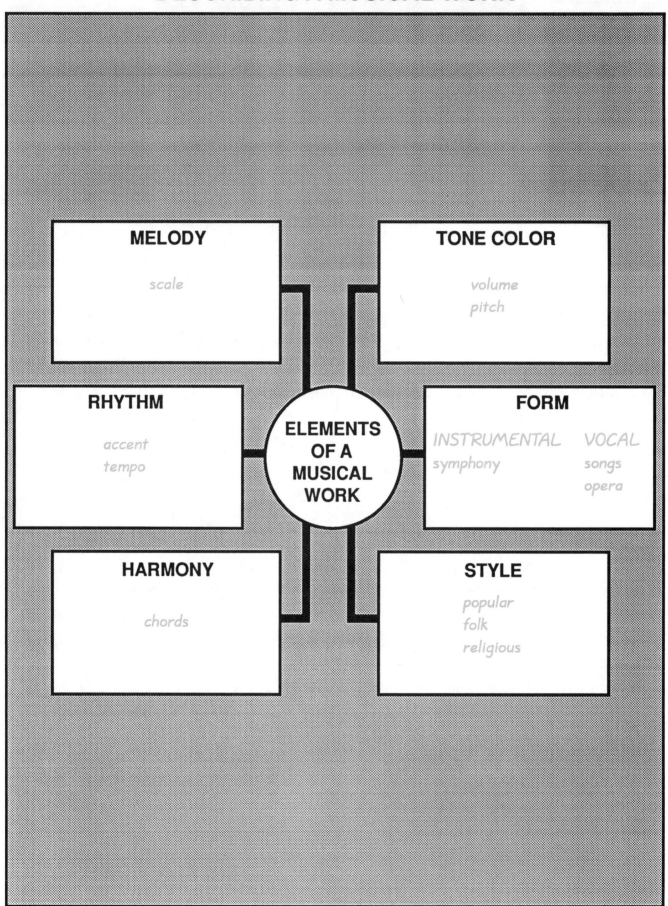

ELEMENTS OF DESIGN

NOTE: This is one of two lessons to develop students' abilities to describe works of art. These lessons help students clarify common terms used to describe elements of design and use them when describing a given picture or comparing two or more pictures. This lesson requires no specialized knowledge of art. It may also be used as a critical reading lesson and for a writing-across-the-curriculum activity.

THINKING SKILL: Verbal classification

CONTENT OBJECTIVE: Students will use a branching diagram to classify words which describe basic elements of design: color, shape, line, texture, and pattern.

DISCUSSION: TECHNIQUE—Use a transparency of the branching diagram to record students' responses as they discuss elements of design. Review the five elements of design before assigning the student activity. Confirm that students understand the terms in the exercise before students sort them independently.

Identify the terms that appear in more than one element. Discuss how the same term when used to describe different elements has a similar effect; i.e., a soft color and a soft texture both suggest lightness or calm.

DIALOGUE—Encourage students to apply these terms to specific pictures.

How does knowing the terms that describe design elements help you understand what to look for in a picture? How does knowing what to look for change the way you appreciate art?

Because we do not commonly discuss pictures with elementary school children, we expect that picture analysis is too difficult or too abstract for them. Young children, however, enjoy having words to describe what they see and sense. These terms can also be used to examine buildings, furnishings, photographs, sculptures, magazine graphics, bridges, etc.

RESULT—Knowing the words that people use to describe a picture helps one appreciate and understand it more thoroughly.

WRITING EXTENSION
• **Describe the elements that make up a picture. Explain how these elements contribute to the general effect of the picture. What would happen if one of the elements changed?**

THINKING ABOUT THINKING
• **How did using the diagram help you relate words you already knew to the elements of design? How did the diagram help you understand the differences between the various elements of design?**
• **Suggest another lesson in which classifying information on a graph would help you understand what you are learning.**
• **Design another diagram that would help you learn terms to describe pictures.**
• **What other things might you organize quickly with a branching diagram?**

SIMILAR ENRICHMENT LESSONS
• To classify music, art, architecture, or dance according to era, culture, purpose, or type.
• To select music, art, flowers, decorations, or fashions appropriate to an occasion.
• To classify instruments by type or location in the orchestra.

ELEMENTS OF DESIGN

DIRECTIONS: Sort the following terms by the element of design which each describes. Terms may be used in more than one box.

bright, circle, coarse, curved, dull, fuzzy, irregular, oval, rectangle, regular, slick, smooth, soft, straight, thick, thin, triangle, wavy, zigzag

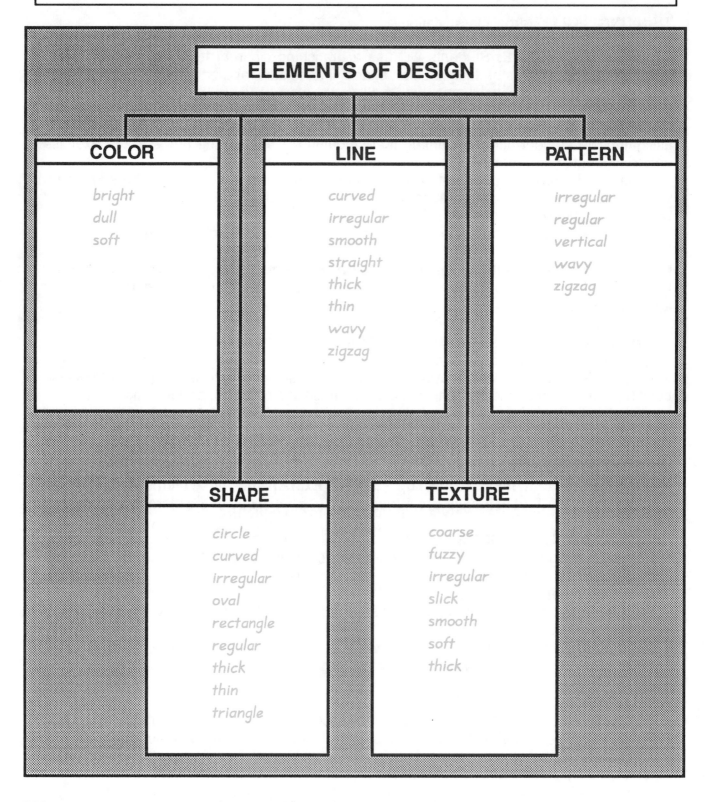

ELEMENTS OF DESIGN

COLOR
bright
dull
soft

LINE
curved
irregular
smooth
straight
thick
thin
wavy
zigzag

PATTERN
irregular
regular
vertical
wavy
zigzag

SHAPE
circle
curved
irregular
oval
rectangle
regular
thick
thin
triangle

TEXTURE
coarse
fuzzy
irregular
slick
smooth
soft
thick

DESCRIBING A PICTURE

NOTE: This is the second of two lessons to develop students' abilities to describe works of art. These lessons help students clarify common terms used to describe elements of design and to use these terms to describe a given picture or to compare two or more pictures.

THINKING SKILL: Verbal classification

CONTENT OBJECTIVE: Students will use a central idea graph to describe elements of a picture: color, line, shape, texture, pattern, and perspective. The art objectives are at the 2nd grade level; readability level is 4th grade. Use orally with younger children.

DISCUSSION: TECHNIQUE—Students must be able to examine a large, high-quality reproduction as they discuss the elements of design in the picture. Vincent Van Gogh's *A Starry Night* was used to provide the sample answers. Use a transparency of the central idea graph to record responses as students apply elements of design to describe a picture.
    DIALOGUE—Encourage students to apply these concepts in examining pictures.

How does the information on the diagram help us understand what to look for in a picture? How does the information on the diagram help us understand the differences between different pictures? How does knowing what to look for in a picture help us appreciate it differently? How does the diagram help us describe the design of the picture, the effect of the picture, and the components of the picture?

    Select a picture that students relate to or one that demonstrates these elements clearly, like *A Starry Night*. Help the class discuss the painting, or ask students to write about it as an individual assignment. Discussing pictures is also an excellent Think/Pair/Share activity. Because we do not commonly discuss pictures with elementary school children, we expect that picture analysis is too difficult or abstract for them. In practice, however, children enjoy knowing words to describe what they see and sense. These terms can also be used to examine other works such as buildings, furnishings, photographs, sculptures, magazine graphics, bridges, etc.
    RESULT—Knowing the terms to describe the characteristics of a picture helps one describe it more clearly.

WRITING EXTENSION
- Describe the elements of style that you look for in a picture.
- Use the elements of design to describe a picture of your choice.

THINKING ABOUT THINKING
- How did using the graph help you understand the elements of a picture? How did using it help you look at or understand a picture differently? Why?
- Suggest another lesson in which depicting information on a central idea graph would help you understand what you are learning.
- Design another graph that would help you describe pictures.

SIMILAR ENRICHMENT LESSONS
- To classify music, art, architecture, or dance according to era, culture, or type.
- To select music, art, flowers, decorations, or fashions appropriate to an occasion.
- To describe patterns in clothing design or clothing from different historical periods.

DESCRIBING A PICTURE

DIRECTIONS: Read the passage carefully. After each element is described, look for that characteristic in the picture you are looking at. For each element (color, line, shape, texture, pattern, and perspective), write details in each box on the diagram to describe that characteristic and its effect in the picture.

Five elements make up the uniqueness of a picture: **color, line, shape, texture,** and **pattern,** When we discuss a picture, we describe both the characteristic and the effect of the characteristic. For example, when discussing color we would describe what the colors seem like or how they make you feel.

To describe **color,** name the colors and how they are combined. If primary colors in a picture are next to each other on the color wheel (such as red, purple, blue), the blending of the colors seems more calm. If colors are opposite each other on the color wheel (such as red and green), the colors contrast with each other. The reds stand out from the greens. The effect is active and exciting.

Colors can also suggest objects, ideas, or attitudes. Red, yellow, and orange seem warm; blue, green, and purple seem cool. Blue and green give the appearance of water and plants. They suggest woods, oceans, sky, quiet, and harmony. Red and orange suggest fire, speed, or energy.

We describe **line** in a picture by describing what the lines look like. Are they straight, curving, wavy, or zigzag? Each type of line has its effect. Straight lines seem firm and strong; wavy or curving lines seem graceful or soothing; jagged or zigzag lines seem active or sharp.

Shape in a picture may be described by the type of geometric figure used (circles, squares, trapezoids, triangles, spirals, or rectangles). Shapes have a special meaning. For example, heart or four-leaf clover shapes suggest happiness.

Texture is what the surface looks like (how the surface would feel if we touched it): rough, scratchy, hard, smooth, soft, or wet. Texture can also suggest meaning: rough textures seem strong and bold; soft textures seem gentle and peaceful.

We describe **pattern** as the arrangement of shapes and lines in a picture. Repeating shapes create a rhythm in a picture the same way that repeating sounds create rhythm in music. Regular rhythm seems calm but irregular ones suggest confusion.

Select a picture and describe it using the elements above. Isn't art more interesting when you know what to look for?

DESCRIBING A PICTURE

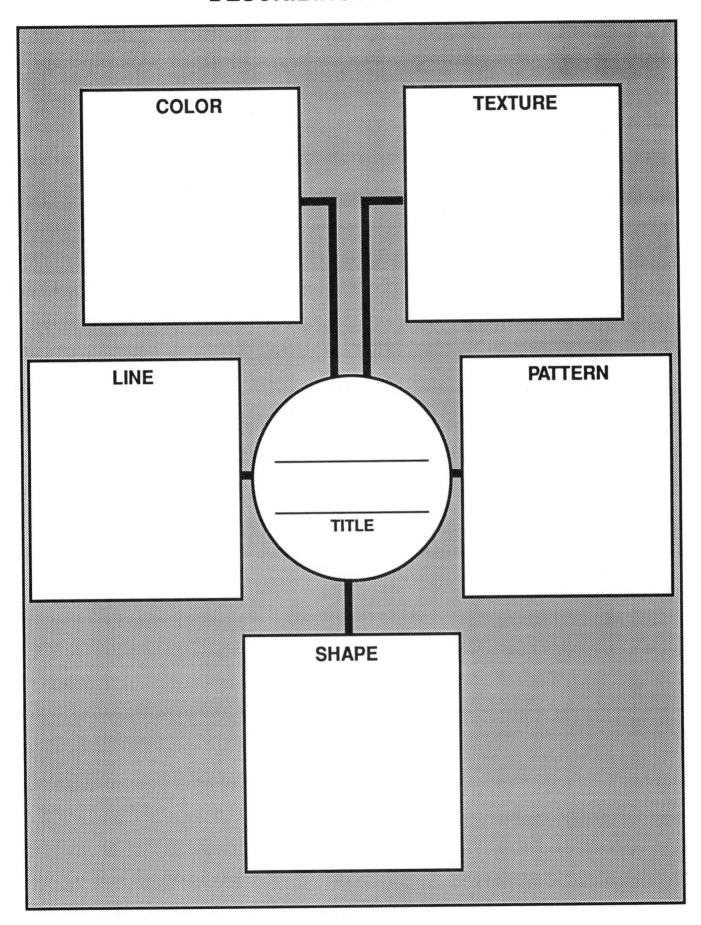

COLOR

TEXTURE

LINE

PATTERN

TITLE

SHAPE

CHAPTER 8—PERSONAL PROBLEM SOLVING

SHORT- AND
LONG-TERM GOALS
(branching diagram)

EFFECTS OF
WATCHING TOO MUCH
TELEVISION
(central idea graph)

REDUCING LUNCHROOM
WASTE
(central idea graph)

DO I REALLY KNOW IT?
(flowchart)

SHORT- AND LONG-TERM GOALS

THINKING SKILL: Compare and contrast, planning

CONTENT OBJECTIVE: Students shall identify short- and long-term goals.

DISCUSSION: TECHNIQUE—Use a transparency of the compare and contrast diagram to describe how short-term and long-term goals are alike and how they are different. Because young students don't understand that people have goals, they tend to believe that people act randomly or that they are controlled by schedules.

DIALOGUE—Discuss the difference between short-term and long-term goals. **Short-term goals** are those actions which can usually be done with less time, effort, and planning. They give us an immediate sense of having finished the task and being satisfied with it. **Long-term goals** usually require more effort, time, and planning, but are usually of greater value and personal significance. They usually require more reflection to decide whether the goal has been satisfied. Students often do not understand this distinction and, therefore, fail to set long-term goals in favor of short-term satisfaction. Identify short-term and long-term goals commonly held by students in your class.

Short-term goals are often a step toward a long-term objective. Use the following diagram to project the long-term goal for each short-term goal in this lesson.

Clean my room   ⟶   Organize my stuff so I can find it
                                      Keep on the good side of Mom or my roommate

Meet a new kid ⟶ Have more friends

Study for a test on Friday ⟶ Get better grades / Understand the subject better

Visit a friend ⟶ Have more good friends

Encourage students to identify the long-term goal for which their short-term goal is a step. Similarly, identify some short-term goals which may be necessary to fulfill a long-term goal.

Why is it important to know the difference between short- and long-term goals? How does knowing the difference help you understand what to do first?

RESULT—Perceiving the difference between short- and long-term goals helps us identify the types of goals we set and understand what may be required to satisfy them.

WRITING EXTENSION
- **Describe how short- and long-term goals are alike and how they are different.**

THINKING ABOUT THINKING
- **How did using the diagram help you understand short- and long-term goals more clearly?**
- **Suggest another decision in which you think that using this graph would be helpful.**

SIMILAR PERSONAL PROBLEM SOLVING LESSONS
- To compare or contrast desirable or undesirable habits or alternatives and their consequences.
- To compare or contrast choices, responsibilities, privileges, and courses of action.

SHORT- AND LONG-TERM GOALS

DIRECTIONS: Goals are results we want to happen. Short-term goals can be done with less time and effort and give us good feelings right away. Long-term goals take more time, effort, and planning, but usually mean more to us in the long run. Use the branching diagram to sort the list of goals given in the box.

Clean my room	Meet a new student
Get better grades	Run faster
Get in good physical condition	Study for a test
Learn to use a computer	Visit a friend

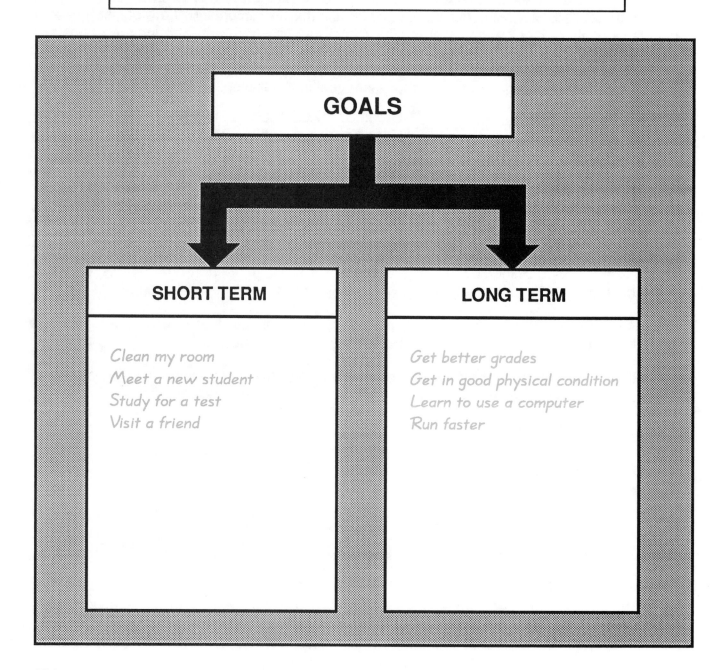

GOALS

SHORT TERM

Clean my room
Meet a new student
Study for a test
Visit a friend

LONG TERM

Get better grades
Get in good physical condition
Learn to use a computer
Run faster

THE EFFECTS OF WATCHING TOO MUCH TELEVISION

THINKING SKILL: Verbal classification, prioritizing, cause and effect

CONTENT OBJECTIVE: Students will identify the consequences of prolonged television watching.

DISCUSSION: TECHNIQUE—Compile a class list of consequences and mark each consequence with the number of students who identified it. Record the four most cited consequences on a transparency of the central idea graph.

DIALOGUE—Encourage your students to draw inferences regarding the effects prolonged television watching may have on them personally, as well as what other things they may be missing because their time is spent watching television.

We have identified some consequences of too much television viewing. What else are you missing by spending some of your time watching television? (This discussion is effective as a Think/Pair/Share activity, followed by a class discussion to summarize results.) **As you read the list of consequences, are there some types of consequences that are more obvious than others?**

How much viewing is too much? (Survey the class to find a class standard.) **Experts in this field recommend one hour per weekday and a total of four hours on the weekend. How can you decide what programs to watch?** (Answers: Review all the shows in the weekly television listings, decide which are most appealing, and circle only those which add up to the time limit. Review the shows you watch now and eliminate those you like least. Make a criteria list of what makes a television show worthwhile and review the weekly television listings for shows that are likely to match that. Decide which type of shows you like and select only from those. Start watching television and stop when you have reached the time limit.)

RESULT—By recognizing the effects of too much television viewing, one can decide whether its entertainment value is worth the consequences. We can decide whether what we are missing by long hours of viewing may be more important than seeing the shows. We can decide how much viewing is appropriate and how we may alter our viewing habits.

WRITING EXTENSION
- **Describe the effects of too much television viewing.**
- **Describe how you would plan your television viewing.**

THINKING ABOUT THINKING
- **How did using the diagram help you understand the effects of prolonged television viewing?**
- **Why is it important to understand as many consequences of a decision or activity as possible?**
- **Suggest another lesson in which depicting information on a graph would help you understand the consequences of an activity.**
- **Design another diagram that would help you recognize consequences of an activity.**

SIMILAR PERSONAL PROBLEM SOLVING LESSONS
- To illustrate factors leading to a personal or classroom conflict or issue.
- To illustrate the consequences of personal or class decision making.

EFFECTS OF WATCHING TOO MUCH TELEVISION

DIRECTIONS: What are the consequences of your spending so much time watching television? Are there more important things that you could be doing?

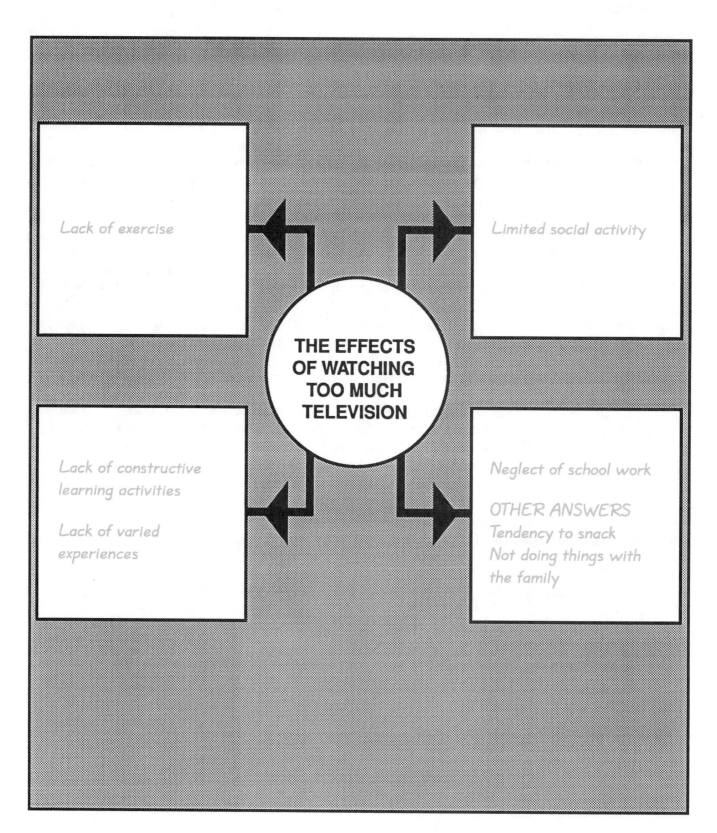

Lack of exercise

Limited social activity

THE EFFECTS
OF WATCHING
TOO MUCH
TELEVISION

Lack of constructive
learning activities

Lack of varied
experiences

Neglect of school work

OTHER ANSWERS
Tendency to snack
Not doing things with
the family

REDUCING LUNCHROOM WASTE

NOTE: This lesson models practical problem solving processes which can be used for student consideration of problem situations within the school. Decide as a group whether lunchroom waste is a problem in your school. If it is not, use the three graphics to discuss the factors which explain an existing problem, its consequences, and alternative solutions.

THINKING SKILL: Establishing causes, predicting consequences, evaluating solutions

CONTENT OBJECTIVE: Students will use the central idea graph to propose ways of reducing lunchroom waste.

DISCUSSION: TECHNIQUE—Have students brainstorm causes for food waste in the lunchroom. List as many suggested causes as possible on the chalkboard. Poll the class marking each cause with the number of students who agree with each suggestion. On a transparency of the central idea graph, record the six causes which the class selects as the most likely or most significant ones.

Repeat this process, asking students to identify the consequences of lunchroom waste. In each case identify the school personnel and operations most affected by the waste and the direct and indirect financial cost to the school.

Repeat the process again as students propose solutions to the problem of wasted food. Encourage them to be specific again as students propose consequences of wasting food and produce as many solutions as possible.

Sample answers provided on the graphs will not necessarily be the answers suggested by the class. Students may well arrive at different causes, effects, and solutions to the problem.

DIALOGUE—This lesson simulates individual problem solving to resolve a school condition. Individual problem solving in this case involves generating causes and consequences for the purpose of suggesting possible solutions to the school staff. This lesson also alerts students that their own individual behavior over which they have immediate control may be contributing to the problem.

In solving any problem, why is it important to identify as many causes as possible? Why is it important to evaluate whether a suggested cause is a likely one? What evidence do you have or must you find to know whether the cause is a likely one? Why is it important to evaluate whether a suggested cause is a significant one? Identify a cause that may be a likely, but not significant, one. Why would you think of as many causes as possible, then limit your problem solving to a small number?

To evaluate the consequences of wasted food, examine the cost of the problem in terms of money and time. Examine how students may be affected, directly or indirectly, by the problem. Identify choices, materials, or activities that students may be missing because of the costliness of the food waste.

To evaluate solutions to the wasted food problem, examine each suggestion's acceptability to all people involved: cafeteria staff, principal, teachers, students, janitorial staff, and parents.

What kind of information would you need to determine whether lunchroom waste is a problem in this school? What action might you take as a result of examining this situation? (Actions may include approaching the principal with the results of your discussion, deciding as a class and as individuals what you can do to reduce wasted food, or conducting further research to estimate the extent of the problem.)

RESULT—Identifying the causes and consequences of and the potential solutions to a problem establishes a starting point for the solution. It is important to identify evidence of likelihood in discussing causes and consequences and to limit the factors to a manageable number.

WRITING EXTENSION

- Explain why it is important to identify the causes and consequences of and the possible solutions to a problem.
- Identify other school or individual problems that can be better understood using this process.

THINKING ABOUT THINKING

- How did using the diagram help you think of good ideas and select the most significant ones?
- What effect did listing the causes and consequences have on your awareness of the problem?
- Design another diagram that would help you identify or evaluate causes, consequences, and possible solutions.
- Suggest another problem in which using this graph would help you understand causes, consequences, and possible solutions.

SIMILAR PERSONAL PROBLEM SOLVING LESSONS

- To illustrate the consequences of personal or group decision making.
- To illustrate the consequences of local, state, and federal government decision making.
- To illustrate factors leading to a personal or group conflict or issue.
- To illustrate factors leading to a local, state, or national conflict or issue.

REDUCING LUNCHROOM WASTE

DIRECTIONS: Each day, school cafeteria personnel must dispose of large quantities of food which students leave uneaten. Write on the central idea graphs the answers to the following questions:

What explains the amount of food that students leave uneaten?
What are the consequences of wasting food?
What can be done to reduce lunchroom waste?

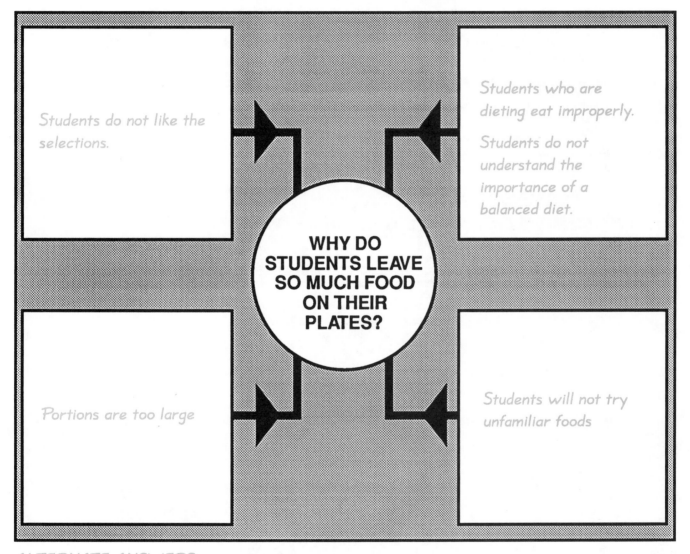

Students do not like the selections.

Students who are dieting eat improperly.

Students do not understand the importance of a balanced diet.

WHY DO STUDENTS LEAVE SO MUCH FOOD ON THEIR PLATES?

Portions are too large

Students will not try unfamiliar foods

ALTERNATE ANSWERS
Food may be cold, overcooked, over- or under-seasoned
Lack of choice — "all or none"
Students rush out to play
Students are not hungry
Many lunches are "pre-packaged"
Not enough time to finish the meal
Snacking on less nutritious foods
Food allergies

REDUCING LUNCHROOM WASTE

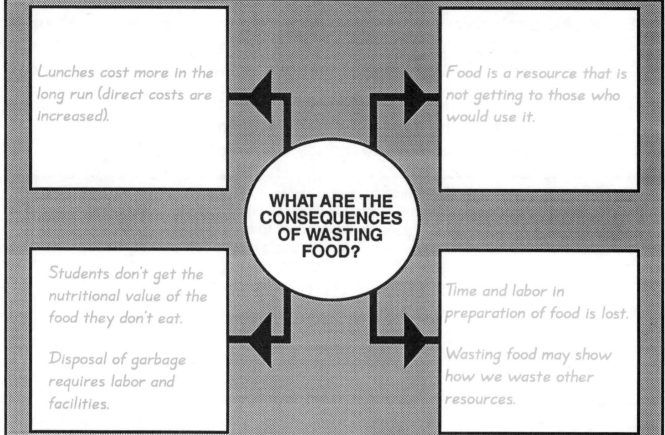

Lunches cost more in the long run (direct costs are increased).

Food is a resource that is not getting to those who would use it.

WHAT ARE THE CONSEQUENCES OF WASTING FOOD?

Students don't get the nutritional value of the food they don't eat.

Disposal of garbage requires labor and facilities.

Time and labor in preparation of food is lost.

Wasting food may show how we waste other resources.

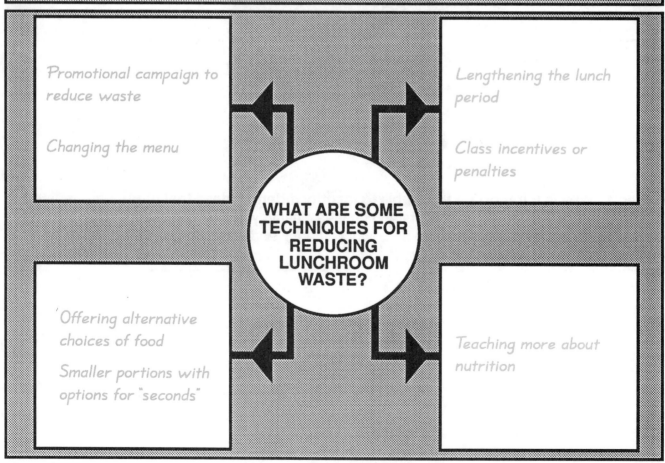

Promotional campaign to reduce waste

Changing the menu

Lengthening the lunch period

Class incentives or penalties

WHAT ARE SOME TECHNIQUES FOR REDUCING LUNCHROOM WASTE?

Offering alternative choices of food

Smaller portions with options for "seconds"

Teaching more about nutrition

DO I REALLY KNOW IT?

THINKING SKILL: Verbal sequences, verbal classification, identifying attributes

CONTENT OBJECTIVE: Students will use a flowchart to confirm their clear understanding of a concept. This process helps students "check" how well they understand key concepts and can be used to review concepts in any discipline.

DISCUSSION: TECHNIQUE—Use a transparency of the flowchart to record student responses as they review how clearly they understand key concepts. This process may be used to introduce significant concepts or to review concepts before a unit test. Design a bulletin board display of this process to remind students how to review for a test.

This lesson introduces students to the six steps of Hilda Taba's concept-development model. The Taba model is usually used by the teacher to explain a new concept effectively. The purpose of this lesson, however, is to teach students how to confirm their understanding of important ideas. It is the responsibility of the student to be certain that he or she understands a concept clearly. This review technique is an effective memory tool and promotes students' confidence in their ability to take tests.

Ask students to think about a recently-learned concept and to write phrases on the flowchart on the right to record what they remember about that idea. Then discuss why each question is helpful in understanding any new concept.

DIALOGUE—Encourage students to identify why each step in the process is important in clarifying whether they truly understand an idea.

Step 1: **Why is it important to identify what kind of thing or idea this concept is?** The category to which the concept belongs will be included in its definition. Accurately stating the category reduces confusion about the concept.

Step 2: **Why is it important to be able to name some examples?** Examples help you remember the concept.

Step 3: **Why is it important to be able to identify some similar ideas?** You usually learn new ideas by tying them to something that you already know well. A similar idea, even one not in the same field, becomes a "mental peg" on which to hang the new concept.

Step 4: **Why is it important to be able to identify different ideas that might be confused with this one?** If you do not understand an idea clearly, you may confuse it with something else. By recognizing ideas that are somewhat different and identifying why they are different, you can clearly distinguish this key idea from others.

Step 5: **Why is it important to identify the important characteristics of the concept?** Important characteristics will be included in a definition of the concept. If you do not know the important characteristics of a concept, then you really do not have a clear understanding of it and are likely to confuse it with other ideas.

Step 6: **Why is it important to be able to define a key concept?** A good definition is the precise expression of what something is and how it is different from other similar things. A good definition demonstrates how clearly you understand a concept. When you combine the category in Step 1 with the significant characteristics in Step 5, you have formed a precise definition.

RESULT—You can be sure that you know what something is if you can name what kind of thing it is, give some examples, identify some things that are similar to and different from it, name the significant characteristics, and write a full definition of it.

WRITING EXTENSION

• Describe the steps for checking how clearly you understand a concept.

THINKING ABOUT THINKING

• In what situations is it important to be sure you understand a concept?
• Why is it important for you to be confident about your understanding?
• Design another graphic organizer that will help you review a concept effectively.

SIMILAR PERSONAL PROBLEM SOLVING LESSONS

• To depict the steps in instructions, information retrieval, study skills procedures, and independent study.

DO I REALLY KNOW IT?

NOTE TO TEACHERS: The following is an example of possible responses to a language arts topic for primary students. The responses are detailed for your information.

EXAMPLE: Poem

WHAT KIND OF AN IDEA IS IT?

A short piece of writing (as compared to a novel or play)

CAN I NAME SOME EXAMPLES?
Horton Hatches The Egg
Fog
The Song of Hiawatha

WHAT ARE SOME SIMILAR IDEAS?

Words of a song

WHAT ARE SOME DIFFERENT IDEAS THAT MIGHT BE CONFUSED WITH THIS ONE?

Television commercial, novel, dictionary, atlas, melody

WHAT ARE ITS IMPORTANT CHARACTERISTICS?

A poem is a shorter piece of writing than a novel. A poem usually has a special beat or form.

CAN I GIVE A FULL DEFINITION?

A poem is a short piece of writing that has rhythm or rhyme.

DO I REALLY KNOW IT?

NOTE TO TEACHERS: The following is an example of possible responses to a social studies topic for primary students. The responses are detailed for your information.

EXAMPLE: _____ Money _____

WHAT KIND OF AN IDEA IS IT?

Objects that people give to each other to buy things (medium of exchange)

CAN I NAME SOME EXAMPLES?

Pennies, nickles, dimes, quarters, dollar bills

WHAT ARE SOME SIMILAR IDEAS?

Tokens (used for bus or subway rides), coupons, passes

WHAT ARE SOME DIFFERENT IDEAS THAT MIGHT BE CONFUSED WITH THIS ONE?
Checks, credit cards (these are used to make purchases, but they are not a standard unit and they do not have to be accepted for payment; they are not produced and supported by the national government), barter (no token represents a value, services and goods are exchanged)

WHAT ARE ITS IMPORTANT CHARACTERISTICS?
Money represents a standard amount that people recognize. It must be accepted for purchases made within its country. Money is produced and given value by the national government.

CAN I GIVE A FULL DEFINITION?
A metal or paper object of standard value which is exchanged for goods or services. Money must be accepted for payment and is produced and supported by the national government.

DO I REALLY KNOW IT?

NOTE TO TEACHERS: The following is an example of possible responses to a science topic for primary students. The responses are detailed for your information.

EXAMPLE: Dinosaur

WHAT KIND OF AN IDEA IS IT?

A dinosaur is any of a group of reptiles that lived millions of years ago.

CAN I NAME SOME EXAMPLES?

Brontosaurus, tyrannosaurus, triceratops

WHAT ARE SOME SIMILAR IDEAS?

A steam shovel (see compare and contrast lesson "The Steam Shovel," p. 98)

WHAT ARE SOME DIFFERENT IDEAS THAT MIGHT BE CONFUSED WITH THIS ONE?

Alligators (a reptile that lives today), mammoth (an extinct mammal), fossils (remains of plants and dinosaurs or other animals)

WHAT ARE ITS IMPORTANT CHARACTERISTICS?

A dinosaur is a reptile that disappeared from earth millions of years ago. There were at least five thousand kinds of dinosaurs. They did not all live at the same time.

CAN I GIVE A FULL DEFINITION?

A dinosaur is a reptile that fossil records indicated lived, and died out, millions of years ago.

DO I REALLY KNOW IT?

NOTE TO TEACHERS: The following is an example of possible responses to a science topic for primary students. The responses are detailed for your information.

EXAMPLE: Amphibian

WHAT KIND OF AN IDEA IS IT?

An animal with a backbone (vertebrate) that can live on land or in water.

CAN I NAME SOME EXAMPLES?

Frogs, toads, salamanders

WHAT ARE SOME SIMILAR IDEAS?

A scuba diver can spend time on land or stay underwater a long time.
An amphibious landing craft can travel on land or water.

WHAT ARE SOME DIFFERENT IDEAS THAT MIGHT BE CONFUSED WITH THIS ONE?

Reptiles such as snakes, alligators, and lizards never have gills like amphibians. Fish can never live out of water. Neither reptiles nor fish change form as they mature as amphibians do.

WHAT ARE ITS IMPORTANT CHARACTERISTICS?

- Cold-blooded
- Vertebrates
- Most hatch from eggs
- Have moist soft skin

• Immature form looks different from the adult—immature amphibians have gills which are replaced by lungs as they develop and grow legs when they mature

CAN I GIVE A FULL DEFINITION?

An amphibian is a vertebrate that is cold-blooded, hatches from an egg, changes form as it grows up, and has soft, moist skin

DO I REALLY KNOW IT?

DIRECTIONS: Think about a plant, animal, object, or idea that we have studied. Check out how well you understand it by answering the questions on the chart.

EXAMPLE: _____

WHAT KIND OF AN IDEA IS IT?

CAN I NAME SOME EXAMPLES?

WHAT ARE SOME SIMILAR IDEAS?

WHAT ARE SOME DIFFERENT IDEAS THAT MIGHT BE CONFUSED WITH THIS ONE?

WHAT ARE ITS IMPORTANT CHARACTERISTICS?

CAN I GIVE A FULL DEFINITION?

© 1992 Critical Thinking Press & Software • P.O. Box 448, Pacific Grove, CA 93950